# DEVELOPING COGNITIVE AND CREATIVE SKILLS THROUGH ART

# DEVELOPING COGNITIVE AND CREATIVE SKILLS THROUGH ART

## Programs for Children with Communication Disorders or Learning Disabilities

**Rawley A. Silver, Ed.D., A.T.R.**

Honorary Life Member
American Art Therapy Association

AN AUTHORS GUILD BACKINPRINT.COM EDITION

AN AUTHORS GUILD BACKINPRINT.COM EDITION

Published by iUniverse.com, Inc.

For information address:
iUniverse.com, Inc.
620 North 48th Street, Suite 201
Lincoln, NE 68504-3467
www.iuniverse.com

Originally published by Ablin Press

Updated with a new epilogue

ISBN: 0-595-08886-4

Printed in the United States of America

# Contents

List of Tables ........................................... viii
List of Figures .......................................... x
Preface .................................................. xv
Acknowledgments ....................................... xvii

**Part One   The Role of Art**

Chapter 1   Cognition ................................... 5

Nonverbal Thinking .................................... 5
Organizing and Representing Experiences ............... 9
Left and Right Hemisphere Thinking .................... 10
Establishing Patterns for Language to Follow .......... 11
Learning New Words .................................... 14
Activating or Reinforcing Language .................... 16
Transfer of Learning .................................. 18
Imaginary Play ........................................ 20
Abstract Thinking ..................................... 21
Recall ................................................ 25

Chapter 2   Adjustment ................................. 29

Fulfilling Wishes Vicariously ......................... 29
Testing Reality ....................................... 29
Expressing Unacceptable Feelings in an Acceptable Way ... 33
Obtaining Relief from Tension ......................... 35
Self-Monitoring ....................................... 38
Personal Involvement .................................. 39
Experiencing Control Over People and Events ........... 42
Transfer of Behavior .................................. 43

Chapter 3   Assessment ................................. 49

Clues to Perception of Self and Others ................ 51
Clues to Interests and Concerns ....................... 53
Clues to Assessing a Child's Development .............. 57
Clues to Change ....................................... 59

Chapter  4  Expectations ...............................   63

Miguel ................................................   64
Paul ..................................................   65
David .................................................   66
Ralph .................................................   68
Charlie ...............................................   69
Maureen ..............................................   74

Chapter  5  Creative Skills .........................   79

First Study: Handicapped Children in Four Schools ........   80
Second Study: A Demonstration Project For Hearing-Impaired
    Children and Adults .................................   84
Third Study: State Urban Education Project for Children with
    Language and Hearing Impairments ...................   97

Part Two   Developing Cognitive and Creative Skills

Chapter  6  Issues, Objectives, and Methods ...............   105

Questions at Issue ......................................   105
Working with Any Child or Adult ........................   108
Working with Handicapped Children and Adults ...........   111

Chapter  7  The Cognitive Skills Under Consideration .......   117

Chapter  8  Ability to Associate and Represent Concepts
            Through Drawing From Imagination ............   121

Rationale ..............................................   121
Testing Procedures .....................................   122
Remediation ...........................................   138
Results ................................................   139

Chapter  9  Ability to Order Sequentially and Conserve
            Through Painting, Modeling Clay, and Predictive
            Drawing .....................................   141

Rationale ..............................................   141
Testing Procedures .....................................   143
Remediation ...........................................   148
Results ................................................   151

Chapter 10  Ability to Perceive and Represent Concepts
            of Space Through Drawing From Observation ...   161

Rationale ..............................................   161
Testing Procedures .....................................   166
Remediation ...........................................   172
Results ................................................   175
Observations ..........................................   176

Chapter 11   Case Studies .............................   179

   Burt....................................................   179
   Vito....................................................   188
   Stroke Patients .......................................   193

Chapter 12   Statistical Analyses .......................   203

   State Urban Education Project for Language- and Hearing-
      Impaired Children ...............................   203
   Art Program for Children with Learning Disabilities .......   225

Chapter 13   Discussion and Conclusions...................   231

   Cognitive Abilities ...................................   231
   Creative Ability ......................................   233
   Conclusions...........................................   236

Epilogue, 1986 .........................................   237

   Stimulus Drawings....................................   237
   A Drawing Test ......................................   237
   National Institute of Education Project...................   239
   Subsequent Research .................................   243

Epilogue, 1989 .........................................   249

   Gender Differences in the Emotional Content of Drawings    249
   Relationships Between Strongly Negative Responses and
      Depressive Illness ...............................   251

Epilogue, 1999 .........................................   255

   The Cognitive Content of Responses
   to Simulus Drawing Tasks ............................   255
   The Emotional Content of Responses
   to Stimulus Drawing Tasks............................   258

References..............................................   263

Index ..................................................   269

# List of Tables

Table 1 Results of questionnaire for educators of the deaf and other specialists 82

Table 2 Results of questionnaire for art educators 83

Table 3 Comparison of deaf and hearing populations as measured by the Torrance Test of Creative Thinking (Figural Form A) 87

Table 4 Comparison of paintings by twenty-two deaf and twenty-two hearing art students as judged by three university professors of art 88

Table 5 Comparison of portfolios by sixteen deaf students with the work of hearing art students as judged by thirteen art educators 90

Table 6 Comparison of deaf and hearing art students by eleven teacher-observers 91

Table 7 Questionnaire and responses regarding the interest of deaf children in art 93

Table 8 Questionnaire and responses regarding interest of deaf teenagers and adults in art 94

Table 9 Questionnaire sent to handcraftsmen and employers in various art fields 96

Table 10 Responses to questionnaires addressed to craftsmen, employers, and administrators, regarding vocational opportunities for the deaf in the visual arts 97

Table 11 Scoring form for drawing from imagination 125

Table 12 Scoring form for predictive drawing 145

Table 13 Scoring form for manipulative tasks 146

Table 14 Scoring form for drawing from observation 169

Table 15 Scoring form for manipulative games 176

Table 16 Children in the top and bottom 10% in test of spatial concepts 177

Table 17 Profile evaluation of Burt 180

Table 18 Burt's performance on project tests 186

Table 19 Cognitive skills of stroke patients 195

Table 20 Scoring form, Fall program posttest of cognition 206−207

Table 21 Results, drawing from imagination by experimental, control, and normal children 208−209

Table 22 Results, predictive drawing test by experimental and control children 212−213

Table 23 Raw data, predictive drawing test by experimental and control children 214

Table 24 Raw data analysis, predictive drawing test. Comparison of experimental group pre- and posttest scores 214

Table 25   Raw data analysis, predictive drawing test. Comparison of experimental to control group on pretest   214

Table 26   Raw data analysis, predictive drawing test. Comparison of Spring program control group on pre- and posttest   215

Table 27   Raw data analysis, predictive drawing test. Comparison of experimental group posttest to control group pretest   215

Table 28   Results, predictive drawing test by normal children   216

Table 29   Results, drawing from observation test by experimental, control, and normal children   219–220

Table 30   Scoring form used by university professor of art and art therapist-painter   221

Table 31   Results, evaluation of art works by university professor of art   222–223

Table 32   Results, evaluation of art works by art therapist-painter   224–225

Table 33   Results of art program for children with learning disabilities taught by graduate students at College of New Rochelle. Fall 1974   227

Table 34   Results, questionnaire sent to parents of fifteen children who attended art classes (with total of responses indicated)   228

### *Epilogue*

Table E1   Results, Interscorer Reliability Study   247

Table E2   The Means and Standard Deviations of the Ratings for Each Set of 12 Response Drawings   247

Table E3   Comparing Responses to the Draw-a-Story Task by Depressed, Normal, Emotionally Disturbed, Learning-Disabled and Deaf Children, Adolescents, and Adults   254

# List of Figures

Figure   1   "Frankenstein"   7
Figure   2   Man in the abstract?   8
Figure   3   "The monkey got away from the bear and went into the building"   8
Figure   4   Mother's grave   9
Figure   5   Eric's first fisherman   12
Figure   6   Eric's "House by the river"   13
Figure   7   Eric's second fisherman   14
Figure   8   Eric's "Peace"   15
Figure   9   Eric's last fisherman   15
Figure  10   Barbed wire   16
Figure  11   "He is killing the bees"   17
Figure  12   "Pohweh"   18
Figure  13   "The End"   19
Figure  14   "$90,000 I have more money"   19
Figure  15   "Sad or Happy"   20
Figure  16   Near and far   20
Figure  17   "It was stollen car/the helicopter shoot car pop"   21
Figure  18   "The Walking Bug"   22
Figure  19   Eddie Cantor   22
Figure  20   "Ghostman"   23
Figure  21   Children playing   24
Figure  22   "I love you children"   24
Figure  23   "Chinese Girl in China and Hawaiian Girl in Hawaii"   25
Figure  24   "Rusty Nosed Boat"   26
Figure  25   "Brances"   26
Figure  26   Kenneth and friend on motorcycle   30
Figure  27   Kenneth and motorcycle, #2   31
Figure  28   Mourning the death of a dog   31
Figure  29   "Help! Help!"/"O.K."   32
Figure  30   "I love you"/"Oh Thank You"   32
Figure  31   Slaying a dragon   33
Figure  32   Man overboard   34
Figure  33   Dynamiting a sergeant   34
Figure  34   Michael's angry man   35
Figure  35   Mark's car crash, #1   36
Figure  36   Mark's car crash, #2   36
Figure  37   Larry's man and woman   37
Figure  38   "The lady got a pencil in her eye . . ."   38
Figure  39   Splashdown of a smiling astronaut   38

Figure  40  Man with eyepatch    39
Figure  41  Woman with eyepatch    40
Figure  42  Farm scene, cat about to land on dog    41
Figure  43  Grandmother in coffin, self in pool    41
Figure  44  Robbing the safe    42
Figure  45  Putting the spook behind bars    43
Figure  46  "A girl or boy in the spring?"    44
Figure  47  Eugene's family portrait    44
Figure  48  Eugene's devil    45
Figure  49  Eugene's butterfly    46
Figure  50  Eugene's Black Beauty as leader    47
Figure  51  Terry's family portrait, tree isolating self    50
Figure  52  Tree isolating girl    50
Figure  53  Maureen's family portrait    51
Figure  54  ·Robert's family portrait    52
Figure  55  Lucy's family portrait    53
Figure  56  "Daddy, my house is on Frie/Help me"    54
Figure  57  "Help Daddy"/"I'm Coming"    54
Figure  58  Moon base by Billy    55
Figure  59  Moon base by newspaper artist    56
Figure  60  Hypodermic needle and other drug equipment    56
Figure  61  "Pancakes on a Plate with Butter"    57
Figure  62  "Atomic Uses?"    58
Figure  63  "What no one else knows"    58
Figure  64  Michael's family portrait    59
Figure  65  Michael's abstract painting    60
Figure  66  Michael's witch with fingers    60
Figure  67  Michael's birds with claws    61
Figure  68  Michael's "Play Ball'    61
Figure  69  Michael's last painting    62
Figure  70  Miguel's first drawing    64
Figure  71  Miguel's second drawing    64
Figure  72  Miguel's third drawing    65
Figure  73  Painting produced in Miguel's fourth class    66
Figure  74  Painting produced in Miguel's fifth and sixth classes    67
Figure  75  Paul's painting    67
Figure  76  David's painting    68
Figure  77  Ralph's first drawing    69
Figure  78  Ralph's painting of a ship caught on an iceberg    70
Figure  79  Ralph's painting of a ship being bombed    71
Figure  80  Ralph's painting of warfare in outer space    71
Figure  81  Charlie's first painting of flowers, age eleven    72
Figure  82  Charlie's second painting of flowers, age eleven    73
Figure  83  Charlie's shout in silence, age eleven    73

Figure  84    Charlie's shout in silence, age fourteen      74
Figure  85    Charlie's imaginary landscape, age fourteen      75
Figure  86    Charlie's imaginary landscape, age eleven      75
Figure  87    Charlie's imaginary landscape, age twenty-four      76
Figure  88    Painting that received highest score      89
Figure  89    Painting that received award in open juried show      92
Figure  90    Kinetic Family Drawing by stroke patient      114
Figure  91    "I made a witch"      115
Figure  92    "Hotel/2 Pools"      116
Figure  93    Stimulus cards, set A      123
Figure  94    Stimulus cards, set B      123
Figure  95    Selecting at the functional level      126
Figure  96    "Man Kissl a . . ."      127
Figure  97    Combining at the level of proximity      128
Figure  98    "Spring Day/Sonny and Cher"      129
Figure  99    Combining at the level of a unified whole      130
Figure 100    Daisy's first drawing      131
Figure 101    Daisy's second drawing      131
Figure 102    "Wedding Presents"      132
Figure 103    Cat and mice      132
Figure 104    Cat and garden      133
Figure 105    Ruth's first drawing      133
Figure 106    "NO BODY ON THE BEACH in Puerto Rico"      134
Figure 107    Nobody at home      135
Figure 108    Randall's gorilla      136
Figure 109    Confrontation      136
Figure 110    "A king on his birthday with a cake and icecream cone steps
              to the door to his castle"      137
Figure 111    "The Babies Sitter"      138
Figure 112    Predictive drawing test      144
Figure 113    Matrix ordering test      147
Figure 114    Conservation test, part one      148
Figure 115    Conservation test, part two      148
Figure 116    Painting equipment      149
Figure 117    Series ordering with paint      149
Figure 118    Testing out predictions      151
Figure 119    David's first predictive drawing      152
Figure 120    David's painting of someone fishing      152
Figure 121    David's second predictive drawing      153
Figure 122    David's last predictive drawing      154
Figure 123    Ralph's pretest and posttest      154
Figure 124    Ralph's painting of someone fishing      155
Figure 125    Paul's predictive drawing      155
Figure 126    Lucy's predictive drawing      156

Figure 127    One adult's predictive drawing        157
Figure 128    Another adult's predictive drawing        158
Figure 129    Ralph's first drawing from observation        162
Figure 130    Ralph's second drawing from observation        162
Figure 131    Ben's first drawing from observation        163
Figure 132    Ben's second drawing from observation        163
Figure 133    Ben's third drawing from observation        164
Figure 134    Dan's first drawing from observation        164
Figure 135    Dan's second drawing from observation        165
Figure 136    Dan's third drawing from observation        165
Figure 137    David's landscape drawing        166
Figure 138    David's first drawing        166
Figure 139    David's third drawing        166
Figure 140    Reuben's first drawing        167
Figure 141    Reuben's second drawing        167
Figure 142    Reuben's third drawing        167
Figure 143    Photograph of the arrangement        168
Figure 144    Drawing scored for ability to represent spatial
                    concepts        168
Figures 145−146    Drawings showing lack of the ability to represent
                    depth        170
Figures 147−148    Drawings showing lack of the ability to represent
                    depth        171
Figure 149    Drawing showing the ability to represent accurately in all
                    dimensions        172
Figure 150    Painting showing interest in form        174
Figure 151    Painting showing interest in content        174
Figure 152a    Burt's first drawing, man with knife in his stomach        181
Figure 152b    Closeup, Figure 152a        182
Figure 153    Burt's drawing of airplanes dropping bombs        183
Figure 154    Burt's nurse on crutches        184
Figure 155    "No cars, no people, rain all over," etc.        185
Figure 156    Burt's drawings from observation        186
Figure 157    Burt's predictive drawing pretest        187
Figure 158    Burt's drawing from imagination        187
Figure 159    Burt's predictive drawing posttest        188
Figure 160    Vito's first drawing        189
Figure 161    "Mouse, bug"        189
Figure 162    "Vito me"        190
Figure 163    "Otiv"        190
Figure 164    Vito's magician        191
Figure 165    Vito's landscape        191
Figure 166    "Vito, Vito, Vito"        192
Figure 167    Vito's dinosaur        193

Figure 168    "Dreaming about a Dune Buggy"    194
Figure 169    Gary's drawing from observation    196
Figure 170    Mrs. Verne's first attempts to draw    196
Figure 171    Mrs. Verne's second attempt to draw    197
Figure 172    Mrs. Moore's drawing from observation    198
Figure 173    Mrs. Moore's predictive drawing    198
Figure 174    Mrs. Moore's first drawing from imagination    199
Figure 175    Mrs. Moore's second drawing from imagination    199
Figure 176    Mrs. Jensen's first drawing from imagination    200
Figure 177    Mrs. Jensen's second drawing from imagination    201

## Epilogue

Figure E1    Stimulus Drawings    238
Figure E2    Mean Scores for Experimental and Control Groups on Pre and Posttests, 1980 Project    240
Figure E3    "The Killier" (sic) by Joey, age 8, Pretest Drawing from Imagination    242
Figure E4    Pretest Drawing from Observation by Joey    243
Figure E5    Posttest Drawing from Observation by Joey    243
Figure E6    "The Dog Chasing the Cat" by Joey, Posttest Drawing from Imagination    243
Figure E7    "The Dying Bride" by Caroline, 14    245
Figure E8    "The Father is Yelling at the Boy" by Omar, 7    245
Figure E9    "Close but yet so far away" by an Art Therapy Student    245
Figure E10    "The Painter and his Son" by Jim, 8    246
Figure E11    "Going to the Malt Shop" by Sarah, 14    246
Figure E12    "Midnight Break" by Art Therapist    246
Figure E13    Type of Score by Sex Interaction    248
Figure E14    Sex and Age Differences in the Emotional Content of Drawings    250
Figure E15    "Man Escapes Danger" by George, 8    251
Figure E16    "The Tiger Chases the Chick to Eat It" by Anna, 8    252
Figure E17    "Prey" by Sam, 13, Depressed    253
Figure E18    Comparing Strongly Negative Responses to the Draw-a-Story Task (Scored 1 Point) by Depressed, Normal, Learning-Disabled, Emotionally Disturbed, and Deaf Children, Adolescents, and Adults    254

# Preface

The main purpose of this book is to call attention to art procedures found useful in developing concepts of space, of sequential order, and of class or group of objects. Although concept formation is usually associated with language, it is also evident in the visual conventions of drawing.

The procedures were developed in studies of children with hearing impairments, language impairments, or learning disabilities. In the studies children improved significantly in the ability to represent concepts of space, order, and class, as measured both by tests developed in the studies and by tests adapted from experiments by Jean Piaget, Jerome Bruner or their associates. Although these investigators were concerned with typical rather than handicapped children, and with verbal rather than nonverbal communication, their observations about stages of cognitive development can be applied not only to what a child says but also to what he draws.

The studies also found that subtle cognitive skills seem to be relatively independent of communication disorders and verbal-analytical skills. Some handicapped children had higher scores than unimpaired children, and some highly intelligent adults did not do as well as the handicapped children in performing the tasks.

The second purpose of this book is to provide art techniques for evaluating cognitive and creative skills of children and adults who cannot communicate well verbally. The third purpose is to reconcile different points of view. Some art educators feel that using art for therapeutic purposes will interfere with learning in art. On the other hand, some art therapists feel that structuring art experience will inhibit spontaneity. In a study designed to develop cognitive skills, handicapped children developed art skills and expressiveness to a degree that was statistically significant, indicating that art experience can be educational and therapeutic concurrently, and that we do not have to sacrifice one developmental need for another.

Part One is concerned with the roles art can play in cognition, adjustment, and assessment. It is also concerned with the need to re-examine low expectations of intellectual and artistic ability, and to demonstrate that the handicapped can be truly gifted.

Part Two is concerned with art procedures found useful in remediating cognitive deficits and in identifying cognitive skills. These include the ability to associate and represent concepts through drawing from imagination, the ability to perceive and represent concepts of space through drawing from observation, and the ability to order sequentially through painting, modeling clay, and predictive drawing.

The book is illustrated with drawings and paintings produced in experimental art classes for handicapped children and adults. It is addressed to educators, therapists, psychologists and physicians.

# Acknowledgments

I want to thank the handicapped artists, children and adults, for making this endeavor possible. I am particularly indebted to the young man called "Charlie" and his family, whose courage, talent, and devotion to one another impelled and sustained the work reported here.

In addition, I would like to express my gratitude to those who evaluated the drawings and paintings produced in the experimental art classes: Mildred Fairchild, Ed.D., Emeritus Professor of Art, Teachers College, Columbia University, and Jane Field, Registered Art Therapist-painter; also, Marilyn Slapikas, Andrea Stein, and Ruth Weissmann, teachers of special education; and Laura D'Amico, Joann O'Brien, Martha Geller, Judy Itzler, Mary Simons, and Phyllis Wohlberg, graduate students at the College of New Rochelle.

I am also grateful to the art therapists and educators who made it possible to develop norms for the Silver Test by administering the test to handicapped and normal children. They include Doris Arrington, ATR, Thomas J. Bamrick, Jr., Janice Bell, Eldora Boeve, Paul Chaltas, Harriet Cohen, Sylvia Corwin, Marilyn Crawley-Shields, Joan Delany, Ena P. Ellwanger, Phyllis Frame, ATR, Lucrezia A. Fusco, Elizabeth Gayda, Lisa Irving Halprin, Marilyn Hawkins, Karen Hayes, Judith Itzler, ATR, David F. Johnson, Georgianna Khatib, Janeen Lewis, Carole McCarthy, Eileen McCormick, ATR, Deborah Mack, Nancy Margulies, Lauren Marks, Constance Naitove, ATR, Jo-Ann Lizio O'Brien, ATR, Norma Ott, Sr., Martha Otterstedt, Carol Paiken, Anah Pyte, Sr., Miriam Saumweber, ATR, Patricia Schachner, Fred Spinowitz, Timothy Sugrue, D. Wayne Van Tassell, Niru Dewan Terner, Ronald Topping, Robert Vislosky, ATR, Simon Willoughby-Booth, Phyllis Wohlberg, and Diane Young.

To Ed, Paul, and Jon

"The words or the language, as they are written or spoken, do not seem to play any role in my mechanism of thought. The psychical entities which seem to serve as elements in thought are . . . in my case, the visual and some of muscular type. Conventional words or other signs have to be sought for laboriously only in the second stage."

—*Albert Einstein*

# DEVELOPING COGNITIVE AND CREATIVE SKILLS THROUGH ART

# Part One

# The Role of Art

# Introduction

When children have handicaps that interfere with learning, we are often so preoccupied with their limitations that we lose sight of their strengths. Some skills can be developed in spite of impairments, such as teaching language-impaired children to read. We do not expect them to read as well as unimpaired children, and what is notable is not that they read particularly well but that they are able to read at all.

Other skills develop *because* of impairments, not in spite of them, and can equal and even excel those of any normal child. As Rene Dubos has observed, one of the most important laws of biology is that the many potentials of a cell usually become manifest only when it is compelled to use them. The many potentials of a handicapped child may also become manifest only when disabilities compel their use.

One such potential, often overlooked, is the ability to represent thoughts and feelings through visual forms. There is evidence that imagery is a basic instrument in thinking for some normal adults. For the child who has difficulty learning language, imagery may serve to bypass verbal weaknesses and capitalize on visual strengths. Another such potential is the ability to generalize from experiences, and to transfer learning from one situation to another.

Can handicapped children learn through art the concepts that are usually learned through talk? Can they express through drawings the thoughts and feelings they cannot put into words, and can their drawings provide useful clues to what they know and how they think or feel? Do they have as much aptitude for art as unimpaired children? Can educators use art to stimulate their cognitive or emotional growth without neglecting their creative growth? The answers to these questions may lie in special opportunities in art for educating children in general and handicapped children in particular.

The aim of Part One is to call attention to these opportunities and to demonstrate how art experience can answer the questions raised. The drawings and paintings on these pages were made by students, including some adults, in experimental art classes. Some were called learning-disabled. Some were called language- and hearing-impaired. Some had learning problems resulting primarily from hearing handi-

3

caps, and some were emotionally disturbed. All were impaired to a degree that prevented them from using language freely in reading, writing, talking, or understanding what was said. Regardless of their handicaps, some were also gifted. The children attended special schools. Because sign language was not allowed in the schools, pantomiming and drawing were used in the art classes when verbal communication failed.

# Chapter 1

# Cognition

Children who cannot learn language in the usual way are often deficient in intellectual functioning. Their education traditionally centers around language development. It is generally assumed that the cause of their deficiency is language retardation, but this may be misleading. Language is obviously related to thinking, but whether or not language is essential to thinking is open to question.

## NONVERBAL THINKING

There is considerable evidence in recent scientific literature that language and thought develop independently, that language follows rather than precedes logical thinking, and that, even though language expands and facilitates thought, high level thinking can and does proceed without it.

A recurrent theme in the writing of Jean Piaget is that logical thinking exists before the appearance of language, which occurs around the middle of the second year. By the beginning of the second year a child is capable of repeating and generalizing his actions. If he has learned to pull a blanket to reach a toy on top of it, he is capable of pulling the blanket to reach anything else. He can also generalize by using a stick to move a distant object or pulling a string to reach what is attached.

Furth reviewed over fifty empirical studies comparing performances of deaf and hearing populations on conceptual tasks involving both abstract and concrete material, as well as tasks involving memory and visual perception. He concluded that intellectual ability is largely independent of language. He also observed that learning language does not require high intelligence, since a four-year-old child can master language, even though some individuals deaf from birth do not acquire competence (Furth, 1966, pp. 51–54).

Sinclair-de Zwart, a linguist who originally thought that the operational level of children would reflect their linguistic level, performed two experiments to determine the relationships between these levels in children ages five to eight. She established two groups: conservers, who realized that when liquid was poured from one glass to a glass of another shape the quantity did not change; and nonconservers, who judged the quantity according to the appearance of the containers. In her first experiment she asked the children to describe simple objects. She found that the conservers kept in mind both objects at once while the nonconservers failed to do so. In her second experiment she taught the nonconservers to describe the objects in the same terms used by the conservers, then examined them to see whether this training had affected their development. In every case there was only minimal progress after linguistic training, and she concluded that language is not the source of logic, but is on the contrary structured by logic (Sinclair-de Zwart, 1969, p. 325). If so, the usual assumption of causal relationships may be reversed. It is usually assumed that improving a child's language will improve his thinking, but higher levels of thinking may be the cause as well as the consequence of improved language skills, and nonverbal procedures may cause levels of language to rise.

In the thinking of a normal child, the function of language is primarily to pin down his perceptions, organize his experiences, and understand and control his environment, according to Strauss and Kephart. By labeling his perceptions with a word, the hearing child can make them usable again and again. In addition, language opens up the whole field of vicarious experience. When he cannot obtain a desired result he can substitute words for the unsuccessful activity, and by symbolizing it, obtain it imaginatively without having to lift a finger, so to speak. Furthermore, by hearing about the experiences of other people he can obtain information that otherwise he would have to obtain by himself. He can compare himself with others, and use the experiences of others, without having to have the experiences himself (Strauss and Kephart, 1955, p. 91).

Can art symbols take over some of the functions of language symbols in the thinking of a language-impaired child? Like language symbols, art symbols are a way of labeling perceptions and imagining experiences. They can represent particular subjects or classes of subjects. For example, a painting of a man can represent the painter's father, or authority figures in general, or Man in the abstract, or all three, just as the word "man" can represent each or all of these ideas, depending on the verbal context. The child with inadequate language is handicapped in representing his thoughts effectively, but even though his capacity for language may be impaired, his capacity for symbolizing may be intact, and he may be able to represent his thoughts nonverbally by drawing them. Figures 1 and 2 are offered as examples.

"Frankenstein" (Figure 1) was painted by twelve-year-old Ralph, who had language and hearing impairments. Since he labeled his paint-

Figure 1.  "Frankenstein"

ing, he intended to represent a particular person, but Frankenstein could also be someone else in disguise, consciously or unconsciously. The lightning and Frankenstein's wound could also represent what Ralph would like to do to people in general, or perhaps to himself.

Symbols have meaning beyond their visible form. Art symbols may have many possible meanings simultaneously at different levels. Figure 2 was painted by a deaf young man of sixteen who did not want to talk about his painting. Although what he had in mind is not known, his painting is highly suggestive. It may represent a particular man or be a statement about Man as small, alone, and unprotected, but with arms upraised, perhaps defiant or asking for help.

Figure 2.   Man in the abstract?

Children too young to represent the subjects they have in mind sometimes talk as they scribble, using words to convey ideas they cannot draw. Some older children with communication disorders do the same. Dan, for example, explained his painting (Figure 3) as "the monkey got away from the bear and went into the building." Dan, age

Figure 3.   "The monkey got away from the bear and went into the building"

eleven, with an IQ of 65 (Nebraska Scale), was in a school for language-
and hearing-impaired children. He seemed to hear normally and speak
fluently, but was unable to read or to write from dictation, and his
visuo-motor coordination was poor.

While some language-impaired children seem retarded in the ability to represent their thoughts through drawings, others seem pre-
cocious. Fred, also age eleven, and in the same school, produced
Figure 4. With an IQ of 82 (Leiter Scale), Fred had receptive and
expressive language impairments, as well as hearing loss from menin-
gitis at the age of two. Fred said the face in the drawing was his
father's, the tree was himself, and the name on the tombstone was his
mother's. Since he had also written on the tombstone the numbers
"30" and "1972," a teacher, pointing backward over her shoulder,
asked him if his mother had died. Fred, pointing forward to the future,
shook his head, "No." Nothing further was volunteered or asked, and
we can only speculate about whether his drawing represented the fear
of her death or a wish for it.

## ORGANIZING AND REPRESENTING EXPERIENCES

It may be useful to try a new approach to evaluating the cognitive skills
of these children, and to start by defining cognition as Bruner has

Figure 4.  Mother's grave

explained it—a way of organizing the barrage of stimuli from the out-side world. We reduce the complexity of the barrage by constructing models, imaginary representations. We match a few milliseconds of new experience to a stored model, then predict what will happen next from the model. For example, we may glimpse a shape and a snatch of movement, then respond to the model we happen to match—night watchman, or burglar.

In other words, thought is carried out by representing reality vicariously and economically. As Bruner points out, we represent with the aid of "intellectual prosthetic devices," such as language, but there are pictorial devices as well. "It is still true that a thousand words scarcely exhaust the richness of a single image" (Bruner, 1966b, pp. 16–19).

A child's drawing is a pictorial device that can represent reality vicariously and economically, and thus reflect his thinking. The child with inadequate language is deprived of many opportunities to repre-sent his experiences. Without language he lacks our major device for constructing models of reality. This alone could account for cognitive deficiency. But if his visuo-spatial capacities are intact he may be able to construct visual models of reality, and represent his experiences nonverbally by drawing images of them.

## LEFT AND RIGHT HEMISPHERE THINKING

Language disorders are associated with damage to the left hemisphere of the brain while visuo-motor disorders are associated with damage to the right hemisphere. Lesions in the left hemisphere tend to affect ver-bal learning, while lesions in the right hemisphere tend to affect visuo-spatial learning.

The left hemisphere of the brain seems to be specialized not only for language, but also for analytical and sequential thinking. It is associated with concepts and intellect, science and mathematics, logic and history. With most adults, talking, writing, reading, and under-standing verbal messages are accomplished more effectively through the left hemisphere.

The right hemisphere of the brain seems to be specialized not only for spatial thinking and visuo-motor skills, but also for processing in-formation simultaneously or holistically. It is associated with intuition and creativity, art and metaphor, music, poetry and dance. With most adults, manipulating objects and recognizing faces and patterns are accomplished more effectively through the right hemisphere.

Although our society values more highly the verbal and analytical skills of left hemisphere thinking, we need and make use of both the thinking hemispheres. Physicists, for example, often use graphical methods to simplify complicated mathematical calculations.

In studies of children, left hemisphere specialization for language is present at least by five years of age, according to Witelson, but there is virtually no information concerning right hemisphere specialization for the processing of spatial information in childhood. (Her own recent studies have found evidence of right hemisphere specialization for processing spatial information in children as well as in adults (Witelson, 1976, p. 245)).

Witkin and his associates suggest that styles of thinking are related to individual patterns of adaptation, that preferred modes of thinking are established early in life, and that, for some, imagery is the preferred mode (Witkin, 1962, p. 375).

Arnheim observed that we use different modes in solving problems. For example, it is now 3:40 p.m. What time will it be in half an hour? One person translates the problem into arithmetical quantities $(40 + 30 = 70; 70 - 60 = 10)$. Another translates it into images, visualizing the face of a clock, with its minute hand advanced halfway around from 8 to 2 (Arnheim, 1969, p. 17).

## ESTABLISHING PATTERNS FOR LANGUAGE TO FOLLOW

Both hemispheres of the brain share much of their information through nerve fibers that cross over from one hemisphere to the other. Learned patterns and incoming information are relayed widely throughout the brain. According to Masland, large areas of the brain, called association areas, have no direct connection with incoming sensory channels, but serve as integrating centers to which information may be relayed. He postulates that events occurring in temporal relationship to each other interact, and that later experiences, involving only part of a total pattern, may activate the larger pattern because of previously established interactions. As he also postulates, "Every experience that we have, and all of the training and conditioning which occur throughout the lifetime, result in the establishment of activation patterns through which our sensations are interpreted and related to associated information and to the appropriate response" (Masland, 1969, p. 94).

If so, it may be that art experience can establish activation patterns for language to follow, or reinforce patterns set by language. Would drawing pictures enable a child to sustain thoughts he cannot verbalize or to associate them with past experiences, or would they trigger new associations? Can art procedures bypass language disorders and lead a child to the fundamental mathematical or logical ideas that are usually learned through language?

In search of answers, some Piagetian tasks were presented to ten language-impaired children in a pilot study. They were asked to predict the way water would look in a tilted bottle, the way a fishing line would look on a tilted pole, and the way a house would look on a steep mountain slope. They were invited to check their predictions with a bottle half-filled with water and a weighted string tied to a stick, then asked to draw pictures of someone fishing on a mountain. This task is described in detail in Chapter 9.

The most interesting response was made by Eric, age ten, with an IQ of 59 (Stanford-Binet), who had marked verbal deprivation. He had receptive and expressive impairments and a bilateral hearing loss of 30–40 dB. He lived with his mother, who was deaf, and his grandmother, who was hard of hearing. Their native language was not English.

In his first drawing (Figure 5) the water is not horizontal, the fishing lines are not vertical, and the fisherman seems about to slide down the hill. Nothing was said or done to call Eric's attention to these flaws.

The following week a different task was presented, but it did not

Figure 5.   Eric's first fisherman

interest Eric. Instead, he painted Figure 6, showing a vertical house on a horizontal surface.

The third week, Eric experimented with another new task, but the fourth week he returned to fishing on the mountain. In Figure 7 the fishing line is vertical and the fisherman stands squarely on the hill.

With time for another painting, Eric wrote "Peace" twice (Figure 8), adding in pencil with an arrow, "Eric did this."

In his fifth and final art class, Eric returned to the first task again (Figure 9). The fishing line is vertical, the fisherman stands upright on the hill, and for the first time the surface of the water appears horizontal. In this painting, however, Eric seemed less interested in representing the real world than in creating a fanciful world of his own. He painted the water in stripes of red, orange, blue, and yellow, the fisherman in blue, and the hill in black. His sun, larger than ever, has blue rays.

This series of paintings suggests that Eric learned the concepts of horizontality and verticality, that he learned them without instruction, and that he did so without learning words to label the concepts. Apparently he was intrigued by the tasks and solved them by returning again and again, spontaneously, to experiences he could not verbalize but could think about as he painted his pictures.

Figure 6.  Eric's "House by the river"

Figure 7.  Eric's second fisherman

## LEARNING NEW WORDS

Drawings can uncover the words that have special appeal to a particular child, and perhaps kindle a desire to learn them. In the experimental art classes, children often asked for the names of what they had drawn, or asked how to spell a particular word. I would say the words and write them on the blackboard, and often the children would incorporate them into their drawings.

To the extent that a child's drawings enable others to know which words label his experiences, he can be given the words he needs to integrate new information with what he already knows, or perhaps ask questions about the things that puzzle him.

Figure 10 was made by a sixteen-year-old in a class for slow learners in a school for the deaf. His classroom teacher happened to visit the art room just as he was drawing the barbed wire in the lower left corner. Knowing that this was a new word for him, she taught it to him then and there, placing his hand on her cheek as she said "barbed wire," while he repeated the words, again and again, until both were satisfied.

Figure 8.   Eric's "Peace"

Figure 9.   Eric's last fisherman

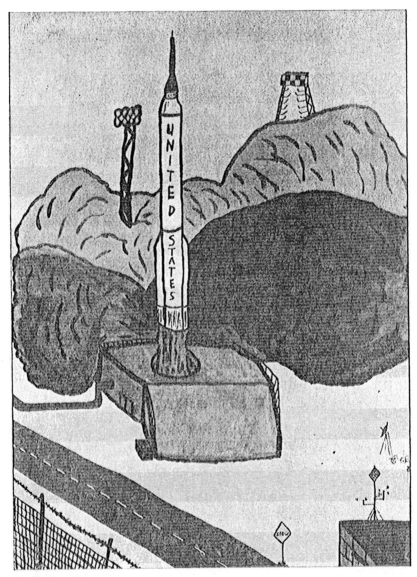

Figure 10.   Barbed wire

## ACTIVATING OR REINFORCING LANGUAGE

In the experimental art classes, language-impaired children often wrote messages on their drawings and paintings even though they were not asked to do so. In one program, fifty-eight of the 172 drawings and paintings produced included written messages. Perhaps this is because communication is a special problem for these children, and language is uppermost on their minds. Perhaps it is because we all want a name to go with a familiar tune or face, and for these children it may be particularly gratifying to be able to label experiences.

This natural inclination to associate drawing with language can provide unique opportunities to make use of words learned previously and all but forgotten. Figure 11 was made by an eleven-year-old who had very little intelligible speech and relied heavily on gestures. He had receptive language impairment, a hearing loss of 100 dB in his better ear, an IQ estimated at 74, and a "short attention span." He worked on this drawing for 50 minutes and then began talking about it. I could not understand him but his classroom teacher did and began to write his comments on his picture: "It is poison. The bees are afraid. He is killing the bees. He is going to run for his horse. The rabbit is looking all around at everything." When she had finished writing, he went over her penciled writing carefully with a black pen.

Figure 12 was made by a thirteen-year-old whose greatest difficulties were recalling information, integrating new information with information previously learned, and fixing his attention for more than five minutes. He had multiple handicaps, including disorders of the central nervous system, profound hearing loss, and cardiac disorders requiring frequent hospitalizations. He, too, had very little speech, and his class-

Figure 11.   "He is killing the bees"

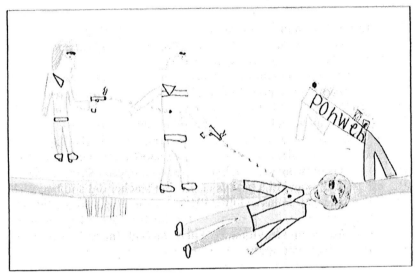

Figure 12.   "Pohweh"

room teacher was delighted to find that he know the word "power," even though he spelled it phonetically.

The boats heading for disaster (Figure 13) were made by an eight-year-old described as "hyperactive and severely aphasic." His performance score on the WISC Scale was 117; his verbal score, 92. Asked why it was "the end," he replied, "because I finished."

"$90,000 I have more money" (Figure 14) was painted by a twelve-year-old with language and hearing impairments and an IQ estimated to be normal.


## TRANSFER OF LEARNING

One goal in education is the transfer of learning, to give students understanding beyond what is taught directly so that they can use their knowledge elsewhere.

Transfer of learning has been explained in terms of survival value. If an organism is prevented from reaching its norm or goal in the ordinary way, it will be resourceful and try another way. "The end rather than the means seems to be the important thing" (Sinnott, 1961, p. 33).

If so, we can expect a handicapped child to want to develop his skills, and if disabilities prevent him from developing in the ordinary way, we can expect him to try to find alternatives. He may try drawing to help himself learn.

Learning has been defined as using new information appropriately in a new situation, in one's own way, for one's own purposes (Stratemeyer, 1957, p. 80). To the extent that a child spontaneously

Figure 13.   "The End"

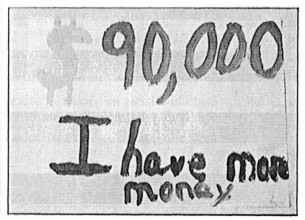

Figure 14.   "$90,000 I have more money"

draws a picture about something he has learned elsewhere, he is using that information in his own way for his own purposes and applying it appropriately in a new situation. Particularly for the child deficient in language skills, drawing and painting pictures about his experiences can serve to integrate new information and demonstrate what has been learned. To the extent that art experience provides this new situation, it can provide an opportunity for transfer of learning. In the experimental art classes, children were often free to work in their own ways for

Figure 15.   "Sad or Happy"

their own purposes. Figure 15 was made by Carmen, age twelve, in a school for language- and hearing-impaired children. By chance, her classroom teacher saw her drawing and asked if I had suggested the topic. (I had not.) She said that earlier in the day she had been trying to teach Carmen about alternatives and opposites.

In Figure 16, note the small airplane in the upper left. This drawing also came as a surprise to a teacher who said she had been trying to teach "near" and "far." The drawing was made by the multiply handicapped child who drew "Pohweh" (Figure 11).

### IMAGINARY PLAY

It is often said that the deaf child lacks imagination, which is fundamental in abstract thinking. It may be more accurate to say that he

Figure 16.   Near and far

lacks opportunities to put his imagination to work. The child who is deficient in language is severely restricted in imaginary play, in contrast to the hearing child, who can talk about being a cowboy or a lion as well as listen to stories.

When a child does not or cannot talk fluently about imaginary experiences, he may spontaneously engage in imaginary play while drawing and thereby possibly sustain or prolong the imaginary play.

The child who drew the cops and robbers fantasy about a helicopter chase (Figure 17) was a twelve-year-old deaf child. Although he has written an explanation ("it was stollen [sic] car/the helicopter shoot car pop"), it does not tell his story very well.

The painting of the walking bug (Figure 18) was made by Robert, another deaf child, age twelve.

Robert painted Figure 19 after watching a movie about Eddie Cantor, whose figure can be seen halfway up the right side and whose eye is on the bottom of the painting. Robert also painted Figure 20.

## ABSTRACT THINKING

If a child who cannot talk about a hypothetical event were to draw a picture of an event that deals with possibilities, or that classifies

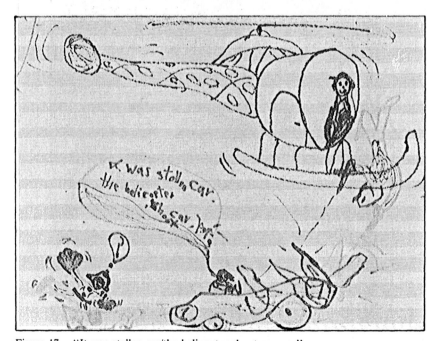

Figure 17.    "It was stollen car/the helicopter shoot car pop"

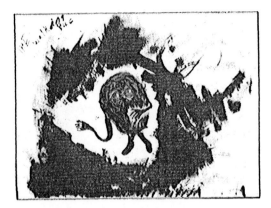

Figure 18.   "The Walking Bug"

Figure 19.   Eddie Cantor

Figure 20.  "Ghostman"

according to abstract principles, or that discerns similarities within differences, then he would be using an ability to grasp abstract ideas, and
there would be evidence of his ability to deal with abstract concepts.

The drawing of children playing (Figure 21) was made by a deaf
girl, age eleven, who selected activities suitable for a particular location at a particular time of year, and drew them as a verbal child might
have written a list. This seems to be a picture of a hypothetical event in
which the various activities have elements in common.

The painting of a skull and bones (Figure 22) was made by a
twelve-year-old boy who seems to be making the wry observation that
people say one thing, but mean another—an abstract idea, a statement
of affection meaning the absence of affection. The words deny the
symbols for poison, but (insincere) they reinforce the warning of the
image. Richard was below average academically and very poor in language skills for a deaf child his age (he asked for help with the spelling),
but he is evidently bright. If his language ability was used to judge his
intelligence, it might appear otherwise.

The painting of "Chinese girl in China and Hawaiian girl in
Hawaii" was made by Ira, age nine and deaf (Figure 23). Apparently
he notices differences within similarities, and vice versa.

Figure 21.   Children playing

Figure 22.   "I love you children"

Figure 23.  "Chinese Girl in China and Hawaiian Girl in Hawaii"

## RECALL

We remember details more easily when we organize them into structured forms such as sentences, averages, or mathematical formulas. It is easier, for example, to recall the words in a sentence than to recall those same words when seen at random on a list. Like a sentence, a drawing or painting is a structured form, and it too can help preserve what might otherwise vanish.

A child cannot portray an object until he recalls what it looks like, and he cannot make it recognizable to others until he clarifies impressions and evaluates his work. He makes repeated decisions in the effort to embody his ideas and communicate them to others, selecting tools and materials, revising and clarifying, continuing to guess and to experiment until he decides that his work is finished.

If an inarticulate child were skilled in the visual arts, his pictures could give him not only a means of pinning down and organizing his thoughts, but also a way to structure them.

When Ira first drew the "Rusty Nosed Boat" (Figure 24), he did not identify the fish, but he had given his boat its remarkable name. He

Figure 24. "Rusty Nosed Boat"

took this drawing home with him, and when he returned it some weeks later, for an exhibition, the names of the fish had been added. Ira's knowledge about dolphins, as distinguished from eels, swordfish, and sharks, is evident without the labels. By putting his knowledge into

Figure 25. "Brances"

concrete form, either writing or drawing, he had to recall and to associate what he had learned previously.

Many of the drawings and paintings produced in the experimental art classes seemed inspired by a desire to think about and pass along some information. Figure 25 is Lisa's message about "brances" [sic] —how much they cost, how long they must be worn, and how they look both off and on the teeth.

# Chapter 2

# Adjustment

Drawing and painting, like dreams and daydreams, can tap the unconscious—condensing, symbolizing, and expressing experiences. Language is the usual medium of psychotherapy, and talk about drawings is the usual medium of art therapy, but art experience can be healing in itself without talk, if need be, by fulfilling wishes vicariously, ventilating feelings, reducing isolation, and providing opportunities to cope with problems and to adjust to disappointments.

## FULFILLING WISHES VICARIOUSLY

One way that art experience can be therapeutic is through fantasied gratification. Daydreams or dreams that represent wishes as fulfilled actually do provide partial gratification, according to the psychiatrist Charles Brenner. A thirsty dreamer, dreaming of quenching his thirst, goes on sleeping (Brenner, 1974, p. 66).

Some children seem to use their drawings to obtain in imagination what they cannot obtain in real life. The drawings made by Kenneth (Figures 26 and 27) seem to have served this purpose. Kenneth, age fourteen, was conspicuously small for his age, but once, when angry, he picked up and threw a school desk. He had receptive and expressive language impairment, bilateral hearing loss, and motor handicaps suggesting cerebral palsy. In his drawings, motorcycles, flags, and military uniforms were recurrent themes. In Figure 26 he has a glamorous companion. In Figure 27 he rides alone. His drawings seem to have served the function of giving him, vicariously, power and strength.

To the extent that art experiences can enable a child to identify with heroes, it can diminish the energy of repressed wishes, enhance ego strength, and provide gratification.

## TESTING REALITY

Children try to experience a broad range of events vicariously. The usual procedure, according to Bruner, is to substitute words and sentences in place of events in order to have a trial run on reality (Bruner 1966a, p. 58).

Figure 26.   Kenneth and friend on motorcycle

Language-impaired children sometimes use drawings in place of words to have trial runs of their own. The scene in the graveyard, mourning the death of a dog (Figure 28), was made by the child who dictated his fantasy about killing the bees (Figure 11).

The girl who had more than $90,000 (Figure 14) also had fantasies about romance. In her first drawing, the boy rescues the girl in the water, while back on the beach, unaware, others are having a picnic (Figure 29).

In the girl's next drawing, the boy and girl sail away under a cloudless sky. John declares his love and Jackie replies, "Oh thank you" (Figure 30).

Figure 27.   Kenneth and motorcycle, #2

Figure 28.   Mourning the death of a dog

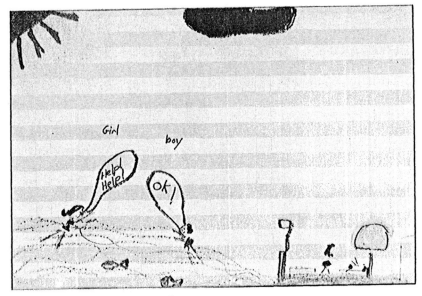

Figure 29.   "Help! Help!"/"O.K."

Figure 30.   "I love you"/"Oh Thank You"

## EXPRESSING UNACCEPTABLE
## FEELINGS IN AN ACCEPTABLE WAY

According to Brenner, repressing unwanted thoughts and feelings makes them unconscious, and each repression diminishes ego strength, since it requires an expenditure of energy to maintain the repression and to keep thoughts under control (Brenner, 1974, p. 81). To the extent that art experience can help children project anger or fear indirectly through symbols, it can help them express unwanted feelings. Symbols do not state directly, as Jung observed. They well up from the unconscious and are vague, unknown, never fully explained. Signs are linked to conscious thought and simply denote the objects to which they are assigned. Symbols express indirectly by means of metaphor (Jung, 1974, p. 43).

Drawings can enable a child to release energy indirectly rather than repress unwanted feelings or act them out. In Figure 31, Michael, age eleven, used the metaphor of slaying a dragon.

In Figure 32 a murder is taking place. The victim is being shot and thrown overboard at the same time, while from above him on the ship a cannonball is aimed at the man who shoots.

In Figure 33, done by a fourteen-year-old, sticks of dynamite are tied to a tough sergeant, and the fuse is lit. One little soldier salutes the sergeant.

In Figure 34, Michael, age eleven, seems to have symbolized anger itself. He was always cheerful in the art class, and I had no idea

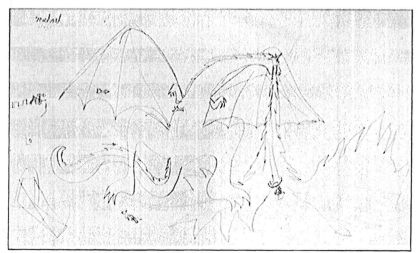

Figure 31.    Slaying a dragon

Figure 32.   Man overboard

Figure 33.   Dynamiting a sergeant

Figure 34.  Michael's angry man

of his behavior elsewhere until I read school records that described him hitting children without apparent provocation, being rude to adults indiscriminately, and recently sticking the point of a pencil into his finger.

Some children depicted scenes of violence almost as soon as they realized they could draw what they wished. Mark liked to paint traffic accidents (Figures 35 and 36).

## OBTAINING RELIEF FROM TENSION

Children who have difficulty verbalizing anger have difficulty ventilating frustrations, and, without some expression, anger can turn into

Figure 35.   Mark's car crash, #1

Figure 36.   Mark's car crash, #2

Figure 37.   Larry's man and woman

rage. Like the tragic dramas of ancient Greece, drawing and painting
can serve as catharsis, restoring inner harmony and balance.

Some children in the experimental classes followed up angry
drawings with drawings that seemed to reverse the action. In Figure
37, for example, Larry made a pencil drawing of a man and woman,
then painted wounds on their faces, and finally painted stitches on their
wounds. If he had repressed his anger at the people he represented, he
might have turned it upon himself. If he had expressed his anger directly, he might have been punished. The fact that he undid the damage
suggests that his anger had been spent, at least for a while.

Otto explained his drawing (Figure 38) as follows: "The lady got a
pencil in her eye. It is covered with tape. The man is a priest. He was
smoking a cigarette which got smashed." Making this picture apparently provided some relief: immediately afterward he depicted a
smiling astronaut climbing out of a spaceship following a splashdown
(Figure 39).

Giving form to feelings does not necessarily relieve tension.
Underlying problems remain. Using the same symbols repeatedly may
indicate that the problems are deep-seated and unresolved. Otto drew
people with eyepatches in two other paintings (Figures 40 and 41).

Figure 38.   "The lady got a pencil in her eye . . ."

Figure 39.   Splashdown of a smiling astronaut

## SELF-MONITORING

Comparing our thoughts and feelings with the thoughts and feelings of others is a continual activity, important in regulating behavior and in maintaining emotional stability. Since language usually plays a major role in self-monitoring, the child who has difficulty understanding what is said, or making himself understood, has difficulty in monitoring himself. To the extent that art experience can enable a child to com-

Figure 40.  Man with eyepatch

pare himself with others, and find himself adequate, it can help him control his behavior and maintain emotional balance.

John, a deaf child, age nine, was described by his teacher as average in intelligence, below average in self-esteem, and very poor in social attitudes, with much difficulty in relating to children and adults. In the art class he did not join in social exchanges. He was usually preoccupied with drawing, and with eating candy bars, which he did not offer to share.

He worked on his drawing of a farm (Figure 42) for ninety minutes. When he had finished, he rapped on the table for attention, and held his drawing up for all to see. He pointed to the cat about to land on the dog and acted out the impending fight. This behavior suggests that he used his drawing to elicit the approval of his classmates, and to assure himself that he deserved their admiration and respect.

## PERSONAL INVOLVEMENT

Painting is sometimes thought of as withdrawing into a private world, but it can also be an act of involvement, engaging the painter in at least three kinds of relationships. First, he relates himself to the viewer. Child or adult, he usually paints with the expectation that his painting will be seen and understood.

Second, the painter relates pictorial elements—colors, forms, and subjects, if any. He does not need green paint, for example, in order to

Figure 41.   Woman with eyepatch

represent grass. He can suggest grass with yellow or blue, depending on neighboring colors. He can even use black and white. If he is very young, he makes his more important subjects larger regardless of their actual size. Even if he is not young, but can allow his feelings to predominate, he may also relate pictorial elements symbolically.

Third, the painter relates to his subjects by identifying with them. In ancient China the painter was taught to lose himself in what he portrayed, to imagine himself to be a pine branch, for example, in order to capture the essential quality of pines. Similarly, the African sculptor and the contemporary expressionist try to go beyond physical appearance to essence. Their works of art not only represent ideas, they *are* the ideas.

Figure 42.    Farm scene, cat about to land on dog

Figure 43.    Grandmother in coffin, self in pool

In the visual arts, subjectivity is highly esteemed. The works of Picasso or Rouault can be identified at a glance, but the works of a distinguished scientist can rarely be identified by his expressive style. It is the nature of art experience to invite subjectivity, as it is the nature of science to be objective at all costs.

Children identify with their subjects spontaneously (if they are free to choose their subjects themselves). In one of the classes a little girl often drew flying birds. Each time, just before drawing them, she made little flying gestures with her shoulders, elbows, and wrists. The ten-year-old who drew Figure 43 used gestures and two words to convey a message—she was in the swimming pool and her grandmother was in the coffin.

The drawing of the burglar robbing the safe (Figure 44) was made by a sixteen-year-old whose only relative, his grandmother, was terminally ill. Like the safe, his own safety seems threatened.

## EXPERIENCING CONTROL OVER PEOPLE AND EVENTS

The child who is inarticulate has difficulty persuading others or even letting his wishes be known, but as a painter he can be powerful. He can punish villains and reward heroes, change painful experiences into pleasant ones, and alter the appearance of objects at will.

Figure 44.   Robbing the safe

The painting of the spook (Figure 45), by ten-year-old Lisa, seems to be an attempt at control by altering an actual experience—riding through a tunnel in an amusement park and suddenly arriving at a frightening tableau. The small figure at the bottom is herself, saying, "Help me." In putting her spook behind bars, she changed a frightening situation into a safe one.

The drawing titled "A girl or boy in the spring?" (Figure 46) was made by a thirteen-year-old with language and hearing impairments. I overheard her classroom teacher asking her if she had ever seen a tree trunk that color, and, if not, why on earth had she used an *orange* crayon. In coloring the tree trunk orange she was imposing her will on the world, and with the boy saying, "Jean where Jean/very sad," was perhaps improving on reality with a little romance.

## TRANSFER OF BEHAVIOR

The physiological basis for transfer lies in the adaptability of our nervous systems. A variety of stimuli can provoke us to make a particular response, and we can achieve a particular goal through a variety of means, as ethologist S. A. Barnett has pointed out. We can identify a melody regardless of the key in which it is played or the musical instrument that produces it. We recognize certain patterns as

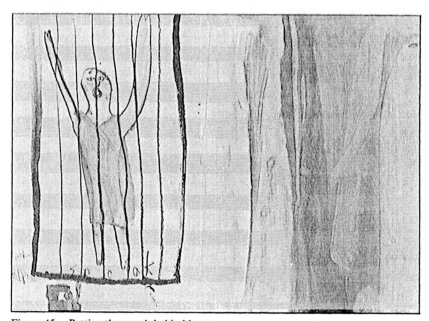

Figure 45.   Putting the spook behind bars

Figure 46.   "A girl or boy in the spring?"

"the same"—auditory or visual or tactile—because they have relationships in common. We also generalize in response. A man who has
learned to write with one hand can learn to write with the other, or
even with his foot. This tolerance of variation in recognizing stimuli

Figure 47.   Eugene's family portrait

and responding to them develops with experience, and one of the most remarkable facts about it is that learning to do one task improves our skills at other, similar tasks (Barnett, pp. 11–12). We are also apt to generalize the effects of an unpleasant experience, or a pleasant one, to all the surrounding circumstances (Barnett, 1967, p. 176).

Can the gratifications in art experience, and the energy generated, carry over to other school situations? Eugene's behavior seems to show a transfer of attitudes that developed in the art class and subsequently became evident in his home classroom. He was a ten-year-old whose diagnosis was obscured by multiple emotional problems. He was thought to be deaf, but might have been language- or learning-impaired. Although his IQ score on the Otis scale was 89, a psychological report found average or above average intelligence, with high potential. It described him as pugnacious, inclined to withdraw when thwarted, and unable to work persistently. His teacher said he had little concept of right or wrong. The day before the art program began, his classmates went to the zoo, but Eugene had to remain in school because his behavior was so unpredictable. He lived with his mother and three siblings, his father having disappeared.

Figure 48.   Eugene's devil

Figure 49. Eugene's butterfly

In our first meeting I asked him to show me who lived in his house with him, but I was unable to make him understand my request. I made a quick sketch of my own family, pointing out myself. He produced Figure 47. Where his father might be expected to stand beside his mother, there is, instead, a picture on the wall.

In our third meeting he painted the devil (Figure 48). Our room happened to have a glass-paneled door and was directly across the hall from Eugene's classroom. Furthermore, our meetings ended just as lunch time began. His classmates formed a line in the hall outside, admired his devil extravagantly, and escorted him away to lunch in triumph.

In our fourth meeting he painted the butterfly (Figure 49). When his teacher saw it, she mentioned that he had found a small dead moth in the classroom just before the art period began, and had been excited by the discovery.

In our fifth meeting he painted the group of horses galloping in a paddock (Figure 50), led by Black Beauty. (Eugene is black.)

Figure 50.   Eugene's Black Beauty as leader

In our seventh meeting a classmate, arm around Eugene, asked if he might accompany Eugene to the art class, and his teacher gave her consent. His painting was an abject imitation of Eugene's painting, step by step.

With our eighth meeting the art program ended, and Eugene's teacher completed the following questionnaire:

Have you noticed any changes in Eugene's behavior during the past few months? _yes_

In relation to other children: _Eugene still fights easily but is showing some improvement in helping th. other children with art_

In classroom attitudes: _he seems more attentive, and is showing slight improvement in being a better sport_

Self-confidence: _he is especially proud of his art work and there is some carry over of this confidence_

Expressiveness: _definite improvement in ability to complete sentences (speaking)_

Other: _Eugene has a very difficult home situation and is hurt by neglect of the father. The special attention he gets for his talent is aiding slightly this lack of attention at home_

These modest changes in behavior suggest that Eugene's accomplishments in art had given him new status among his peers, and that he had monitored himself through his paintings. At any rate, he was put in charge of class lines, responsible for keeping his classmates in orderly rows. Since reward in learning is said to stimulate the expenditure of energy in further learning, it may be that Eugene's experiences in art helped motivate him to seek attention through approval rather than disapproval. It may also be that an improvement in self-image, developed through art, had transferred to other school situations.

This experience with Eugene impressed me with the need for objective instruments for assessing changes in behavior that might result from art experience. Even though drawings and paintings are essentially subjective, they have elements that can be quantified.

# Chapter 3

# Assessment

Communication is a problem not only for those persons who have language disorders, but also for those who work with them. It is sometimes difficult to know if a test of intelligence is testing anything more than the ability to understand directions. To illustrate, an attempt to match experimental and control children in the program for children with language and hearing impairments, described in Chapter 12, involved a painstaking search through records and produced a mass of confusing data. Twelve children had been tested with the WISC scale, receiving IQ scores between 72 and 106. The child who received the highest score, 106, nevertheless received the low score of 66 on the Stanford-Binet test. A child who was scored 77 on the Stanford-Binet scale received a score of 96 for performance and 65 for verbal IQ on the WISC scale. Two children could not be scored. The Stanford-Binet test had been used with six other children, three of whom were scored between 50 and 70, and three were unscored. Other tests employed included the Peabody, Leiter, Merrill-Palmer, Hiskey, Bender-Gestalt, Goodenough, and Arthur Point Scale. Many were unscored for reasons such as "did not respond" or "verbal communication nil." In addition, some children had multiple disabilities, with cerebral palsy a frequent diagnosis. After reviewing the data, we decided to use a preliminary tentative match based on sex, age, class assignment, and diagnosis as expressive or receptive (or both) language impairment.

Studies of deaf populations have produced contradictory results and interpretations. Some studies have found deaf children less intelligent than hearing children. Some studies have found deaf children to have normal intelligence with difficulty in abstract thinking, and some studies have found them to have normal intelligence and normal ability to think abstractly with the same broad range in ability that is found in hearing populations.

Even for the hearing in a literate society, verbal language is often inadequate. We communicate without it and in spite of it, like the hostess who urges her guests to stay and then yawns. We read facial expressions and posture, and when they seem to contradict what is said we tend to rely on the nonverbal message. The visual arts have

Figure 51.  Terry's family portrait, tree isolating self

Figure 52.  Tree isolating girl

been relied on throughout history to communicate across languages and cultures, across distance and time. Even without subject matter, art forms can be meaningful, and some meanings are easier to convey through images than through words. A caricature or a captionless cartoon can be eloquent.

Children draw people, animals, trees, and even houses in much the same way all over the world. They draw before they can write, and they associate their drawings with thought even before they can draw anything recognizable. They also associate their drawings with feelings, distorting subjects symbolically and providing clues that might be inaccessible otherwise.

## CLUES TO PERCEPTION OF SELF AND OTHERS

Some inarticulate children are eloquent in drawing even when they lack artistic skill. Terry, for example, age fourteen, deaf, and described by her teacher as below average in academic achievement, motivation, and social attitudes, drew a family portrait (Figure 51). She drew her mother, father, and sister, and then added herself at the right edge of her paper, isolated by a tree and much smaller than the others, even though she was at least 5'6" tall.

Figure 53.  Maureen's family portrait

Terry seems to see herself as separated in some way from her family, and in the light of her teacher's evaluation there is reason to suppose that Terry's sense of alienation carries over to her life at school. Her teacher's impatience comes through in her words:

> Though still very obstinate, she will attempt to do her assignments . . . She now realizes that "homework" must be done . . . She occasionally contributes orally to class discussions . . . She now realizes that there are class duties or responsibilities and she usually accepts her job . . . She has shown a slight improvement in her attitude toward adults and their requests.

It is interesting to note that Terry often used the tree as a metaphor or symbol of isolation. In Figure 46 the tree isolated a boy reaching

Figure 54.   Robert's family portrait

toward a girl on the other side of it and saying, "Jean where Jean/very sad." In Figure 52 the tree isolates a girl, wearing a hat, who may be waving goodbye.

In Figure 53 Maureen separates herself from other members of her family with a red and yellow flame-like shape.

Robert, on the other hand, uses a line (Figure 54).

Lucy does not isolate herself symbolically, and seems to have a higher opinion of herself, since she is the tallest and largest in her family group (upper right). Even so, the group seems to have been composed without her. She is the only one without arms and legs (Figure 55).

## CLUES TO INTERESTS AND CONCERNS

The two drawings of buildings on fire (Figures 56 and 57) were made by Ben, age fourteen. In the first drawing he is saying, "Daddy my house is on frie [sic]/help me," and Daddy replies, "Don't cry/pull the fyre alarm box."

In his second drawing Ben calls for help again, and Daddy replies, "I'm coming."

Ben hears and understands, but has expressive language impairment and poor motor coordination. His IQ on the Stanford-Binet scale is 70. He has no friends, is very shy, polite, and withdrawn. When his

Figure 55.  Lucy's family portrait

Figure 56.   "Daddy my house is on Frie/Help me"

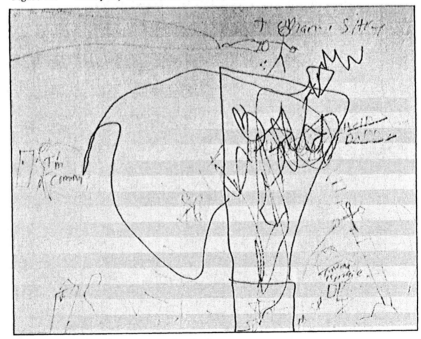

Figure 57.   "Help Daddy"/"I'm Coming"

parents were divorced he went to live with his mother. Although these drawings were shown to the school's consultant psychiatrist, they were not taken seriously until Ben was found walking in a traffic lane on a city bridge.

The painting of a moon base (Figure 58) was made by Billy, age sixteen, several years before the moon landings actually took place. Although his IQ was 157 (Arthur Point Scale), he was in a class for slow learners in a school for the deaf. He was among the weakest readers in his class, very poor in lip reading, and poor in writing as well. His teachers described him as easily bored and not one for routine. His tolerance for frustration was low, and when faced with difficulty he tended to withdraw.

Several weeks after the art program ended, an artist's conception of a moon base appeared in a newspaper (Figure 59). The landscape, spaceships, and uniforms closely resemble those in Billy's painting. Since he had no notes, he must somehow have acquired technical information. Or else, if he had seen the photograph before, he must have had an ability to recall details, an ability as unexpected as any technical knowledge. In either event, Billy's teacher was surprised by his interest in space flight. With these clues to a vocabulary having particular meaning for him, she might possibly build a desire for language that could close the gap between his low educational achievement and high intellectual endowment.

Figure 58.   Moon base by Billy

Figure 59.  Moon base by newspaper artist

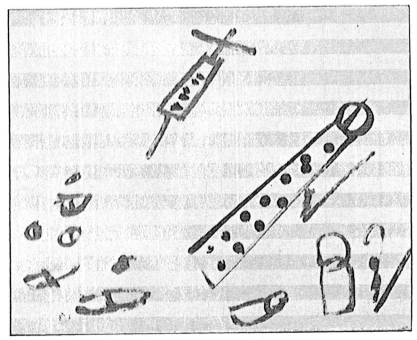

Figure 60.  Hypodermic needle and other drug equipment

Another drawing that provided clues to unexpected knowledge is the drawing of a hypodermic needle and other equipment associated with drugs (Figure 60). No one had been previously aware that this child knew so much about drugs.

Another drawing that revealed a special interest was made by Stewart. In his first class he asked what he should paint. The answer was, "Paint whatever you like." The result was Figure 61, "Pancakes on a plate with butter."

## CLUES TO ASSESSING A CHILD'S DEVELOPMENT

A drawing titled "Atomic Uses?" (Figure 62) was a spontaneous drawing that seems to reveal understanding of the abstract issues involved in the use of atomic power. Beneath the word "you," under the large question mark, is a sign with arrows pointing left and right. The left side, labeled "war," points to a group of armaments; the right side, labeled "peace," points to hospital and power plants. Translated into words it might read, "Will atomic power be used for war or for peace? It's up to you."

This drawing was the work of Ernest, age seventeen, who attended a school for the deaf. He was a good student, with an IQ of 128,

Figure 61.   "Pancakes on a Plate with Butter"

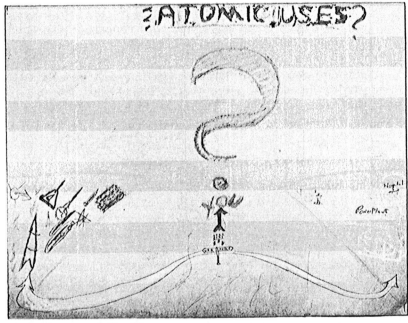

Figure 62.   "Atomic Uses?"

and had been saving money from a paper route in order to go to college.

By way of contrast, Figure 63 was made by a twelve-year-old girl in a school for language- and hearing-impaired children. She could hear and speak with no evidence of difficulty, but had organic disorders of the central nervous system. She painted this picture in response to

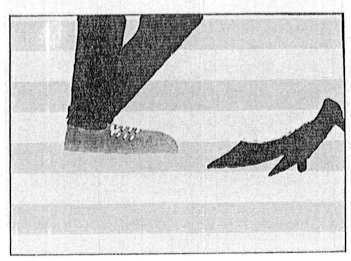

Figure 63.   "What no one else knows"

my suggestion—draw something that you know and no one else knows. This seems to be an unusually literal response.

## CLUES TO CHANGES

A sequence of drawings and paintings by Michael, age nine, showed changes that paralleled his increasing effort to make contact with others. With a diagnosis of "chronic brain syndrome and motor and auditory aphasia," he was above average in intelligence, but below average in self-esteem, according to his teacher, and painfully shy. He usually drew people without hands or fingers, as in his family portrait (Figure 64). Although the members of his family stretch out their arms, only two of them touch.

Michael continued to draw people without hands or fingers until our tenth meeting, when he made a nonobjective painting, stabbing and scrubbing furiously with his brush (Figure 65).

After that, he painted the witch with fingers (Figure 66), and then the birds with claws (Figure 67), and, in our last meeting, "Play ball" and the nonobjective painting (Figures 68 and 69).

Figure 64.  Michael's family portrait

Figure 65. Michael's abstract painting

Figure 66. Michael's witch with fingers

Figure 67. Michael's birds with claws

Figure 68. Michael's "Play ball"

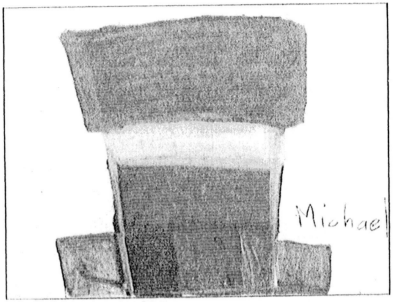

Figure 69.   Michael's last painting

# Chapter 4

# Expectations

We tend to have low expectations of handicapped children. We often equate language with intelligence, and expect that an inarticulate child will lack intelligence as well as other abilities.

Few expect the deaf to have an interest in art. When planning the project described in Chapter 5, I was advised by a vocational specialist that I would have difficulty finding deaf students willing to attend art classes. Another warned that those who enrolled would ask to be paid for their trouble. The classes were filled from the beginning, however, and there was a waiting list thoughout the program. With hindsight, it is not surprising that an art class for deaf students would have wide appeal. Deafness is isolating, and art can be a way of sharing experiences without the need for talk.

Few look for ability in the visual arts among the deaf. In drafting the project proposal I was asked to delete this sentence: "Students who show talent will be encouraged to apply to art schools for vocational training in industrial design, commercial art, or fine arts." Administrators of the sponsoring agency saw some merit in art as a hobby, but not in art as a possible vocation. As it turned out, three of the children in the program are now in art schools, and two of the adults have had solo shows.

When art educators were asked to be on the panel of twenty judges to evaluate.artwork produced in the project classes, two art supervisors declined. The reason, they wrote, was that it was unfair to deaf children to compare their paintings with the work of hearing children.

Parents of six of the children who enrolled in the project classes had tried previously to enroll their children in art classes, but only one child had been accepted. We tried to find art classes for the children when the project ended, but, although we approached twenty-three art programs for children, no classes were found for five of the eight deaf children. As for teenagers, the director of a museum art school said he would not admit them unless their mothers stayed with them in the art class. And the mother of one of the teenagers, when she saw his work on exhibition, said, "Don't tell me *you* did that. You *couldn't* do that. Your teacher must have done it for you."

Unfortunately, expectations can affect the evidence of aptitude. Creative ability is often repressed, as Torrance has found. Highly creative children conceal their ability when they fear rejection or failure (Torrance, 1962, p. 126). Expectations can also be self-fulfilling. This has been demonstrated in a study in which eighteen teachers were told that certain children in their classes had unusually high potential for intellectual gains. The "unusual" children had actually been chosen at random. Eight months later, however, all the children were tested again, and this time the so-called unusual children actually did show statistically significant greater gains in IQ (Rosenthal and Jacobson, 1968).

## MIGUEL

What might we expect from a deaf child, age eleven, who produced Figures 70, 71, and 72 in his first three art periods? Miguel worked very slowly and showed little evidence of aptitude for art.

Figure 70.   Miguel's first drawing

Figure 71.   Miguel's second drawing

Figure 72.   Miguel's third drawing

In our fourth meeting, however, he worked quickly, covering the 18 × 24″ paper with colors he mixed himself: grey for the background, brown for the hair, and tan for the face (Figure 73).

In our fifth meeting he started Figure 74, and finished it the following week.

The great difference in ability between Miguel's first drawings and his last one, produced a few weeks later, suggests that a child who is outwardly dull and submissive may be inwardly sensitive and independent.

## PAUL

What might we expect from a ten-year-old with a short attention span, an IQ estimated at 62, receptive and expressive language disorders, and peripheral hearing loss? As his teacher described Paul, "He wants to achieve and tries very hard, but is very easily discouraged. At times he is lazy and will copy rather than think for himself." She also found him below average for a deaf child in academic achievement, language, memory, and self-confidence.

In Figure 75, Paul mixed subtle colors—mauve, sienna, pink, and pale yellow—from poster paints in the three primary colors and black and white. He worked so intently that when a classmate tried to attract his attention he waved her away without looking up. His classroom teacher was so impressed that she allowed him to stay on in the art room until he lost interest. He worked steadily for ninety minutes.

Figure 73.   Painting produced in Miguel's fourth class

## DAVID

What might we expect from a sixteen-year-old whose parents charged that he was an unmanageable delinquent and asked that he be placed away from home? David had been referred to a school for the deaf by a probation officer, who reported that his parents appeared quite rejecting. "One cannot help but discredit the allegation of a boy who is very short, about 5′ tall, hitting his father, who is almost 6′ tall and powerfully built."

In his school, David resented being placed in a class of younger children who were at his academic level. His IQ score was 120 (Arthur Point Scale). He was often belligerent, and I was told to expect disturbances in the class. He was consistently gentle and eager in the art

Figure 74.  Painting produced in Miguel's fifth and sixth classes

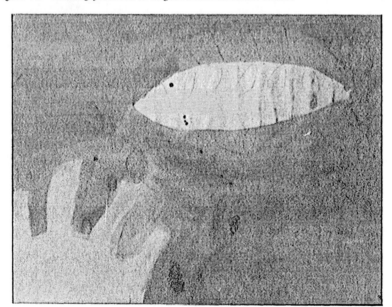

Figure 75.  Paul's painting

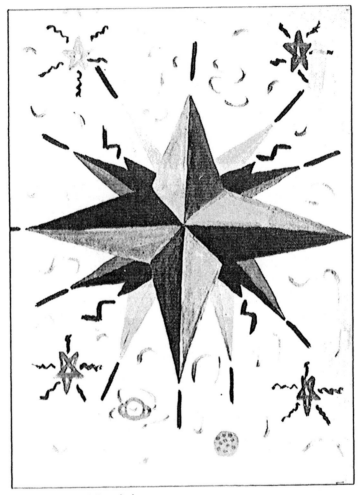

Figure 76.   David's painting

class, however, and worked on his painting (Figure 76) for three
periods. Soon after, he was expelled from the school when a switch-
blade knife was found among his possessions.


## RALPH

What might we expect from a child who hears, but has difficulty following directions and answering questions, who forgets a word as soon as
he hears it, according to his teacher, and cannot recognize it even after
frequent exposure? Ralph, age twelve, performed at the third grade

level in mathematics, and at the first grade level in reading. He was very talkative, but confused verbs and subjects, dropped final syllables, and used the wrong pronouns. When he was seven years old his father was imprisoned for attempting to kill his mother.

Although his IQ was estimated at 77, Ralph was able to do all the tasks described in Part Two, indicating that his conceptual, sequential, and spatial abilities seemed to be intact. This will be evident in his drawings, which are presented in Chapters 9 and 10 (Figures 123, 124, 129, and 130). When he was free to work as he wished he usually painted fantasies of adventure. He drew Figure 77 in his first art class, and painted Figures 78, 79, and 80 in the order in which they are presented. He also painted Frankenstein (Figure 1, Chapter 1).

## CHARLIE

What might we expect from an eleven-year-old who seemed to have no language whatever in the art class? Charlie had spent a year in a mental hospital when he was six, but the following year, when he was enrolled in school, a psychiatrist found him "not psychotic, not schizophrenic, not autistic." He was found to have receptive and expressive language impairment, with a high degree of selectivity for excluding sounds. We communicated through pantomime, and Charlie never had to be shown art techniques twice. His gesture for pleasure was kissing his fingertips in salute, and he often saluted his brushes and paints.

Figure 77.   Ralph's first drawing

Figure 78.    Ralph's painting of a ship caught on an iceberg

One day I brought spring flowers to the art class. Charlie gave them his salute, put them in a milk bottle, and painted Figure 81, changing the milk bottle into a vase and inventing the tulip and pussy willow. He then painted Figure 82, using a palette knife, in just a few minutes.

His drawing (Figure 83) suggests what it must feel like to shout in silence.

Charlie and I met again three years later in another experimental art class. At fourteen, Charlie was much subdued. He now attended another school for handicapped children, where he had been placed in a special class for slow learners. His sister said he was unhappy in the new school, and his drawing (Figure 84), similar in theme to Figure 83, now shows tears and the word "cry."

Charlie's landscape (Figure 85), drawn at age fourteen, is bleak and wintry, and broken branches and bare trees predominate. It is in sharp contrast to the landscape he had painted when he was eleven (Figure 86).

One day our art class visited a museum to try one of the taped acousti-guide tours. As we walked to the various paintings discussed on the tape, we followed a diagram of the galleries provided by the museum. Although I am quick with maps and diagrams, Charlie was quicker. Even with the diagram upside down in my hand as we walked, he knew the direction to take.

I was so impressed that I tried to interest several psychologists in testing him, but failed. I then wrote to three prominent specialists,

Figure 79.   Ralph's painting of a ship being bombed

Figure 80.   Ralph's painting of warfare in outer space

Figure 81.    Charlie's first painting of flowers, age eleven

asking for guidance. One did not reply. Another suggested that Charlie be tested, and the third, E. Paul Torrance, sent his Test of Creative Thinking, advised how to administer it, and offered to score the results.

Charlie's performance on the nonverbal test was "truly outstanding," as Dr. Torrance wrote, "the product of a mind of considerable power." He had scored in the upper 0.5% in originality, the upper 3% in fluency, the upper 10% in flexibility, and in the last category, elaboration, his score was "almost unexcelled." His performance "reflected a high order of ability to acquire information, form relationships, and, in general, to think."

The scores and Dr. Torrance's letter were sent to Charlie's school, but, as I was told, they "changed nothing because language comes first" and "there is a limit to what you can do without language." Charlie remained in the class for slow learners until he graduated.

When Charlie graduated from school he found employment in a greenhouse, and recently built, by himself, a greenhouse of his own.

Figure 82.   Charlie's second painting of flowers, age eleven

Figure 83.   Charlie's shout in silence, age eleven

Figure 84.    Charlie's shout in silence, age fourteen

He continues to draw, mostly landscapes from imagination and memory. Figure 87 is an example of his recent work, done at age twenty-four. The landscape seems less depressed than the one he produced at age fourteen. Although one tree is down, and two branches are broken, other trees are intact and again leafed out.

## MAUREEN

What might we expect for a deaf young woman with an ambition to study sculpture and teach art to deaf children? Maureen had just graduated from a public high school that had a special program for deaf students. Although she had received A's in art, she was advised by her guidance and vocational counselors that she could not meet the

Figure 85.   Charlie's imaginary landscape, age fourteen

Figure 86.   Charlie's imaginary landscape, age eleven

Figure 87.  Charlie's imaginary landscape, age twenty-four

academic requirements of art schools, and should aim for beauty cul-
ture or clerical work instead. She refused.

She was one of the first to enroll in our art class for deaf adults.
She also asked if she could help me teach the children's class. She felt
she could offer special skills in communicating with deaf children because her younger brother was also deaf. I was immediately convinced
that I needed an assistant, and Maureen was engaged. As the weeks
went by, it became clear that she was competent, enthusiastic, quick to
learn, and excellent with children. She was never once absent or late.
As an art student she showed exceptional ability.

I was so impressed with Maureen, I spoke with admissions officers
in several art schools, describing her abilities as I saw them. They felt it
was inadvisable for her to apply for admission to their schools. However, the director of a school specializing in ceramics expressed interest
in seeing her work. Maureen brought three pieces of sculpture, and was
not only accepted for admission, but received scholarships in both
ceramics and sculpture.

As a recent graduate of her high school, Maureen was eligible for
aptitude tests, which she took, and when the time came to discuss the
results with her school counselor, she asked me to accompany her. I
did, and I told him what she had accomplished during the year in art
school and as my student and assistant. He said I had been wasting my
time and giving Maureen false hopes. He advised her to become a
laboratory technician, and when she said she had no interest in this
field, he advised her to go to a public library and read a book on

vocations for high school graduates. When she had found a suitable vocation, she should write him a letter telling him what she would like to be and why.

When the art project ended, Maureen continued teaching children, part-time, in a school for the deaf that had no art teacher. At her art school she became an assistant, helping to fire clay and teaching in exchange for tuition, and received two honorable mentions in juried shows. She went on to earn an associate degree in ceramics, married, and now teaches, with her husband, in an industrial arts program. She also teaches art privately to handicapped children.

# Chapter 5

# Creative Skills

Educators of handicapped children look for ways to stimulate imagination, but they usually have in mind verbal stimulation and they usually overlook art. Very little verified knowledge is available about aptitudes for art and other creative abilities of children, or adults, who have language and hearing handicaps.

Myklebust measured deaf children with tests of mechanical aptitude and artistic judgment. He found them within normal limits, and concluded that concerted effort should be given to the diagnosis of various aptitudes, as well as to training, in order to capitalize on special aptitudes and develop potential abilities (Myklebust, 1960, p. 369).

Pintner, working with 700 deaf students, also concluded that there is little difference between the deaf and the hearing in artistic judgment. He had thought it advisable to explore the question of artistic capacity "not with a view of showing that the deaf have special capacity in this area, but rather with the hope of finding that they are less handicapped in this area than in others, so that wise educators of the deaf may be able to utilize better those capacities in the total education and training of the deaf" (Pintner, 1941, p. 223).

Although Pintner's expectations were low, the wise educators he addressed had even lower expectations, apparently, for few if any schools for the deaf have explored the question of artistic capacity. A survey of forty-six schools found that 20% did not provide *any* art education. Among the schools that did have art programs, only 54% employed art teachers, and less than half (46%) allowed students who were sixteen years old or older to attend a class in art or crafts (Howell, 1967).

Lampard evaluated paintings made by twenty deaf children over a period of six years, starting with their entry into school at the age of four. The paintings were evaluated with respect to their subject matter and technique, and were found to differ from the work of hearing children: "There seems to have been very little involvement and painstaking interest . . . planning, organization or care. . . The work is not always careless. It is sometimes slow, painstaking and rigid" (Lampard, 1960, pp. 419−420). The greatest deviation was found in subject matter. Lampard described the paintings as ". . . empty of subject matter, of imagery, or narrative . . . there are not many people or animals nor is there much action or interaction . . . The pictures do not seem to have been painted with any idea of telling a story or indeed of making any comment on the world around them" (Lampard, 1960, p. 421). Lampard's findings suggest that deafness is the cause of retardation in art expression. The possibility that the cause might lie elsewhere was not considered, nor were objectives or methods of teaching described.

A recent study by Singer and Lenahan suggests that deaf children lag behind hearing children in originality, imagination, and abstract thinking. In the study, twenty deaf children were asked to make up stories and to answer questions about their dreams, fantasies, and play. Their answers were found to be unimaginative and concrete, even less rich in fantasy than the answers of hearing children three to five years younger. "None mentioned any games such as . . . cops and robbers . . . For the most part, the fantasies . . . related experiences they had actually encountered rather than some they wished to encounter. . . . All suggest greater concreteness and lack of originality than shown in responses by their normal peers" (Singer and Lenahan, 1976, p. 47).

These findings were based on *verbal* responses. To generalize from them would be a serious error, for deaf children do *not* in fact lag behind when verbal expression is bypassed and nonverbal instruments are used to assess these capacities. Evidence supporting this claim may be found in three studies. Since the studies have been reported elsewhere, their findings are summarized here.

## FIRST STUDY: HANDICAPPED CHILDREN IN FOUR SCHOOLS

This study had several goals: among them, to determine whether or not deafness necessarily impedes development of creative skills, and to determine whether or not unfavorable comparisons between deaf and hearing students can be eliminated, or at least reduced, by a particular approach to teaching art (Silver, 1966). Another goal was to determine whether or not art teachers can try to stimulate communication, cognition, and adjustment at the same time that they pursue the objectives of art education.

To obtain answers to these and other questions, experimental art classes were taught at three schools for deaf children, and at a school for language- and hearing-impaired children. Twenty-five children, ages eight to seventeen, were selected by administrators of their schools. Thirteen were deaf and twelve were diagnosed as aphasic. They attended weekly art classes of approximately one hour for approximately eleven weeks.

Since the time was limited, it was felt advisable to restrict the children to drawing and painting from imagination. Subject matter originated with the children, except for the request for family portraits in the first art class for children whose communication skills were particularly poor. The artwork produced in the classes was evaluated by two panels of judges by means of questionnaires.

## Evaluations by a Panel of Twenty Educational Specialists

The judges included psychologists, psychiatrists, school administrators, educators of children who were either deaf, learning-impaired, or unimpaired, and university professors of special education. Among the questions asked were: whether or not they found evidence that art afforded opportunities to imagine, associate, and express thoughts and feelings; and whether or not they found evidence that would be useful in assessing interests, abilities, attitudes, or needs (as indicated in Table 1). Of the 337 answers, 93% affirmed that the paintings did provide such evidence, 2% denied it, and 5% of the answers were qualified.

## Evaluations by a Panel of Twenty Art Educators

Twelve of the judges had taught in universities or colleges, and eight either taught or supervised art teachers in elementary or high schools. Judging the same paintings and drawings as did the panel of educational specialists, they compared the pictures with the work of hearing art students, and evaluated them for subject matter and technique, for sensitivity to art values, and for technical skill.

The questions were phrased in terms used in the Lampard study in order to facilitate comparisons between the findings of the two studies. Of 260 answers, 243 (or 93%) were affirmative, one answer was no, and sixteen answers were qualified (as indicated in Table 2). All found evidence of storytelling, spontaneity, and the use of people and animals. Nineteen found evidence of action and interaction in subject matter; seventeen found painstaking interest in technique. These findings differed from the findings of the Lampard study, which noted that there were not many people or animals, nor much action or interaction, and which found a shutting out, rather than a working out, of anxiety-provoking images and ideas.

This study has suggested that an appropriate goal in art education is to help students become sensitive to art values and articulate in art expression, and that, with this goal, art teachers are not restricted to teaching art. They can try to stimulate communication, cognition, and adjustment at the same time that they try to make their students sensitive to art forms and skillful in art techniques. The final question raised was whether or not these goals conflict. The judges apparently did not

Table 1.   Results of questionnaire for educators of the deaf and other specialists

|  | Answers | | |
|---|---|---|---|
| Questions | Yes | No | Other |
| Do you or do you not find evidence in the pictures that art afforded opportunities to— | | | |
| 1. Imagine | 19 | 0 | 1[a] |
| 2. Remember | 20 | 0 | 0 |
| 3. Generalize | 18 | 0 | 2[a,a] |
| 4. Associate | 20 | 0 | 0 |
| 5. Evaluate | 17 | 1 | 2[a,a] |
| 6. Express ideas | 20 | 0 | 0 |
| 7. Express emotions | 20 | 0 | 0 |
| 8. Find success | 18 | 1 | 1[a] |
| 9. Realize capacities | 17 | 1 | 2[a,a] |
|  | 169 | 3 | 8 |
| Do you or do you not find evidence that would be useful in assessing the deaf or aphasic child's— | | | |
| 10. Interests or concerns | 20 | 0 | 0 |
| 11. Knowledge or ignorance | 19 | 1 | 0 |
| 12. Educational needs, such as vocabulary | 16 | 3 | 1[a] |
| 13. Attitudes toward himself | 18 | 0 | 2[a,b] |
| 14. Attitudes toward others | 18 | 0 | 2[a,b] |
| 15. Emotional needs, such as referral for guidance | 16 | 1 | 3[a,a,b] |
| 16. Ability to think independently | 20 | 0 | 0 |
| 17. Ability to think abstractly | 19 | – | 1[a] |
|  | 146 | 5 | 9 |

[a] Qualifying answer such as "sometimes."
[b] Unanswered.

feel so. Asked if they found evidence of sensitivity to art values, seventeen of the twenty art educators answered "yes." Of the remaining three, one answered "sometimes," another wrote "yes and no," and the third, who answered with a question mark, made this comment:

> I find the best work extremely sensitive, but lacking the rather shallow sophistication of comparable work by hearing children of the same ages.

Asked if they found evidence of technical skill, sixteen answered "yes"; the remaining four answered: "yes and no," "sometimes," "no, in most cases," and "evidence not as strong here." Of the total of sixty answers to questions dealing with aptitude for art, fifty were "yes," one was "no," and nine were qualified answers. Fifteen of the art educators answered "yes" to all questions dealing with subject

Table 2.   Results of questionnaire for art educators

|  | | Answers | | |
| --- | --- | --- | --- | --- |
| Questions | | Yes | No | Other |
| Do you or do you not find evidence in the pictures of— | | | | |
| I.  Subject matter:[c] | | | | |
| a. storytelling | | 20 | 0 | 0 |
| b. information giving | | 20 | 0 | 0 |
| c. action and interaction | | 19 | 0 | 1 |
| d. people and animals | | 20 | 0 | 0 |
| e. desire to communicate | | 20 | 0 | 0 |
| f. commenting generally | | 18 | 1 | 1[a] |
| II.  Technique:[c] | | | | |
| g. painstaking interest | | 17 | 0 | 3[a] |
| h. involvement | | 20 | 0 | 0 |
| i. planning | | 18 | 0 | 2[a] |
| j. spontaneity | | 20 | 0 | 0 |
| k. pleasure | | 18 | 0 | 2[a] |
| III.  Sensitivity to art values | | 17 | 0 | 3[a] |
| IV.  Technical skill | | 16 | 0 | 4[a] |
| If you have taught hearing children, do you find differences between— | | | | |
| V.  The best pictures in this exhibition and the pictures of talented hearing children of about the same ages, in aptitude for art | | 6 | 9 | 1[a] |
| VI.  These pictures and the pictures of an average group of hearing children of about the same ages | | 9[b] | 8 | 0 |

[a] Qualifying answers, such as "sometimes."
[b] Seven found hearing children superior, two found deaf superior.
[c] Since one of the purposes of the questionnaire was to compare the results with the findings of the Lampard study, the questions concerning subject matter and technique are phrased in terms borrowed from the Lampard study.

matter, technique, sensitivity to art values, and technical skill. One of them made this comment:

It is clear to me, judging from this exhibition, that aesthetic values do not degenerate when art is taught to deaf and aphasic children. Moreover, the tremendous value and deep felt need to express makes the experience of art in this particular situation immeasurably important.

It should be noted that subject matter was not suggested to the children, except for the family portraits, and that limitations of time and space made it necessary for both panels of judges to evaluate the same group of drawings and paintings. Consequently, most of the artwork evaluated for aesthetic qualities had been selected not for skill, but for evidence of adjustment or cognition. The fact that none of the children attended more than eleven classes may also be relevant. Given more time, some may have shown greater progress.

Nevertheless, the evaluations of the twenty art educators were far more favorable toward the deaf than the evaluations in the Lampard study. This suggests that deafness does not necessarily interfere with aptitude for art, and that reasons for the unfavorable findings of the Lampard study may lie elsewhere. The findings also suggested that art educators *can* try to stimulate communication, cognition, and adjustment, without neglecting or interfering with the development of sensitivity to art values and skill in art techniques. It was thought that further investigation would be useful, and the second study was undertaken.

## SECOND STUDY: A DEMONSTRATION PROJECT
## FOR HEARING-IMPAIRED CHILDREN AND ADULTS[1]

The main objectives of this project were to obtain information about the aptitudes of hearing-impaired children and adults, and about vocational opportunities for the deaf in the visual arts. Another objective was to identify effective methods of teaching these students (Silver, 1967).

As in the previous study, I taught experimental art classes and panels of judges evaluated the drawings and paintings produced. Unlike the first study, the judges did not know that they were evaluating the artwork of handicapped students. It was felt that if they had this knowledge, they might be influenced either favorably out of sympathy or unfavorably because of low expectations. There were two hypotheses: 1) Given an adequate introduction to studio experiences and to the offerings of museums, deaf students can be expected to have as much aptitude and interest in the visual arts as do hearing students, and 2) vocational opportunities for the deaf in the visual arts are generally underestimated.

Notices were sent to schools and other agencies in the New York City area announcing forthcoming free instruction in painting and sculpture, as well as free field trips, for a limited number of deaf children and adults. Students were not selected for ability in art but were accepted in the order in which their applications were received.

[1] This study was supported by a grant from the United States Office of Education Bureau of Research.

Weekly classes were held at a society for the deaf. The children's class was limited to eight students each term, and the adult class (which included teenagers) was limited to fifteen students each term. There were fourteen classes in each of the two terms. The children met for one hour on Saturday mornings and the adults met for two hours on Saturday afternoons.

Although the project called for a new population of students in the second term, three children, three teenagers, and four adults from the first term also enrolled in the second term because they could not or would not find art classes elsewhere. Consequently, an additional class was taught at a school for language- and hearing-impaired children during the second term, where administrators chose eight children. Thus there were fifty-four participants, of whom seventeen were adults, thirteen were teenagers, and twenty-four were children. Of these, nineteen were deaf (nine children, four teenagers, six adults). and nine were hard of hearing (three teenagers, six adults). The rest were believed to have language impairments caused by disorders of the central nervous system. To compare these students with hearing students, four assessments of aptitude were made: the Torrance Test of Creative Thinking, and three evaluations by panels of judges. In addition, a painting produced in one of the art classes was submitted to an open juried art exhibition.

## Comparison of Deaf and Hearing Populations
## as Measured by the Torrance Test of Creative Thinking

This test is concerned not with creativity in art but with creativity in general. Its nonverbal form (Figural Form A) was administered to twelve students, without a time limit but with a record of the time consumed. This was suggested by Dr. Torrance, who, with his associates, scored the results. The test was administered to the eight children in the second-term children's class, and to three teenagers and one adult from the adult class.

The test consists of three tasks. These tasks involve the ability to acquire information, to form relationships, and to return to the same stimulus repeatedly, perceiving it in different ways. The results are evaluated for fluency, flexibility, originality, and elaboration. In the first task subjects are asked to draw a picture in which a pear shape (made of colored paper with adhesive backing) is an integral part. In the second task subjects are asked to draw pictures by adding lines to ten incomplete figures. In the third task they are asked to draw pictures using thirty pairs of parallel lines. In each task the directions urge the subjects to think of interesting pictures or objects that no one else will think of, and to give them names or titles. It was impossible to convey this idea to the children and to one of the teenagers, but it was probably understood by the other three students, who were able to read the directions. The students were asked by the testers to add titles to their pictures, as directed by the test, but this was not insisted on.

*Results*    The twelve students had a very high level of performance, as indicated in Table 3. Their average scores were in the 99th percentile in both originality and elaboration, in the 97th percentile in fluency, and in the 88th percentile in flexibility. Eight students had scores that placed them in the 99th percentile. The composite average score of all twelve placed them in the 96th percentile.

In commenting on the results, Dr. Torrance observed that there were quite a number of outstanding performances, and that almost all the deaf students were especially good on elaboration. He also pointed out that their attention to elaboration of ideas did not seem to interfere with their originality, but that in a few cases low flexibility, or ability to shift from one idea to another, had inhibited originality. He added that the students were able to use expansive energy and that there "should certainly be plenty of ways of capitalizing on such 'gifts' or 'skills' as these."

When the results were in, I mistakenly assumed that the schools the children attended would be interested in them, especially since the indications are for creativity in general, not specifically in art. I sent the children's scoring worksheets to the three schools for the deaf, together with Dr. Torrance's interpretations, and information about the availability of the test.

There were no acknowledgments. Some weeks later I met psychologists from two of the schools. One said that the Torrance Test would hold no interest in her school because there was no interest in developing creative ability, only in developing ability to understand and to retain what was taught. The other psychologist expressed doubt that twelve children taken at random could do so well on any test. It seems to me that the students who took the Torrance Test were not a random group. All had shown interest in art, since they had enrolled in the art program when it was announced, and seven of the twelve had attended art classes from October to April when they took the test. Furthermore, all were deaf and could be expected to compensate with greater visual sensitivity.

## EVALUATIONS BY PANELS OF JUDGES

In addition to the Torrance Test, there were three assessments of ability based on evaluations by panels of judges. In the visual arts, ability and aptitude are usually rated subjectively rather than by means of objective scores. Painters, sculptors, printers, and craftsmen usually

Table 3. Comparison of deaf and hearing populations as measured by the Torrance Test of Creative Thinking (Figural Form A)

| Student | Age | Composite total score[a] | Percentile | Fluency | Flexibility | Originality | Elaboration |
|---------|-----|--------------------------|------------|---------|-------------|-------------|-------------|
| A. | 12 | 74 | 98 | 74 | 50 | 70 | 100 |
| B. | 12 | 81 | 99 | 74 | 65 | 85 | 100 |
| C. | 8 | 80 | 99 | 74 | 67 | 79 | 100 |
| D. | 12 | 68 | 96 | 50 | 57 | 89 | 77 |
| E. | 18 | 80 | 99 | 74 | 70 | 75 | 100+ |
| F. | 12 | 82 | 99 | 74 | 70 | 88 | 95 |
| G. | 10 | 83 | 99 | 74 | 74 | 91 | 92 |
| H. | 12 | 79 | 98 | 74 | 70 | 88 | 83 |
| I. | 13 | 83 | 99 | 74 | 70 | 88 | 100 |
| J. | 19 | 65 | 91 | 50 | 50 | 60 | 100 |
| K. | 14 | 80 | 99 | 75 | 63 | 82 | 100+ |
| L. | 24 | 80 | 99 | 74 | 53 | 92 | 100+ |
| Average _t_ score | | | | 70.00 | 63.25 | 82.25 | 95.58 |
| Percentiles | | | | 97th | 88th | 99th | 99th |

[a] A score between 40 and 60 is average, a score between 60 and 70 is above average, and a score between 70 and 100 is outstanding.

submit their work to juries, who decide which work will be accepted for exhibition and which will receive awards.

Two objective tests of artistic judgment were available, but I felt they were unsuitable and asked the directors of two leading art schools for their views. One director said that in his school, instead of taking objective art tests, prospective students are asked to draw from imagination, memory, and observation. Their drawings are then judged by members of the faculty. The other director said that his school selected students on the basis of portfolios, interviews, and the recommendations of interested and knowledgeable persons.

In the project, the three panels of judges evaluated drawings and paintings for the following qualities:

1. Sensitivity—defined as keen awareness of and response to colors, shapes, and other visual experiences
2. Expressiveness—ability to embody attitudes or ideas in an image so that they are communicated effectively
3. Originality—imaginative subject matter or unconventional use of tools or materials

## Comparison of Paintings by
## Twenty-Two Deaf and Twenty-Two Hearing Art Students as
## Judged by Three University Professors of Art

To evaluate the paintings made by twenty-two deaf and twenty-two hearing art students, three members of the Department of Art and Education at Teachers' College, Columbia University, were asked to evaluate forty-four unidentified paintings by both deaf and hearing students. The twenty-two deaf students were the total number of students in the project classes during the first term, with the exception of one adult who worked only in sculpture. The twenty-two hearing students had been attending public elementary and secondary schools, or an adult education class in a public high school. Since there were many students in these classes, the teachers of hearing children and teenagers chose students whose artistic ability they judged to be average for their ages. Although all of the hearing adults had previous art experience, their teacher chose students who were comparative beginners. Children and teenagers were matched for age, and each teacher chose one work by each student.

The paintings, identified only by number and, if done by a child, the age of the painter, were rated 1 to 5 points for each of the qualities of sensitivity, originality, and expressiveness, as defined above, with 5 points given to the most ability or aptitude and 1 point given to the least.

**Results**    The average scores of the deaf children and adults were slightly higher than the scores of their hearing counterparts, while the scores of the deaf teenagers were slightly lower, as indicated in Table 4.

The highest score went to Charlie—forty-four points out of a possible forty-five (see Figure 88).

## Comparison of Portfolios of Work by Sixteen Deaf Students With the Work of Hearing Art Students as Judged by Thirteen Art Educators

Portfolios of paintings and drawings by sixteen deaf students were evaluated by thirteen art educators, who were asked to compare them with the work of their own students, and to evaluate them in the light of their own experiences as painters and teachers. The judges were not told that the students were deaf, nor were they told the purpose of the project. It was felt that, if they knew, they might be influenced either

Table 4.  Comparison of paintings by twenty-two deaf and twenty-two hearing art students as judged by three university professors of art

|  | Total | Sensi-tivity | Expres-siveness | Origi-nality |
|---|---|---|---|---|
| 8 Hearing children | 2.33 | 2.54 | 2.50 | 1.96 |
| 8 Deaf children | 2.43 | 2.33 | 2.54 | 2.41 |
| 7 Hearing teenagers | 3.25 | 3.33 | 3.43 | 3.00 |
| 7 Deaf teenagers | 2.89 | 2.86 | 3.05 | 2.76 |
| 7 Hearing adults | 3.00 | 3.29 | 3.05 | 2.67 |
| 7 Deaf adults | 3.08 | 2.90 | 3.24 | 3.10 |

Figure 88.   Painting that received highest score

favorably because of sympathy, or unfavorably because of low expectations. Six of the thirteen judges, who taught art in elementary schools, evaluated the children's portfolios. The seven who taught art in colleges or graduate schools evaluated the portfolios of teenagers and adults.

The deaf students included eight children, three teenagers, and two adults who were participating in the project art program. In addition, they included three seniors from a public high school that had a program for deaf students. These three students had been selected by their teachers for ability in art. Their backgrounds included two or three terms of costume design, two or three terms of art appreciation, and one term of elective art. Each was eighteen years old.

Evaluating the portfolios for originality, sensitivity, and expressiveness, the judges were asked to assume that a score of 3 represented an average student in one of their classes. Thus, 1 point was given to a portfolio that showed very little of a particular quality, 2 points for a below average amount of that quality, 3 points for an average amount, 4 points for an above average amount, and 5 points for an outstanding amount.

**Results**   The combined average scores of the thirteen deaf students from the project classes were above average when compared with hearing students in elementary schools or colleges and beyond. The three deaf students from the public high school were below average when compared with hearing students. Nevertheless, the combined average scores for the total of sixteen deaf students were slightly above average, despite a decided disadvantage—six deaf teenagers were compared with hearing art students in colleges and art schools at the graduate level. The results are shown in Table 5.

Table 5.  Comparison of portfolios by sixteen deaf students with the work of hearing art students as measured by thirteen art educators

|  | Combined average scores | Originality average scores | Sensitivity average scores | Expressiveness average scores |
|---|---|---|---|---|
| Children from project class | 3.53 | 3.40 | 3.52 | 3.74 |
| Teenagers/adults from project | 3.26 | 3.14 | 3.27 | 3.40 |
| Seniors from high school class | 2.53 | 2.23 | 2.83 | 2.43 |
| Total number of deaf students | 3.11 | 2.92 | 3.21 | 3.19 |

In fairness to the three deaf high school students, it should be recognized that they were competing not only with hearing students in college or beyond, but also with deaf students whose art teacher was trying to develop the qualities that were being judged. Their high school art teacher may well have had different objectives, methods, and expectations. Another unknown factor was the effect of being in art classes where most of the students had normal hearing.

## Comparison of Deaf and Hearing
## Art Students by Eleven Teacher-Observers

Invitations to observe the project classes were sent to art schools, schools for the deaf, special educators, and art teachers. Eleven out of twenty-three invitations were accepted. After visiting the classes, the observers were asked to compare the students with their own students in independence, interest in art, and sensitivity, originality, and expressiveness. The judges were also asked to assess differences in teaching the two groups.

*Results*   Nine of the eleven observers found the deaf equal or superior to the hearing in each category. The only observers who found the deaf inferior were two who had experience with deaf students exclusively, and they were not art teachers. They rated the deaf lower in independence, originality, sensitivity, and expressiveness. They thought the deaf were equal only in interest, and in no category did they find the deaf superior to hearing students. These two observers also thought teaching the deaf was more difficult, interesting, and gratifying (as indicated in Table 6).

In sharp contrast, the nine observers who found the deaf equal or superior in all categories were teachers of art, three of whom had experience exclusively with hearing students, while the remaining six

Table 6.  Comparison of deaf and hearing art students as judged by eleven teacher-observers

| Two teachers of the deaf | | | | Nine teachers of both deaf and hearing | | |
|---|---|---|---|---|---|---|
| MORE | SAME | LESS | In comparison with hearing students, these students show: | MORE | SAME | LESS |
| | | 2 | Independence | 4 | 5 | |
| | 2 | | Interest in art | 5 | 4 | |
| | | 2 | Sensitivity | 4 | 4 | |
| | | 2 | Originality | 4 | 5 | |
| | | 2 | Expressiveness | 5 | 4 | |
| 0 | 2 | 8 | | 22 | 22 | 0 |
| MORE | SAME | LESS | In comparison with teaching hearing students, teaching the hearing-impaired is: | MORE | SAME | LESS |
| 2 | | | Difficult | 1 | 7 | 1 |
| 2 | | | Interesting | 2 | 6 | |
| 2 | | | Gratifying | 5 | 4 | |
| 6 | 0 | 0 | | 8 | 17 | 1 |

had taught both deaf and hearing students. One observer thought it was more difficult to teach the deaf, one thought it was less difficult, and seven thought the difficulty was about the same. Two thought it was more interesting to teach deaf students, while six thought it was equally interesting. Five thought it was more gratifying to teach deaf students, while four thought it was equally gratifying.

## SUBMISSION OF A PAINTING TO A JURIED ART EXHIBITION

A painting produced by one of the adults in the project art program was submitted to the annual competition of the Mamaroneck Artists' Guild, open to residents of Westchester County and New York City. The painting was one of sixty paintings and twenty-five sculptures accepted from over 200 entries. It was also one of twelve works that received awards. The painting, titled "The Fisherman," is shown in Figure 89. It is outstanding for its color, but unfortunately it cannot be reproduced effectively in black and white.

## INTEREST IN ART

The children's unusual behavior in the project classes suggested that art had a special attraction for them. They wiped up spills without being reminded, were frugal with paint, and cleaned up willingly at the

Figure 89.   Painting that received award in open juried show

end of the art periods. The adults also seemed to be unusually enthusiastic. They talked about forming an art club when the project
ended, in order to continue working and visiting museums together.
Consequently, we felt it would be useful to know why they had enrolled in the art classes, how much time they spent traveling to and from
the classes, and whether or not they intended to continue studying art
after the project ended.

Questionnaires were prepared for adult students and for parents of
the children. Teenagers who could read well enough answered the
adult questionnaire, while parents answered for those who could not.
There was no questionnaire for eight children who attended the class at
the school for the deaf, since they had not volunteered, but had been
selected at their school.

### Reasons for Attending the Art Classes

According to parent responses, drawing or painting was the chief interest of five of the sixteen children, and among the chief interests of
ten children (as indicated in Table 7). Eleven parents said they wanted
more art experiences for their children than the children were receiving
at their schools. Five parents said their children's schools had no art
teacher. Six said they had difficulty finding an art class that would
accept their children.

Twelve of the sixteen adults and teenagers indicated that they had
enrolled because they wanted to learn more about art classes. Seven of

Table 7.   Questionnaire and responses regarding the interest of deaf children in art

It takes _____ minutes to reach this class from my home.

Name

PLEASE CHECK THE REASONS WHICH BEST DESCRIBE WHY YOUR CHILD HAS BEEN ATTENDING THIS ART CLASS.

__10__ one of his chief interests is drawing or painting

__5__ his chief interest is drawing or painting

__14__ he enjoys drawing or painting

__11__ I feel he should have more art experience than he receives at school

__5__ his school does not have an art teacher for his grade

__6__ I've had difficulty finding an art class which will accept him

__0__ I've had difficulty finding an art class which is satisfactory

_____ other

COMMENTS:

these were interested in art careers, and nine thought art might be an interesting hobby. Another nine painted or sculpted at home and wanted instruction. Nine indicated that the reason for attending the project classes was to learn more about museums and exhibitions (see Table 8).

## Traveling Time

The sixteen children, usually accompanied by their parents, traveled an average of forty-three minutes in order to reach the art class from their homes. Five spent an hour or more traveling to the class. For one child, it was necessary to take two buses and a train each way, and he was present for ten of the fourteen sessions. The adults and teenagers traveled an average of forty-two minutes to reach the class. Four spent an hour or more traveling to the class; one, in her 70s, said it took an hour and twenty-five minutes each way.

## Interest in Continuing in an Art Class After the Project Ended

Since the second term was planned for new students, it was necessary for the original students to find art classes elsewhere if they wanted to continue. To help them find instruction, twenty-three art schools, settlement houses, 'Y's, and adult education programs were approached for catalogs and other information. Their responses varied considerably. The director of one museum-connected art school refused to interview a deaf student or look at his portfolio because the school was "not equipped to handle handicapped students." Another said the second

Table 8.   Questionnaire and responses regarding the interest of deaf teenagers and adults in art

It takes _____ minutes to travel between my home and this class.

_____
                    Name

WHICH OF THESE REASONS BEST DESCRIBES WHY YOU CAME TO THIS ART CLASS? CHECK AS MANY REASONS AS APPLY.

__9__  It seemed a pleasant way to pass the time when there was nothing better to do

__9__  I thought painting or sculpting might be an interesting hobby

__7__  I was thinking of a career in art or a related field

__9__  I paint or sculpt at home and wanted some instruction

__6__  I found it difficult to go to art classes

__12__  I wanted to learn more about art classes

__4__  I found it difficult to go to museums alone or with a friend

__9__  I wanted to learn more about museums and exhibitions

WHICH OF THE FOLLOWING, IF ANY, DESCRIBES YOUR PLANS AFTER THE CLASS ENDS THIS MONTH?

__4__  I may enroll in an art class elsewhere

__3__  I have already enrolled in an art class elsewhere

__11__  I would enroll in an art class only if the students were deaf or hard of hearing

__5__  I expect to paint or sculpt at home

__9__  I am thinking of a career in art or a related field

COMMENTS:
_____

term classes were already filled, one month before the first term ended. The director of another art program said she might interview a deaf student providing he had "intense" interest in art. On the other hand, some welcomed deaf students, and one even offered to help teach in the project.

Each teenager and adult had a choice of several schools, and four enrolled elsewhere: one in an adult education class; another enrolled in two schools, attending three different classes each week; a third enrolled in an art school where she won scholarships in ceramics and sculpture; and the fourth enrolled in a life drawing class where he was recommended for a scholarship at the end of the term.

Eleven adults and teenagers indicated that they would not enroll in an art class unless the students were deaf, and since no such classes were available they continued with the second term. They also formed an art club, following reviews of art exhibitions and visiting the Whitney, Guggenheim, and Brooklyn Museums, as well as the Cloisters.

(During the first term we had visited the Metropolitan Museum, the Museum of Contemporary Craft, and the Museum of Modern Art.) They also planned, hung, and were hosts at an exhibition at the end of the term.

## VOCATIONAL OPPORTUNITIES

Many deaf adults are employed in occupations far below what they are capable of achieving, according to a report prepared for the National Institutes of Public Health Services. It also states that meaningful research is almost non-existent, and that information is needed regarding the kinds of jobs that can be performed by the deaf (National Institutes of Public Health Services, 1969, pp. 69–71).

A case in point was the occupation of one of the adults in the project art class—he earned a pittance working in a factory putting nuts and bolts into bags. He had been so shy about applying for admission to the art class that his sister applied for him, saying that her brother had no background in art but loved to draw and would we consider admitting him (there were no prerequisites, of course). He had exceptional ability, and when the project ended I showed his work to two artist-teachers, who welcomed him into their class. Four years later they gave him a solo show. He continued working at the factory, but has been unable to find employment commensurate with his ability.

In an attempt to obtain useful information about vocational opportunities for the deaf in the visual arts, questionnaires were sent to fifty employers, administrators, and craftsmen in eleven fields. The deaf person was presented as severely impaired in language: "You can assume that in many cases normal written and oral communication would be difficult, and demonstration and pantomime would be the most effective means of communication" (as indicated in Table 9).

Of the thirty-nine responses, thirty-five indicated that a deaf person severely limited in language *could* acquire the skills and knowledge necessary for competency in their fields. Two were undecided and one did not answer this question. Thirty felt that a deaf person severely limited in language *could* earn his living in each of the categories listed. One felt he could not, and six were undecided. Four had known one or more successful deaf craftsmen, designers, or artists (Table 10).

Some of their comments were very interesting. The vice-president and director of a ceramics factory in the South made this observation:

> I should think that teaching people with hearing impairment should be something like teaching in a foreign country in a situation where you do not share a common language. I did this in Taiwan, where I spent four years. Before my Chinese became at all proficient, I communicated almost solely by sign language and by demonstration, and we understood each other quite clearly . . .

Table 9.   Questionnaire sent to handcraftsmen and employers in various
art fields

FIELD_____EMPLOYER 13 SELF-EMPLOYED 22 EMPLOYEE 12

(The term "deaf" as used here refers to those hearing-impaired persons whose
verbal communication is severely limited. You can assume that in many cases
normal oral and written communication would be difficult, and demonstration
and pantomime would be the most effective means of communication. At issue
is whether verbal communication is a crucial aspect of the work in your field.)

I.  Education in This Field

A deaf person could 33, could not 0, acquire the necessary skills and knowledge.

II.  Employment in This Field

A deaf person could 27, could not 1, earn his living as a producing craftsman,
designer, or artist.

A deaf person could 27, could not 0, earn his living producing the designs made
by others.

A deaf person could 27, could not 0, earn his living working under supervision.

The demand for this product is sufficient 19, is insufficient 6, for the average
hearing person to earn his living solely by his output.

COMMENT:


If you know a deaf craftsman, designer, or artist, would you be willing to forward one of these questionnaires to him? If so, please use the reverse side for
your name and address (or his).

A designer and manufacturer of fabrics in the southwestern United
States saw a practical side. Her products are sold to mills and retail
stores, and have received many awards. "I feel that deafness would be
no handicap in the field of hand weaving. . . In my own studio a deaf
person who was a good craftsman-weaver would be an asset because
he would not be distracted by the other conversation going on around
him in the retail part of it." A designer of glass who works for indus-
tries in the East commented: "I have one experience with a 'deaf'
craftsman. He was a talented, capable craftsman who definitely proved
to me he had, indeed, no handicap."

Another comment came from the chairman of a stained glass
studio in a Midwest state: "There is a real opportunity for the handicapped in this craft . . . We have had two other deaf-mutes working in
the studio. One was a talented stained-glass artist-painter, and the
other a lady who did laying out of the glass on easels for the painters,
and similar work." A self-employed craftsman who works in wood
wrote, "Assuming a person has an aptitude for work with the hands

Table 10.    Responses to questionnaires addressed to craftsmen, employers, and administrators, regarding vocational opportunities for the deaf in the visual arts

| Occupation | Number asked | Number answering | Employment[a] | | | Education[b] | | | Demand[c] | | |
|---|---|---|---|---|---|---|---|---|---|---|---|
| | | | Yes | No | ?[d] | Yes | No | ? | Yes | No | ? |
| **First Mailing** | | | | | | | | | | | |
| Hand Bookbinding | 5 | 4 | 4 | | | 4 | | | 3 | | 1 |
| Metalcrafts | 6 | 4 | 4 | | | 4 | | | 2 | 1 | |
| Handweaving | 6 | 4 | 3 | | 1 | 4 | | | 1 | 1 | 2 |
| Blown Glass | 5 | 5 | 3 | | 1 | 5 | | | 1 | 1 | 3 |
| Stained Glass | 7 | 4 | 3 | | 1 | 3 | | 1 | 3 | 1 | |
| Woodworking | 9 | 7 | 5 | 1 | 1 | 5 | | 1 | 5 | | 1 |
| Fine Printing | 2 | 2 | 2 | | | 2 | | | 1 | 1 | |
| Restoration | 1 | 1 | 1 | | | 1 | | | 1 | | |
| Commercial Art | 2 | 2 | | | 2 | 2 | | | 2 | | |
| Store Manager | 3 | 2 | 1 | | | 1 | | | 1 | | |
| Ceramics | 4 | 4 | 4 | | | 4 | | | 2 | 1 | |
| | 50 | 39 | 30 | 1 | 6 | 35 | 0 | 2 | 22 | 6 | 7 |
| **Second Mailing** | | | | | | | | | | | |
| Ceramics | 12 | 9 | | | | | | | | | |
| Store Manager | 1 | 1 | | | | | | | | | |
| Administrator (Art School) | 6 | 6 | | | | | | | | | |
| Deaf Artist, Craftsman | 5 | 0 | | | | | | | | | |
| | 74 | 55 | | | | | | | | | |

[a] Can a deaf person earn his living as a producing craftsman, designer, artist in this field?
[b] Can a deaf person acquire the necessary skills and knowledge for this field?
[c] Is the demand for this product sufficient for the average hearing person to earn his living solely by his output in this field? (Responses to this question indicate that it was ambiguous. As two responses pointed out, a successful hearing craftsman is not "average," but talented.)
[d] Qualified answer, or answered with question mark.

and the ability to visualize three dimensions, then deafness is not a problem. I frequently talk to students in a noisy work shop and must use a minimum of words, relying instead on demonstration."

And, finally, a manufacturer of furniture, and employer, in New York City: ". . . there is now, and apparently will be a growing, shortage of skilled craftsmen . . . " (Other comments may be found in the Appendix.) The questionnaire was also sent to several deaf craftsmen but, curiously, none of them replied.

## THIRD STUDY: STATE URBAN EDUCATION PROJECT FOR CHILDREN WITH LANGUAGE AND HEARING IMPAIRMENTS

The purpose of this project was threefold: first, to help an experimental group of children develop certain mathematical and logical ideas; second, to develop procedures for teaching these ideas through drawing and painting; third, to develop procedures for evaluating cognitive achievements through drawing and painting tasks (Silver, 1973, 1976, 1977).

The children who participated in the project had hearing and language impairments caused by damage to the brain rather than the ear. This type of impairment does not necessarily cause a decrease in auditory sensitivity. It does, however, cause a decrease in auditory comprehension. A child may be able to hear speech but be unable to understand what is said. This impairment takes two fundamental forms—receptive and expressive. Children with the expressive form have difficulty producing language. Children with the receptive form have difficulty comprehending language. The participants in the project had severe receptive or expressive impairments, often both in varying degrees, and many had peripheral losses of hearing as well.

Although aesthetic development was not among the stated objectives of the project, it was of much concern. Some art educators feel that using art for any purpose other than instruction undermines art education and interferes with learning in art. Some art therapists and psychiatrists take the position that instructing or structuring interferes with spontaneous expression.

Since the project was based on the assumption that aesthetic and therapeutic goals do not necessarily conflict, it was concerned with developing art skills and sensitivity to art values. There was another reason for this concern—the general tendency to underestimate the aptitudes of handicapped children.

In an attempt to obtain additional information, the project evaluations included the Torrance Test of Creative Thinking and evaluations of artwork by an art therapist-painter and an art educator.

In the first term, subjects included all children in the first six numerically ordered classes in a school for language- and hearing-impaired children. The experimental group was a randomly selected 50% sample of the six classes, with eighteen children in the experimental group and eighteen serving as controls. Their ages ranged between eight and fifteen years. Art classes were taught two days a week, three classes a day. The eighteen experimental children attended one class a week for eleven weeks, October through December, 1972.

In the second term, subjects included all children in the three remaining eligible classes in the school, as well as the first three eligible classes in another school for language- and hearing-impaired children. Experimental subjects were a 50% sample of the six classes, selected at random. Unselected subjects served as controls. Their ages ranged between eight and sixteen years. Only nine art periods were provided, due to illness of the instructor and unanticipated programming difficulties.

## Torrance Test of Creative Thinking

The results of the Torrance Test were unclear in this study. Unlike the previous study in which the test was presented individually to deaf children and adults, it was impossible to test individually. Instead, the test was presented simultaneously to all the children in a class in the schools for language and hearing impaired. When the results (compiled by the Personnel Press Scoring Service at the University of Georgia) arrived, we were surprised to find that certain children with severe neurological impairment had high scores. We questioned them about the titles they had given their drawings and found that they had not comprehended what was wanted, but had simply filled in the spaces with any words that occurred to them. Thus, their titles did not reflect original or unusual associations—they reflected no association at all. In subsequent testing we tried to verify that the titles were associated with the drawings, but could not be sure, because there were too many children to observe at one time.

On the pretest, children in the experimental group received an average score of 46.67. On the posttest, their scores averaged 48.45. Children in the control group received an average score of 43.52 on the pretest and 46.67 on the posttest. (One child in the experimental group received the unusually high score of 100 in elaboration on both pretest and posttest, accounting, in part, for the difference in scores of experimental and control groups.) There were no significant differences between experimental and control groups on three of the four sections of the test: Fluency, Flexibility, and Originality. On the fourth section, Elaboration, the mean difference was significant on the posttest at the $p < 0.05$ level, although it was not significant on the pretest. Because of the uncertainties, the results of the Torrance Test were not analyzed or incorporated into the findings as were the other tests in this study (see Chapter 12).

## Evaluations by a Registered
## Art Therapist and a University Professor of Art

To compensate for the uncertainties of the Torrance Test, two judges were asked to evaluate three drawings or paintings produced by each child in the fall program experimental group: the child's first work, his last work, and a work produced at midterm. Fifty-four drawings or paintings were identified only by number and shown in random order to conceal the sequence in which they had been produced.

The judges rated each work on a scale of 1 to 5 points for sensitivity and skill, and for the ability to represent objects or events at the level of description (imitative, learned, impersonal), the level of restructuring (going beyond description to elaborate or edit an experience), or at the level of transformation (beyond restructuring, highly personal, imaginative, inventive). The scoring form they used is presented in Table 29 (see Chapter 12).

Of the eighteen children, the first drawings of nine children received the lowest score, 1 point, for commonplace form or content, while their last drawings received the highest score, 5 points, for being highly personal and imaginative, or highly skillful. In skill and expressiveness combined, both judges found improvements to a degree that was statistically significant. The statistical analysis is detailed in Tables 30 and 31, Chapter 12.

## Implications

The findings in these studies cannot be considered conclusive, because they are based on small samples, but they support the belief that objectives in art education and art therapy can be pursued concurrently, and that deafness does not necessarily impede the development of creative skills.

# Part Two

# Developing Cognitive and Creative Skills

# Introduction

In the Singer and Lenahan (1976) study, deaf children were found to be unimaginative when compared with hearing children. In the Lampard (1960) study, paintings made by deaf children were judged inferior to the artwork of hearing children in both subject matter and technique. In the studies discussed in Part One, drawings and paintings by deaf children and language-impaired children were evaluated much more favorably. A possible explanation for these contradictory findings may lie in different approaches to teaching.

It is easy to recognize ability in a good painting, but difficult to say whether a poor painting shows lack of ability or lack of opportunity to develop ability. Art therapists and art educators, like specialists in other fields, differ in their expectations, objectives, and practices. Part Two of this book is concerned with objectives and practices in working with impaired and unimpaired children and adults.

# Chapter 6

# Issues, Objectives, and Methods

What is the purpose of providing art materials and techniques? Is it simply to show students how to draw, paint, or model clay, or how to master some craft? Some educators believe the only appropriate goal of art education is to teach art techniques, art appreciation, or art history. They maintain that to use art for any other purpose is to undermine art education. Some object to representation in art, and others have warned that if art is used for psychotherapy, aesthetic standards will inevitably fall.

On the other hand, some art therapists focusing on mental health say that aesthetics and instruction interfere with diagnosis and therapy. Some students in art education or art therapy are unclear about distinctions between the two fields. Before considering methods, it may be useful to give thought to some questions at issue, and be clear about desired accomplishments.

QUESTIONS AT ISSUE

The Question of Form Versus Content

Some artists and art educators maintain that a work of art has no meaning beyond its physical form, that "to seek, behind form, the emotions of life is a sign of defective sensibility always," to quote Clive Bell. "If a representative form has value, it is as form, not as representation. The representative element in a work of art may or may not be harmful; always it is irrelevant" (Bell, 1958, p. 210).

Others, of course, disagree. Some emphasize emotional content, others emphasize intellectual content, and still others attribute aesthetic value to form and content both: "the noblest poetry is not merely a nice arrangement of consonants and vowels, or stresses and pauses: it is also stained and roughened by a concern for human experience" (Deutch, 1962). According to Kris, it is the number and variety of meanings that provide aesthetic experience. He calls this variety "ambiguity," and he intends not lack of clarity but multiplicity of reference. High ambiguity allows for a wide range of interpretation and acts as a stimulus to the aesthetic response of the viewer. When a work of art is suggestive, it can be understood on several levels simultaneously—intellectually and emotionally, consciously and unconsciously (Kris, 1952, pp. 243–263). If it is true that there is aesthetic value in the expressive or symbolic content in a work of art, as well as in its form, then using art expression as a means of communication with children or adults who have difficulty expressing themselves in words *is* consistent with aesthetic objectives.

Representation has also been called imitation of reality. Kepes calls it "a dead inventory of optical facts" (Kepes, 1944, p. 98), but representation can be so far from imitation that there is no evident resemblance to natural prototypes. Boas, studying primitive art that seemed to be pure design, found that the designs were actually symbolic representations, intended as messages and duly interpreted as such by tribal viewers (Boas, 1955, pp. 88–127).

Like the primitive artist, the child is far from imitative in his representation. In order to make a drawing of a man represent a man, he does not have to make the drawings resemble the man very closely. It is close enough as soon as it *reminds* him of a man. His drawing is a symbol, not an imitation. Lowenfeld demonstrated this in experiments with some 400 children who were asked to draw pictures of themselves picking apples from a branch overhead, just barely within reach. Sixty-nine percent of the nine-year-olds disregarded the size of the tree in relation to themselves. Since only 43% of the ten-year-olds ignored real spatial relationships, Lowenfeld concluded that a typical child disregards what he *sees* and depicts what he *knows*, through symbols, until about the age of ten (Lowenfeld, 1961, p. 18).

## The Question of Therapy Versus Aesthetics

Some art educators object to the use of art by psychotherapists who care little for aesthetic or creative goals. They refer to art classes that have been swamped by maladjusted students, and warn that art standards cannot be maintained if art students find easy and unjustified success.

Success in art does not require indulgence or insincere praise. If quality and skill are critical concerns, originality and sensitivity are no less critical. If a teacher values creativity as highly as skill, he will respect the subjective qualities in his student's work. This is virtually saying that he values and respects the student who can achieve success by being himself. This is not suggesting that individuality produces works of art, but that individuality is one of the prerequisites in art expression and that, in general education, art should be concerned with prerequisites.

If art experience can be reduced to a tool for diagnosing and treating mental illness, it can also be ruined by a professional painter teaching a small class of talented students. A creative atmosphere is no more inherent in an art class than the power to train the mind is inherent in mathematics. A domineering art teacher can be destructive even if he is well informed about art. The quality of an art program depends not only on a teacher's knowledge, but on his objectives and expectations as well. Arbitrary standards of evaluating ability are essential when students are preparing for careers in art, but otherwise it may be better to evaluate ability in terms of individual potentials and growth.

If the objectives of art education were not solely to transmit art information, but were, instead, to develop sensitivity to art values and technical skill *by means of* art knowledge, then art teachers could pursue other objectives at the same time they pursue their traditional goals. They could try to meet the special needs of handicapped individuals without neglecting aesthetic objectives, developing abilities *through* art rather than simply teaching art techniques.

## The Question of Instruction Versus Spontaneity

Some art therapists feel that therapy and instruction do not mix, that structuring art experience will inhibit spontaneity and thus interfere with diagnosis and treatment. Both therapists and educators have said that art and cognition are too far apart to have any bearing on each other.

The studies described in Part Two were based on the beliefs that educational and therapeutic goals do not necessarily conflict, that educators can look beyond art per se to cognitive and emotional goals without neglecting art values and skills, that more than one objective can be pursued at the same time, and that art experience can be structured without sacrificing spontaneity. Structuring here means asking children to do particular tasks, offering them limited subject matter selected from the barrage of stimuli from the outside world, and asking them to focus on particular aspects of the endless stream of their reactions and experiences.

Obviously, some ways of structuring can stifle expressiveness, but on the other hand, if art materials are simply offered and people asked to draw whatever comes to mind, the response may be agonized indecision (particularly in adults). Some structuring seems to stimulate expressiveness rather than suppress it. As both T.S. Eliot and Joseph Heller have observed, when one is forced to write within a certain framework, the imagination is taxed to its utmost and will produce its richest ideas. Given total freedom, however, the work is likely to sprawl.

One way of setting limits without sacrificing spontaneity is to keep the task open-ended; that is, offer options, then relinquish authority, and leave the persons you work with free to make important choices and final decisions. If the task has only one correct response, and it is known in advance, then it is not open-ended. It becomes open-ended only when there are many possible correct responses.

One way to clarify controversial issues is to obtain relevant information that can be quantified. This has been attempted in the studies described in the chapters that follow. It is hoped that the findings will shed some light on the issues under consideration and on the place of representation, therapy, and instruction in art education and art therapy.

## WORKING WITH ANY CHILD OR ADULT

Four objectives are of particular concern: widening the range of communication, providing tasks that invite exploratory learning, providing tasks that are self-rewarding, and reinforcing emotional balance. These objectives seem appropriate both in art education and in art therapy, regardless of whether the students are handicapped or normal, children or adults.

### Widening the Range of Communication

The first objective is to provide an additional channel for conveying thoughts and feelings effectively, to extend communication beyond language to the nonverbal meanings of visual art, to show someone how to draw or paint in order to help him give form to personal experiences. In other words, art knowledge and skills are not ends in themselves, but means to the end of helping us say well what we want to say. By the same token, they can help us learn about others, share their experiences, see the world through their eyes, and help us develop insight into educational and emotional needs.

If this objective is worthwhile, how is it achieved? One way is to elicit rather than instruct, to draw out rather than put in. Idiosyncracies can be encouraged and personal expression invited by suggesting open-ended topics to which each student can respond in his own way. When a task cannot be open-ended, as in drawing from observation, it can be kept short and followed with free-choice activity. Even when the task is to draw a still life, variety of style and interpretation can be encouraged. Consider the difference between apples painted by Chardin and apples painted by Cezanne. Some children use poster paints in thin washes as though they were water colors, while others use them thickly, as though they were oils. Some choose broad brushes while others prefer fine points. Preferences like these deserve respect.

This is not suggesting that freedom is itself the goal. Freedom in education is "the run before the jump," "the tuning of the violin," as Martin Buber once wrote. "Without it nothing succeeds but neither does anything succeed by means of it . . . Independence is a foot-bridge, not a dwelling place" (Buber, 1961, p. 91). Art teachers can guide and instruct while leaving students free to make important decisions. There is a vast difference between freedom and license, guidance and coercion, influence and interference.

## Inviting Exploratory Learning

The second objective is to provide for learning experiences at the other end of the foot-bridge, exploratory learning rather than the passive reception of information. A child can be encouraged to think for himself by presenting tasks in ways that let him make mistakes and correct them, rather than correcting his mistakes or trying to prevent him from making mistakes. This kind of learning can stimulate visuo-spatial thinking as well as verbal-analytical thinking, and can contribute to cognitive, emotional, and aesthetic growth. It can sharpen perception of the way things work, and can intensify awareness of aesthetic qualities.

When opportunities are provided to experiment with art materials and techniques, and to examine objects intensively, art educators are following in the footsteps of the National Art Education Association, which has issued a position paper recommending these practices. When value is placed on originality and creative thinking, students are encouraged to generate their own ideas. The effects of creative thinking in art can transfer to other activities requiring creative thinking, as Torrance has observed; and the sense of achievement that results when others show appreciation may also transfer to other situations.

The distinctive feature of exploratory learning is that it occurs without evident reward. This seems to be true throughout the animal world. According to ethologist S.A. Barnett, cockroaches usually hug corners and shun light, but if given access to a vertical column, they will climb up and down it, and if offered another column once they are used to the first, will explore the new one energetically. The crucial factor is novelty (Barnett, 1967, p. 34).

Exploratory behavior also contributes to the development of intelligence. In laboratory experiments, cats and dogs whose movements were restricted early in life have been compared with animals in control groups without such restrictions. The restricted animals proved to be greatly inferior in their ability to solve problems, to discriminate, and to adapt their behavior to changes in the experimental situation (Barnett, 1967, p. 42).

In general, the approach to teaching in these experimental art classes is indirect rather than direct. Direct instruction is avoided in order to encourage thinking and exploratory learning, to obtain spontaneous responses, and to establish an atmosphere in which independence and initiative would be self-rewarding. Corrections are never made on a student's work. Instead, suggestions are made on a blackboard or scrap paper, and final decisions left to the student.

## Providing Tasks That Are Self-Rewarding

There is evidence that learning is controlled more effectively through reward than through punishment (Hilgard, 1962, p. 325), and that an outstanding characteristic of the school careers of drop-outs is a long succession of failures (Jersild, 1962, p. 286). Success usually leads to higher levels of aspiration, while failure leads to lower levels, and excessive failure leads to abandoning goals altogether. If this is so, educators should provide tasks that are rewarding, which is not the same as saying they should provide rewards. Work that demands the greatest effort can be the most rewarding.

Art experiences can be so rewarding that they are sometimes considered play instead of learning, but beneath the obvious enjoyment are opportunities for becoming deeply absorbed in solving problems. A student must adapt himself to art tools and materials before he can use them effectively. He cannot model stone or carve clay. As he learns what he can and cannot do, he can find the satisfaction of overcoming technical difficulties and losing himself in his work. Painting, for example, becomes most enjoyable when the painter ceases to be conscious of brushes and paint. Play and learning intertwine. Play leads to learning, and learning to play.

The keynote of art experience is enjoyment, or so it seems to me. It is also a time for reflection and the reveries that are so much a part of art experience. Once a child is absorbed in work he should be protected from interruptions, including those of his teacher. A chain of thought is easily broken, and a mood destroyed. The time to intervene is when the child is struggling with a brush that is too large or too small, too wet or too dry, or whenever his teacher can foresee and prevent discomfort or distraction.

## Reinforcing Emotional Balance

The therapeutic goal, according to Jung, is the slow establishment of confidence rather than the demonstration of a clinical theory (Jung, 1974, p. 55).

Art experience provides special opportunities for establishing confidence, as discussed in Chapter 2, but by the same token, instead of building confidence, it provides special opportunities for tearing it down. The subjectivity of painting makes the painter particularly sensitive to criticism of his work. His skill or his teacher's knowledge can both be irrelevant to his sense of failure or success. This is illustrated by an incident that occurred in one of the art programs. A classroom teacher, who had been invited to observe, interrupted a child who was absorbed in painting with a question, "What is your favorite color?" The answer was "White." The visiting teacher replied, "White is not a color. What is your favorite *color*?" This remark would make almost any child unsure of himself. It must have been particularly discouraging to a child whose hearing impairment often required her to accept the perceptions of others when she could not depend on her own. Like enjoyment, self-confidence in art is easily destroyed. Unlike a daydream, a fantasy on paper is vulnerable to anyone who sees it and feels qualified to judge it. The child who feels his work will be judged unsympathetically is likely to keep his fantasies to himself.

Guided by a skillful therapist, however, the art experience can be healing in itself without the interpretation of symbolic images. As Ingmar Bergman observed about acting, the atmosphere is crucially important. The actor cannot perform well if he is scared or insecure. It is only when he feels respected, "watched only by friends," that he "delivers his inner self . . . opens up like a flower" (Meryman, 1971, p. 63). Although a child cannot be made to open up like a flower any more than he can be made talented, therapists and educators *can* provide the atmosphere in which talent and confidence grow.

The practice of art therapy requires training and skill. Without this, there can be real danger in psychiatric interventions, such as attempting to break down defense mechanisms, or interpreting to a student or patient the unconscious meanings in his art. For one thing, interpretations can be distorted by unconscious needs. For another, according to Carl Jung, the meaning of symbols cannot be learned by rote. The same symbols may have different meanings for different individuals, and general rules cannot be laid down (Jung, 1974, p. 59). Even correct interpretations can cause serious harm if handled unwisely. Jung gave up hypnotic treatment because, as he wrote, "I did not want to impose my will on others. I wanted the healing process to grow out of the patient's own personality, not from suggestions by me that would have only a passing effect. My aim was to protect and preserve my patient's dignity and freedom, so that he could live his life according to his own wishes" (Jung, 1974, p. 45).

## WORKING WITH HANDICAPPED CHILDREN AND ADULTS

In the studies discussed in this book, the similarities between handicapped and so-called normal children seemed so much greater than the differences that the same approach was used for both. There were several shifts in emphasis, however, without deviating from principles. Some procedures were stressed and others minimized in order to meet individual needs.

As a rule, children with learning disabilities are differentiated from children whose learning problems are caused by hearing impairment or emotional disturbance or retardation. [The federal definition of learning disabilities defines children with learning disabilities as "those children who have a disorder in one or more of the basic psychological processes involved in understanding or using language, spoken or written, which disorder may manifest itself in imperfect ability to listen, think, speak, read, write, spell, or do mathematical calculations. Such disorders include such conditions as perceptual handicaps, brain injury, minimal brain dysfunction, dyslexia, and developmental asphasia. Such terms do not include children who have learning problems which are primarily the result of visual, hearing or motor handicaps, of mental retardations, of emotional disturbance or of environmental, cultural, or economic disadvantage." (New York Association for the Learning Disabled and its Association for Brain Injured Children. 1977. News. 16 (4): July–August.)] In these studies, however, the differences seemed unimportant. Some so-called learning-disabled children had the same strengths and weaknesses as deaf children (visuo-motor strengths and verbal weaknesses) while other such children had the opposite constellation (verbal strengths and visuo-motor weaknesses). Consequently, the children and adults will here be grouped according to the weaknesses and strengths they seemed to share.

### Verbal Weaknesses and Visuo-Motor Strengths

With individuals who, for whatever reason, have difficulty understanding language or making themselves understood, the first objective can be emphasized—widening the range of communication, stressing content rather than form, meaning rather than elements of design, representational subject matter rather than abstractions. Demonstration can also be emphasized, rather than talk. Art techniques lend themselves to pantomime. Even with hearing students, it is often easier to show a technique than to describe it. With deaf students, abstract ideas can be conveyed by acting out alternatives, such as standing close to a painting, looking puzzled, then stepping back a few paces and coming up with an idea.

To illustrate, it may be helpful to describe the art procedures used in the demonstration project (the second study described in Chapter 5). The first class began with a demonstration of monoprinting. I rolled a brayer over dabs of poster paint on a piece of formica, scratched lines in the paint with a pointed tool, pressed a sheet of onion skin over the paint, and pulled a print. The students were then asked to make prints of their own.

This was the initial procedure for several reasons. It discourages cautious drawing, because poster paint dries very quickly when used this way, and the drier the paint, the weaker the print. One has to work quickly, which discourages self-consciousness, and the results are often dramatic. This initial success was intended to build self-confidence in students who tend to doubt their capabilities. The procedure also establishes a studio atmosphere, each student working independently rather than following the instructor's directions.

The second class began with another demonstration intended to carry over printing techniques to painting. Instead of using formica and a brayer, paint was placed on a paper palette and mixed with a palette knife. Only five colors were used—red, yellow, blue, black, and white. Demonstrations consisted of mixing two primary colors (such as red and yellow, making orange), then adding black (turning the color into brown), and finally adding white (turning it into tan). The demonstration was presented as an experiment to find out what leads to what when combining colors. Students were then asked to choose and mix their own colors on their own palettes, transferring them to paper with either palette knife or brush. Each worked on white paper tacked to a drawing board made of celotex. Some students continued to experiment with colors, while others began to paint representational pictures.

In subsequent weeks additional art materials were introduced. Once their use was demonstrated they remained available, so that by the end of the term, students chose what they wanted from a kind of smorgasbord display.

It should be noted that teaching through demonstration does not necessarily lead to imitation. Whenever a student used tools or materials in a new way, his innovation received recognition and, if justified, praise. Charlie used his breath to direct lines of paint across his paper (Figure 88, Chapter 5). The painting that won the award in the open juried show (Figure 89, Chapter 5) was an innovative mixture of craypas and turpentine.

## Visuo-Motor Weaknesses and Verbal Strengths

With learning-disabled children whose language seems intact, emphasis is placed on the second objective, exploratory learning, on form rather than content, on shapes and colors, rather than subject matter. Language is also emphasized: art activities are reinforced with words.

With severely impaired children, we start with kinesthetic activities rather than drawing, offering modeling clay, monoprinting in

Figure 90.   Kinetic Family Drawing by stroke patient

rhythmic repetitive designs with objects such as corks, and instructional games such as placing objects in given positions. We postpone the more difficult drawing tasks for last.

### Both Verbal and Visuo-Motor Impairment

With stroke patients, and others who are paralyzed and unable to speak, emphasis is again placed on communication—content rather than form, subject matter rather than abstractions, demonstration rather than talk. A major goal is to obtain information about adjustment and intellectual functioning. This kind of information, inaccessible through language, may be available through drawings.

To illustrate, Gary, a fifteen-year-old youth unable to speak and paralyzed on both sides of his body, with movement limited to two fingers of his left hand, was asked to draw the members of his family doing something (the Kinetic Family Drawing technique devised by Burns and Kaufman). He drew his mother cooking at the stove, his father reading in a chair with the family dog at his side, his brother playing an accordian, and himself in his wheelchair, elevated above the others. Although he enclosed his mother and brother in compartments, he drew no barrier between his father and himself. His drawing suggests that, in spite of everything that had happened to him, he still

Figure 91. "I made a witch"

felt supported and loved (Figure 90). His responses to other drawing
tasks are presented in Chapter 11.

## Emotional Disturbance

With disturbed children and adults, emphasis was on building confidence and reinforcing emotional balance. Experiences that might cause
anxiety were avoided, and emphasis was on projective drawing
techniques, such as asking a child to make a large scribble, look for an
image in the scribble, and develop the image into a drawing.

Figure 91 was produced in this way by a twelve-year-old in a
school for emotionally disturbed children. Previously she had spent
her time in the art sessions covering sheets of paper with blue paint. On
this day, presumably, she felt it was safe to relinquish the blue paint
and try a scribble in charcoal. She was very pleased with her drawing,
saying repeatedly, "I made a witch! I made a witch!" Thereafter she
continued to make representational drawings.

Personal expressions cannot be forced. They seemed to appear
spontaneously when pressures were at a minimum, and they seemed to
vanish when pressures were applied. The change in Lisa's drawings
from expressive to noncommittal, then back to expressive, seemed to
be in response to questioning by her classroom teacher. Lisa, age ten,
made the drawing about braces (Figure 25, Chapter 1), the drawing of
her grandmother in the coffin (Figure 43, Chapter 2), and the spook
behind bars (Figure 45, Chapter 2). Her teacher became so interested
that she asked Lisa to bring her drawings to her home classroom after

Figure 92.  "Hotel/2 Pools"

each art period. After a few weeks, Lisa began to draw vases of flowers and other impersonal subjects, and finally, "Hotel/ 2 pools" (Figure 92). Hoping to elicit more, I asked Lisa if anyone could swim in her pools. She answered, "No, the pool is closed."

After that, her drawings remained in the artroom, and soon she was back in form. Her last drawing showed her class picnic, with a classmate being sick in the bathroom, and included her phone number and middle name in her signature. Lisa's behavior suggests that it is unwise to press a child to talk about his drawings before he is ready. A therapist or educator can only invite drawings about personal experiences by being supportive and accepting and worthy of trust.

To summarize, objectives and methods can be the same for all students, handicapped or otherwise, providing therapists and educators remain flexible and emphasize appropriate methods to meet individual needs.

# Chapter 7

# The Cognitive Skills
# Under Consideration

The art procedures described in the following chapters were attempts to develop in the children three concepts related to cognition that are said to be basic in mathematics and reading, as well as important in everyday life. These are: first, the concept of a class or group of objects: second, concepts of space: and third, concepts of sequential order.

Piaget cites three concepts found by the Bourbaki group of mathematicians in their attempt to isolate the fundamental structures of mathematics. They found three independent structures, not reducible to one another, from which all mathematical branches can be generated. One structure is based on ideas of space and applies to neighborhoods, borders, points of view, and frames of reference. A second structure is based on the idea of a group and applies to numbers and classifications. The third structure is based on ideas of sequential order and applies to relationships.

Although these ideas are usually developed through language, they can also be perceived and interpreted visually, and although they may seem highly abstract, Piaget has found them in primitive form in the thinking of unimpaired children as young as six or seven years of age. For example, when asked to copy geometric shapes, they can preserve relationships of inside, outside, and on the border (spatial concepts). They can divide objects into piles according to similarities such as color (concepts of a group or class), and they can put sticks of different lengths in order from shortest to longest (sequential concepts) (Piaget, 1970, pp. 24–32).

The art procedures are based on these three structures as well as on observations by Piaget and Inhelder, and by Bruner and his associates, who have traced the development of cognition through successive stages by presenting children with various tasks. Their tasks were more or less dependent on language, because the investigators were concerned with normal rather than handicapped children, but their tasks can easily be adapted to art activities, and their observations about stages of development enable us to compare handicapped with normal children.

The same three structures found to be basic in mathematics may also be basic in reading. They appear, in slightly different form, in recent studies by investigators concerned with learning disabilities, who seem to be on the same trail, but come from another direction.

One of these investigators, Bannatyne, found that children with dyslexia usually obtain higher scores on certain WISC subtests that, as a group, involve manipulating objects in space without sequencing. He suggested that the three subtests—Picture Completion, Block Design, and Object Assembly—formed a special category, which he called Spatial Ability. Bannatyne also found that dyslexic childen do reasonably well in the WISC subtests that involve the ability to manipulate spatial images conceptually. These subtests—Similarities, Comprehension, and Vocabulary—form his Conceptual category. In one study involving eighty-seven learning-disabled children of ages eight to eleven, he found that 70% had Spatial scores greater than their Conceptual scores. Because the WISC test is standardized, only 50% of normal children would have Spatial scores greater than their verbal Conceptual scores (Bannatyne, 1971, p. 375). He also found that these children almost always do worst on WISC subtests involving ability to sequence (Arithmetic, Coding, and Digit Span subtests—his Sequencing category).

Bannatyne reasoned that it would be useful to regroup the subtests into Spatial, Conceptual, and Sequential categories rather than the traditional Verbal and Performance categories, and subsequent studies by other investigators have confirmed his findings and supported his hypothesis.

Rugel reviewed twenty-five studies of WISC subtest scores of disabled readers, reclassifying the subtests into Spatial, Conceptual and Sequencing categories. He found that disabled readers scored highest in Spatial ability, intermediate in Conceptual ability, and lowest in Sequencing ability, thus supporting Bannatyne's hypothesis (Rugel, 1974, pp. 57–63).

Smith and his associates administered the WISC-R test to 208 school-verified learning-disabled children, recategorizing the subtests in the manner suggested by Bannatyne. The mean Spatial score obtained was significantly greater than the mean Conceptual score, which, in turn, exceeded the Sequential scores (Smith, 1977, pp. 437–443).

These findings suggest that learning-disabled children are characterized by the same pattern of abilities that Bannatyne found for children with dyslexia, and that Rugel found for disabled readers in general (including dyslexia, minimal brain dysfunction, emotional disturbance, and cultural deprivation).

In their discussion of the significance of finding that these children possess in common high visuo-spatial skills, moderate conceptual skills, and low sequential skills, these investigators note that a cognitive approach to diagnosis and remediation has received little attention compared to perceptual and psycholinguistic approaches. They suggest that the time may now be ripe for serious consideration of the cognitive approach.

The time may also be ripe for serious consideration of the role of art in developing cognitive skills. As Bannatyne observed, learning-disabled children have intellectual abilities of a visuo-spatial nature that are not being recognized, allowed for, or trained, since the emphasis is usually on linguistic rather than visuo-spatial education (Bannatyne, 1971, p. 401).

The three main art procedures described in the next three chapters deal with conceptual, sequential, and spatial skills. Drawing from imagination involves the abilities to select, to combine, and to represent ideas in a context. Drawing from observation involves the ability to perceive and represent spatial relationships. Predictive drawing, painting, and modeling clay all involve the ability to represent spatial concepts and to order sequentially. The procedures are designed to stimulate abstract thinking and reasoning, and to develop readiness for mathematics and language. They are based on the hypothesis that children who are deficient in language may be able to use spatial processing to solve problems and develop concepts.

The tasks involved in these procedures were developed initially in the third study summarized in Chapter 5, the State Urban Education Project involving children with language and hearing impairments (Silver, 1973). Subsequently, the tasks were used in a study of children with learning disabilities who seemed to have visuo-motor impairments, but, unlike the first group, their hearing seemed to be intact (Silver and Lavin, 1977). In both studies the children improved significantly as measured by tests developed in the studies and tests adapted from experiments by Piaget, Bruner, or their associates.

# Chapter 8

# Ability to Associate and Represent Concepts Through Drawing from Imagination

## RATIONALE

The ability to form groups on the basis of function or class is one of the three basic structures from which all the branches of mathematics can be generated, as Piaget has pointed out (see Chapter 7). Using the concept of a class, or group of objects, requires the abilities to make appropriate selections, to associate them with past experiences, and to combine them into a context, such as a sentence. These abilities also have particular significance in working with handicapped children, because the two fundamental kinds of language impairment are linked with disorders of verbal selection and combination. Receptive language problems have been called "similarity disorders"—a disturbance of the ability to detect resemblances and make selections, or an inability to analyze or break down a context, such as a sentence, into its constituent parts. On the other hand, expressive language problems are associated with disturbance of the ability to synthesize or to combine the parts into a whole. As might be expected, selecting and combining are said to be the two fundamental operations underlying language behavior (Jakobson, 1964, p. 25).

Although nonverbal behavior is not of much concern to linguists and neurologists, their observations have interesting implications for the visual arts. For, if selecting and combining are the two fundamental operations underlying verbal behavior, they seem no less fundamental in the nonverbal behavior characteristic of art activities. The painter, for example, selects and combines colors, lines, and shapes, and if his work is representational he selects and combines images as well. He combines them into visual contexts that are interesting to look at and may convey meanings that cannot be put into words.

Furthermore, selecting and combining are fundamental not only in language and the thinking that underlies art, but also in creative thinking. The creative individual is often characterized as one who makes unusual leaps in associating experiences not commonly regarded as alike. In other words, he has an unusual capability for selecting and combining, regardless of whether he expresses his thoughts through language, visual art, or some other medium.

Finally, the abilities to select and to combine are fundamental in emotional adjustment. The idea of a group of objects is a concept, and impairment of concept formation is one of the main ways in which neurological and other kinds of damage impinge on thinking. The effects of maladjustment can be discovered earlier in concept formation than in other thought processes, according to Rappaport. He notes that, in verbal concept formation, impairment may escape detection because verbal conventions often survive as "empty shells" even when the ability to form concepts has become disorganized (Rappaport, 1972).

The testing procedures that follow are attempts to bypass verbal conventions and to use drawings instead to evaluate the abilities to select, to combine, and to represent. It is hypothesized that concept formation is evident in visual conventions as well as in language, and that drawings can provide clues to cognitive skills, to thought associations with emotional or unconscious sources, and to changes, if any, in concept formation and adjustment. The remediation procedures are attempts to develop the ability to form associations and to represent them through drawings; that is, to help a child or adult make selections, and deal with them by combining them on the basis of both form and content.

### TESTING PROCEDURES

A series of ink and watercolor drawings on 3 × 5″ cards is presented. They consist of five people, five animals, and five objects, presented in two arrays, as shown in Figures 93 and 94. Materials for this task consist of 8½ × 11″ paper, pen or pencil (without eraser), and the set of fifteen stimulus cards.

The children or adults (individually or in groups) are asked to look over the cards, to select one card from each array, and then to draw a picture about the subjects they select. They are asked to make their drawings tell a story, adding whatever they need to make the story more interesting. They are also asked not to copy the stimulus drawings, but to draw the subjects in their own individual ways. This may seem a difficult idea to get across to children with language and hearing problems, but very few children copied the drawings, and those who

Figure 93.   Stimulus cards, set A

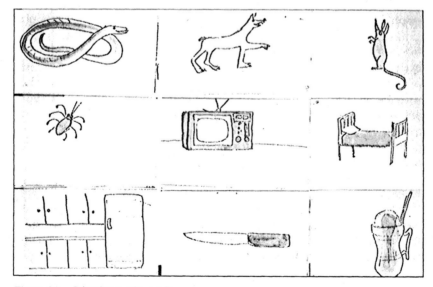

Figure 94.   Stimulus cards, set B

did at first, caught on quickly, and stopped copying when they saw what their classmates were doing. The wish to copy may reflect feelings of inadequacy rather than confusion about directions, however, and we do not ask the children not to copy more than twice.

The intentions are to suggest classes of subjects rather than particular instances of a class, to stimulate thinking about relationships between the subjects selected, and to elicit the associations nonverbally. When his drawing is finished, each child is asked to add a title and to sign his first name to his drawing. If talking is not difficult for the children, they are encouraged to discuss the reasons why they chose their subjects.

Drawing responses are rated on a scale of 1 to 5 points for the abilities to select, to combine, and to represent, with 1 indicating little ability and 5 indicating much ability. Titles and levels of affect are also rated, as well as aesthetic merit and classroom behavior (as indicated in Table 11). The task is used as a pretest and posttest, before and after an art program, in order to note any changes. The scoring form could also be used to evaluate any drawing from imagination.

### Ability to Select (Content)

There seem to be three recognized levels of the ability to select: the lowest level is concrete, the intermediate level is functional, and the highest level is abstract. To illustrate, in experiments with normal children, Olver and Hornsby found that up to the age of seven, a child groups objects on the basis of perceptual attributes, such as color or shape. He takes his first step away from domination by the visible, tangible aspects of things when he takes into account their functions—what they do, or what he can do to them. Gradually, by early adolescence, he develops true conceptual grouping on the basis of class—invisible attributes or abstract ideas. If we ask a child in what way apples and oranges are alike, the young child is likely to say both are round. The older child is likely to say both can be eaten. The adolescent is likely to say both are fruit. In this study it was found that groupings based on perceptible qualities declined steadily from 47% at age six to 20% at age eleven. At the same time, functional groupings increased from 30% at age six to 47% at age eleven (Bruner, 1966a, pp. 70–85).

Olver and Hornsby's experiments called for verbal responses. In one, words were presented on cards and the children were asked how the words were alike. In the other, pictures were presented and the children were asked to select objects that were "alike in some way," and then explain why they were alike. The task used in this study was

Table 11.   Scoring form for drawing from imagination

| Name | Age | Sex | Exceptionality | Date |
|------|-----|-----|----------------|------|

Score from 1 to 5 points (use 2, 3, or 4 for intermediate levels).

A.   Content (ability to select)_____

     1 point:   shows ability to select on the basis of perception; subjects are unrelated in size or placement

     3 points:  shows ability to select on the basis of function; what subjects do or what can be done to them, concrete associations

     5 points:  shows ability to select on the basis of concept or class; goes beyond concrete associations, suggests predetermined idea, imaginary play, abstract thinking; implies more than is visible. Confirm through title (Item E)

B.   Form (ability to combine)_____

     1 point:   shows ability to combine on the basis of proximity and separation; subjects are uncoordinated, floating

     3 points:  shows ability to combine on the basis of a base line (may use bottom of paper as base line)

     5 points:  shows ability to combine into a unified whole; subjects seen from a single point of view, attention to background .

C.   Creativity (ability to represent)_____

     1 point:   shows ability to represent on the basis of imitation; copies stimulus cards or uses stick figures or stereotypes

     3 points: shows ability to restructure; changes or elaborates on cards or stereotypes

     5 points:  shows ability to transform; drawing is inventive, imaginative, personal

The following items are optional. They may be inappropriate in evaluating subjects who have sensory-motor impairments or language disorders.

D.   Aesthetic Merit_____

     1 point:   commonplace form or content

     3 points:  moderate skill or sensitivity

     5 points:  skillful or sensitive expression of a central idea

E.   Title_____ (solicited_____ spontaneous_____) (oral_____ written_____)

     1 point:   descriptive; simply describes what is visible

     3 points:  amplifies; elaborates on what is visible

     5 points:  transforms; meanings are not apparent without title or explanation

an attempt to elicit the same kind of information through drawing, to determine whether an individual selects pictorial elements at the perceptual and concrete level (scored 1 point), at the functional level (scored 3 points), or at the abstract and conceptual level (scored 5 points).

Here are some examples. In drawing Figure 95, Betty selected the stimulus drawings of the girl and the television set, but did not relate them in size or placement. Then she selected the dog and related it to the girl by drawing the dog on a leash. Her drawing was scored 2 points, averaging 1 and 3, for selecting at first on the basis of perception, and later on the basis of function (showing what subjects do or what can be done to them).

Betty, age thirteen, had receptive language impairment as well as severe sensorineural disabilities, including hearing loss of 78 dB in her better ear. Her score on the WISC scale was 64. She also had difficulty with tasks like copying work from the blackboard, and she had emotional problems. She was provocative with other children and had little tolerance for frustration. It was thought that her difficulties revolved around her relationship with her mother, who once wrote, in a letter preserved in Betty's school folder, "I can beat and punish her just so

Figure 95.   Selecting at the functional level

much, but this does not help at all." Incidentally, her mother had had rubella during her pregnancy with Betty.

Figure 96 was the response of Damon, age ten, who had expressive language impairment and a score of 77 on the WISC scale. His drawing received the highest score, 5 points, for the ability to select. Although he did not say much about his drawing, it speaks for itself as a fantasy of violent death. Even his words, with all their mistakes (misspelling "kills" and failing to complete his title, "Man kissl a . . . ") are charged with feeling and conflict (between kill and kiss). Damon had selected the stimulus drawings of the knife, and the head and shoulders of a man. Although he responded to a structured task, his drawing was highly expressive.

It is interesting to note that Damon's diagnosis was *expressive* language impairment, yet his expressive impairment did not carry over to expression through drawing. Betty, on the other hand, was diagnosed as having *receptive* language impairment, which did seem to interfere with expression through drawing.

## Ability to Combine (Form)

The ability to combine was also evaluated on a 5-point scale, based on observations by Piaget and Inhelder, who traced the development of the ability to associate or form groups in spatial as well as logical contexts. They found that before the age of seven a child typically regards each item in isolation, rather than as part of a comprehensive

Figure 96.  "Man Kissl a . . . "

system. Gradually he begins to consider objects in relation to neighboring objects, and to group them on the basis of proximity and separation. The seven-year-old begins to relate objects to an external frame of reference (the bottom of his paper), drawing a parallel line to represent the ground and relating his subjects to one another along this line, or else depicting them on the bottom edge of the paper itself. Gradually his drawings become more coordinated as he takes into account distances, proportion, perspective, and the dimensions of his paper (Piaget and Inhelder, 1967, pp. 430–446).

To evaluate the ability to combine, a drawing receives the lowest score (1 point) if the subjects seem unrelated to each other, or seem related simply on the basis of proximity. A drawing receives the intermediate score (3 points) if it shows a baseline or if the bottom of the paper serves as a baseline. A drawing receives the highest score (5 points) if it shows overall coordination with attention given to the paper as a whole, regardless of whether the drawing is representational or abstract.

Here are some examples. Figure 97 is a drawing by a fifteen-year-old with normal hearing whose impairment in expressive language seems to carry over into impaired visual expression. The drawing seems fragmentary and uncoordinated, with subjects floating in space.

Figure 97.  Combining at the level of proximity

Its meaning is clear enough. To the left someone is watching television. To the right a girl rollerskates on the sidewalk (presented vertically) and a boy rides a bicycle (presented horizontally). A vertical line divides the inside from the outside, with a door at the bottom of the line. The subjects seem to be related at the level of proximity (scored 1 point).

In the drawing titled "Spring Day/Sonny and Cher" (Figure 98) the subjects seem related at the baseline level (scored 3 points). They run along the bottom edge of the paper from one end to the other, a string of flowers between Sonny and Cher like a large family of children.

In the drawing of an urban landscape (Figure 99) the subjects seem related into a unified whole, with attention given to background and to the paper as a whole, all seen from a single point of view. It may seem to be a rather prosaic painting, but it was made by Fred who, later on in the art program, produced the fantasy about his mother's grave (Figure 4, Chapter 1).

## Ability to Represent (Creativity)

A child's concepts of space begin on the perceptual level and continue to the representational level, according to Piaget and Inhelder. It is one thing to perceive an object and quite another to represent it. A child can recognize a circle long before he can draw it from imagination. In order to do so, he must first be able to conjure up a mental image of the circle while the circle is out of sight. At first his concepts of space are

Figure 98.  "Spring Day/Sonny and Cher"

Figure 99.    Combining at the level of a unified whole

imitative and largely passive; then they become intellectually active (Piaget and Inhelder, 1967, p. 37).

In evaluating drawings for ability to represent, a drawing receives the lowest score (1 point) if it passively copies the selected subjects, or follows some stereotypes such as stick figures or cartoon style. A drawing receives the intermediate score (3 points) if the model subjects have been restructured, since restructuring requires thought. Betty, who drew a dog sitting down when the model dog was standing up, had to reconstruct its appearance in her imagination, recalling how a dog might look when sitting, weighing alternatives, making decisions, and changing or elaborating on the dog's appearance.

A drawing receives the highest score (5 points) when it transforms the model and is highly personal, imaginative, or inventive. A child whose drawing transforms the subject seems to have responded to it as an example of a class rather than as a particular object, and then substituted another example of the class that seemed more appropriate. Furthermore, in order to convey a message through his drawing, a child must relate his subjects to one another and to his viewer, and he may relate himself to his subjects as well. This kind of drawing not only gives evidence of thought, but also is often highly personal and inventive.

To illustrate, Daisy, age fourteen, selected the stimulus drawing of the bride, drawing her seated at a table with a wedding cake beside her (Figure 100). To go with the bride she also selected the ice-cream soda, drawing it on the other side of the cake. She seems to have selected on the basis of function (what brides do is eat).

Figure 100.  Daisy's first drawing      Figure 101.  Daisy's second drawing

Daisy then discarded her drawing and started another (Figure 101), replacing the soda with a bridegroom who says, "yes Marry," while the bride says simply, "Marry." She seems to have been thinking as she drew, associating the bride with romance, going beyond the concrete association of her first drawing to fantasy and imaginary play.

This drawing was scored 5 points for the ability to select, 3 points for the ability to combine (she used the bottom of her paper as a baseline), and, because she restructured the bride, 3 points for creativity or the ability to represent. Daisy had receptive and expressive language impairments and a hearing loss of 75 dB in her better ear. The only record of an intelligence test was a mental age of six and one-half years on the Merrill-Palmer scale when her chronological age was seven and one-quarter.

David, age nine, also selected the stimulus drawing of the bride, and with her those of the refrigerator and the television set, titling his drawing "Wedding Presents" (Figure 102). He has transformed the bride (a half-length, three-quarter view in the stimulus drawing), creating a full-length frontal view and inventing a remarkable costume. He also transformed the television set and gave the bride two large refrigerators instead of the modest single one of the model. The judges scored this drawing 5 points for the ability to represent, 3 points for the ability to select (on the basis of function), and 3 points for the ability to combine (along the baseline). David had receptive and expressive language impairments. At the age of two he lost an eye due to retinoblastoma and stopped talking, temporarily, following the surgery. His score on the Merrill-Palmer test at the chronological age of sixty months suggested a mental age of fifty months.

Tom chose the stimulus drawing of the cat to go with that of the mouse, combining them in a way that suggests the mice are in trouble (Figure 103). Although the stimulus drawing showed a whole cat in profile, Tom drew only its head, full face, large, and enclosed with the mice in a border of blue paint. They are grouped into a unified whole on the basis of function and possibly class. Since Tom did not want to talk

Figure 102.  "Wedding Presents"

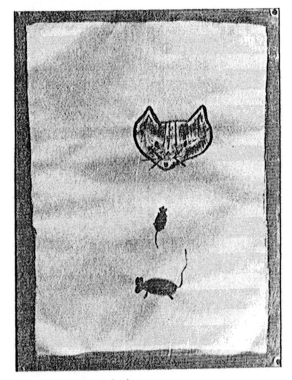

Figure 103.  Cat and mice

about his painting or give it a title, we cannot know whether his visual statement is simply that cats catch mice, or whether his associations had emotional or unconscious sources, symbolizing events in his life.

Ruth also selected the stimulus drawing of the cat, but associated it with flowers rather than mice (with life rather than death). She said her painting (Figure 104) showed "my cat in a garden." In reality she lived in the city and did not have a cat. This painting, scored 5 points in each category, was produced in her last art class. It is interesting to compare it with her first painting, Figure 105, scored 1 point in each

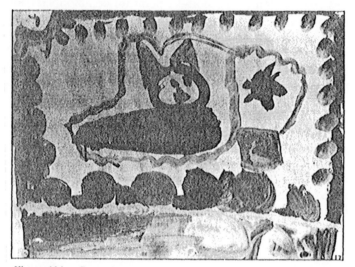

Figure 104.   Cat and garden

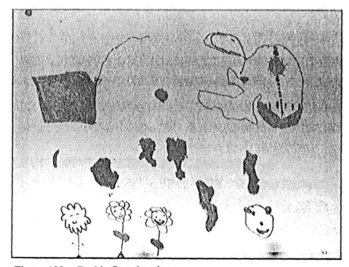

Figure 105.   Ruth's first drawing

category. It is typical of the fragmentary drawings produced by many of the children who seemed unable, at first, to select on the basis of class or function, or to combine their subjects meaningfully.

### Aesthetic Merit

This item on the scoring form for drawings and paintings from imagination seems to need no elaboration. Its purpose is to provide a 5-point rating scale for evaluating the level of art skill and sensitivity to art values, in order to note changes, if any, following an art program.

A drawing or painting is scored 1 point for commonplace form or content, 3 points for moderate skill or sensitivity, and 5 points for the skillful or sensitive expression of a central idea, with 2 or 4 points indicating intermediate levels.

The series of five drawings and paintings by Miguel (see Chapter 4) might serve as an illustration, with his first drawing rated 1 point (Figure 83) and his last painting rated 5 points (Figure 87).

### Affect

The expression of feeling in a drawing or painting can provide clues to concepts of self and attitudes toward others, while changes in expressiveness can provide clues to changes in personality before they are evident in other forms of behavior.

Drawings can be rated for the level of affect, with 1 point for a low level—subjects such as landscapes without people, trees with bare

Figure 106.   "NO BODY ON THE BEACH in Puerto Rico"

branches or no roots, houses with closed or barred windows and doors, isolated individuals, and so forth.

Figure 106, entitled "NO BODY ON THE BEACH in Puerto Rico," and Figure 107, untitled, might serve as examples. They were painted by Tom, age fourteen, who had a hearing loss of 71 dB, which did not seem to explain his other limitations in language, according to school records. Many of his classmates had been transferred to another school and he had asked repeatedly, without success, to join them. His mother had recently moved to California with her other children, leaving Tom behind with his grandmother.

Drawings with highly charged subject matter can be scored 5 points for a high level of affect. Randall's gorilla (Figure 108) and Dorothy's confrontation (Figure 109) might serve as examples.

## Title

The content of a drawing or painting is often obscure without some explanation, particularly when the subject matter refers to abstract ideas. Symbolic meaning goes beyond the form and is, by definition, invisible. Consequently there must be some knowledge of the conscious intent or unconscious meaning behind the drawing before there can be any certainty that the subjects were selected at the level of function or connotation. This is usually determined by verbal association.

Figure 107.  Nobody at home

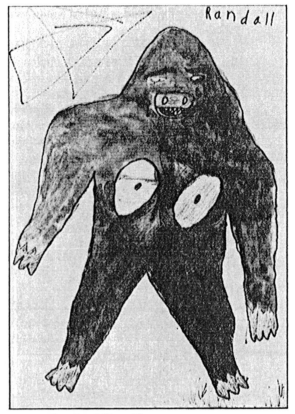

Figure 108.   Randall's gorilla

Figure 109.   Confrontation

Consequently, the scoring form for drawings from imagination asks for a title after the drawing is finished. The title is rated from 1 to 5 points, with 1 point for a title that simply describes what is visible in the drawing, 3 points for a title that elaborates on what is visible, and 5 points for a title that reveals meanings that would not be known without it.

The eight-year-old who painted Figure 110 was highly verbal but did not draw very well. He described this painting as, "a king on his birthday with a cake and icecream cone steps to the door to his castle." The royal ice-cream cone is easily overlooked—it is below and between the cake and the castle tower. Without language, there seems

Figure 110.   "A king on his birthday with a cake and icecream cone steps to the door to his castle"

Figure 111. "The Babies Sitter"

no way of knowing about the imaginary play that accompanied the painting.

## REMEDIATION

Much learning is acquired by association, according to Wilson. He hypothesizes that learning takes place because two things occur together in time. When those same events occur in a similar fashion on several occasions, there is abstraction and generalization. For example, a child screams and gets his way, and eventually sees the relationship between screaming and getting his way. This association is fundamental in both cognitive and affective learning and "probably accounts for the vast majority of learning that most people do" (Wilson, 1971, p. 11).

In asking a child, or an adult, to draw from imagination, the goals are to encourage him to make associations, to put different kinds of subjects together meaningfully in a drawing, to imagine and represent relationships between people, objects, and events that may at first seem to be unrelated.

Other stimulus drawings on 3 × 5″ cards are used for remediation. They include ten drawings each of people, animals, and objects, and four drawings of background scenery. In the first remediation session the stimulus cards are again presented in two arrays—people and large animals at random on one table, objects and small animals on an adjacent table. The stimulus drawings are meant to be suggestive, but vague. What might the children see outside the window? Why is this person angry? Where is the person with the valise going, and why? It was hoped that the stimulus drawings would start a child imagining relationships and events, and then drawing or painting pictures about them.

To encourage a child to extend his imagery, additional stimulus cards included drawings of background scenery—a woodland, a beach, a farm, and the interior of a room. Figure 111 was made by Ruben, age eleven, with receptive language impairment, who tried, without much success, to place his "babies sitter" in the room.

Any drawing or painting from imagination that represents interactions between people or between people and animals or objects, involves association on the basis of class or function. In almost every art period the children were encouraged to draw or paint from imagination. The stimulus cards remained available, but were rarely needed. The children preferred their own ideas.

## RESULTS

These testing and remediation procedures were first used in the State Urban Education Project for children with language and hearing impairments (see Chapter 5) (Silver, 1973).

To compare these children with unimpaired children, the tests were administered once to sixty-three children attending a suburban public school. Sixty-eight unimpaired children participated in the study. The tests were administered over a period of several days during which some children were absent from school. Five children missed the drawing from imagination test, and five missed the drawing from observation test. For this reason the totals of the data reflect only sixty-three scores. The thirty-four children in the experimental classes showed significant improvement after the art program at the $p < 0.01$ level in the combined abilities of selecting, combining, and representing. The thirty-four children in the control groups showed no significant improvement.

The sixty normal children had slightly higher scores than the handicapped children before the art program (but not at a significant level). After the art program, however, the handicapped children in the experimental group had significantly higher scores than the normal children ($p < 0.05$). This project is described in detail in Chapter 12.

The testing and remediation procedures were subsequently used in another study, in which eleven graduate students in the master's degree program in art education at the College of New Rochelle worked individually with eleven handicapped children, under supervision by the course instructor. Comparing scores of the handicapped children before and after the art program, which consisted of ten weekly one-hour art periods, significant gains were shown at the $p < 0.01$ level in the abilities to select, to combine, and to represent (Silver and Lavin, 1977). This study is also discussed in detail in Chapter 12.

# Chapter 9

# Ability to Order Sequentially and Conserve Through Painting, Modeling Clay, and Predictive Drawing

## RATIONALE

Ideas of sequential order are one of the three basic structures of mathematics cited by Piaget (see Chapter 7), and one of the three fundamental categories of the WISC scale, according to Bannatyne (see Chapter 8). In addition, the ability to deal with sequences of stimuli is a skill that has been critically associated with the ability to read, according to Smith and his associates (Smith, 1977).

The painter, mixing tints and shades of paint on his palette, is continually using sequential skills. He usually starts by putting colors on his palette in a certain order, such as warm colors here, cool colors there. With his palette knife he lifts up dabs of green and blue, for example, and mixes them. If the new color is too green, he adds more blue; if it is too blue, he adds more green; if it is too strong, he greys it by adding a touch of its opposite, red; if it is too dark, he lightens it gradually by adding more and more white. Then, when it seems right, he puts a small dab on his canvas, and takes a step backward to judge the effect.

The sculptor is also continually adding and taking away, building up forms with coils and slabs and lumps of clay. Some children intuitively start with small pieces and join them into a collection of separate parts, which become, for instance, the arms, legs, and head of a human figure. Others start with a single mass of clay and pull out the arms, legs, and heads.

Painting and modeling involve children in more than sequential ordering. They involve children in recalling and predicting what leads to what, and can help them learn to conserve. The ability to conserve, to recognize that an object remains the same in spite of transformations in its appearance, is basic in logical thinking. Most rational thought depends on conservation, according to Piaget, and, according to Jerome Bruner the ability to recognize equivalence under different guises is a powerful idea, not only in science but in everyday life.

Up to the age of about seven, children are typically unable to conserve or to order systematically. In one of Piaget's experiments, children were asked to put a series of sticks in order from the shortest to the longest. He found that seven-year-old children tended to develop a systematic approach to solving this problem, first looking for the smallest stick, then for the next smallest, and so on, until they built the whole series. Slightly younger children, who do not have a systematic approach, are able to put all the sticks together in a series, but only through trial and error. Still younger children are unable to coordinate all the sticks together in a single series, although they may make several small series of two or three sticks (Piaget, 1970, p. 29).

The first natural system of reference involves horizontals and verticals, which are the most stable framework of everyday experience, according to Piaget and Inhelder. They state that it is extremely important to find out whether or not a child can spontaneously use such a system of reference (Piaget and Inhelder, 1967, p. 377). As adults, we are so accustomed to thinking in terms of horizontal and vertical frames of reference that they may seem self-evident. The child of four or five, however, has no notion of vertical objects or horizontal planes. Asked to draw trees on the outline of a mountain, the four-year-old child draws them inside the outline. The child of five or six draws them perpendicular to the incline, and only as he reaches the age of eight or nine does he tend to draw them upright. As for horizontal concepts, the four-year-old scribbles a round shape when asked to draw the way water would look in the outline of a bottle. In the next stage he draws a line that remains parallel to the base of the bottle even when the bottle is tilted. Later he draws an oblique line in the tilted bottle. His lines become less oblique and more horizontal until, at about the age of nine, he draws a horizontal line immediately (Piaget and Inhelder, 1967, pp. 375–418).

The development of these concepts has been explored by other investigators using the Piagetian tasks. One study has found that, by the age of twelve, boys tend to understand the principle that the surface of still water remains horizontal, but girls lag behind. It also found that many college women still do not know this principle, and do not readily learn it through observation (Hoben, Jamison, and Hummel, 1973, p. 173). (It should be noted, however, that the procedures they use seem designed to discourage rather than encourage such learning. It may be that the opportunity to observe that was provided lacked the main clue for discovering the principle—a horizontal frame of reference. Horizontality is discovered by noticing parallels, according to Piaget. The child at Stage 2 has noticed that the surface of water in a bottle parallels its base. When the bottle is tilted, he is confused until he links the water to a parallel external to the bottle. Piaget suggests that the bottle be presented at eye level on a table. In the study by Hoben, Jamison, and Hummel the bottles seem to have been presented below eye level, mounted on round discs, judging from the report's illustration.)

What about the handicapped child? In a pilot study we presented similar tasks to children with language and hearing impairments. We invited them to test out their predictions with weighted string and a bottle half filled with water, and then asked them to draw pictures of someone fishing on a mountain. The responses of one of the children, Eric, were shown in Figures 5 to 9 (Chapter 1). In subsequent studies we used the tasks again to evaluate and develop horizontal and vertical orientation through predictive drawing.

Before turning to the tasks, we might consider a recent discovery—a network of particular brain cells that respond selectively to lines received by the eye in different orientations. David Hubel of Harvard Medical School found cells for horizontal orientation, cells for vertical orientation, and cells for diagonal orientation, each of which is stimulated only if lines in the appropriate orientation are perceived. These findings are cited by Carl Sagan, who observes that at least some beginnings of abstract thought have thus been traced to cells of the brain (Sagan, 1977, p. 33).

## TESTING PROCEDURES

### Predictive Drawing

Children, individually or in groups, are asked to fill in outline drawings, showing the way an ice-cream soda would look as the glass is gradually emptied (ordering a series), the way water would look in a tilted bottle (horizontality), and the way a house would look on a steep mountain slope (verticality), as indicated in Figure 112.

*Ordering a Series*    The ability to order sequentially is scored at the highest level, 5 points, when the diminishing soda is represented by a single series of lines without erasures or corrections, indicating a systematic approach. It is scored at the intermediate level, 3 points, when it is represented by a single sequence of lines, but with erasures or corrections indicating that the sequence was achieved through trial

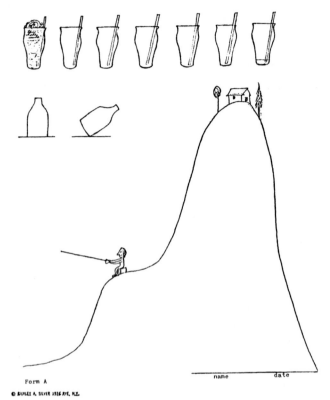

Form A

© BARBARA A. SILVER 1976 RYE, N.Y.

Figure 112.    Predictive drawing test

and error. It is scored at the lowest level, 1 point, when the diminishing soda is represented by two or more sequences of lines or shading (Table 12).

*Horizontal Orientation*    Horizontal orientation is scored 1 point for a line parallel to the bottom or side of the tilted bottle, 3 points for an oblique line not parallel to any line of the tilted bottle nor to the baseline, and 5 points for a line parallel to the baseline (within 5°). Scores of 2 or 4 are used for intermediate levels (Table 12).

*Vertical Orientation*    Vertical orientation is scored 1 point when the drawing shows a house perpendicular to the slope, 3 points when the house is vertical but without visible support, and 5 points when the house is vertical and has visible support, scoring 2 and 4 points for intermediate levels (Table 12).

## Manipulative Tasks

Three additional tests are used when working individually with children. These tasks follow experiments by Piaget, Bruner, or their associates, and serve as pretests and posttests for our studies (Table 13).

Table 12.   Scoring form for predictive drawing

---

*Materials:* pen or pencil and Form A (outline drawings of glasses, bottles, and mountain)

*Procedures:* Ask subjects to fill in the outlines by drawing the way a glass would look as it is gradually emptied, the way water would look in a tilted bottle, and the way a house would look on a steep slope.

For example, "Here is an ice-cream soda (pointing to the first glass at the left), and here it is when the glass is empty (pointing to the last glass at the right). Can you show the way it would look after you ate the ice cream? (pointing to the second glass) and how it would look after you took a few sips, then more sips, and so on until the glass was empty?"

*Score* on the basis of 1, 3, and 5 points (using 2 and 4 for intermediate levels) as follows:

A.   Ordering a series. The diminishing soda is represented by
    1._____two or more sequences of lines or scribbles or shading
    3._____a single series formed through trial and error
            (erasures, corrections, unequal successions of steps, or clusters at either end)
    5._____a single series formed through a systematic approach
            (no erasures or corrections, equal succession of steps)

B.   Horizontal orientation[a]. Water in the tilted bottle is represented by
    0._____a random scribble
    1._____a line parallel to the side or bottom of the bottle
    3._____an oblique line (not parallel to any line of the bottle, nor to the baseline)
    5._____a line parallel to the baseline (within 5°)

C.   Vertical orientation[a]. The house is drawn
    1._____perpendicular to the slope
    3._____on the slope and vertical, but with questionable support
    5._____on the slope and vertical, with visible support

---

[a] The tests of horizontal and vertical orientation are based on experiments by Jean Piaget and Barbel Inhelder as reported in their book, *The Child's Conception of Space,* W. W. Norton and Co., New York, 1967.

**Ordering a Series**   Following the experiment by Piaget described earlier in this chapter, we present the child with a pile of ten sticks and ask him to put them in order from the shortest to the longest. The longest is 4 inches, the shortest is 2 inches.

Responses are scored on a scale of 1 to 5 points, with 1 point for the ability to place three or more sticks in a series without coordinating all into a single series, 3 points for the ability to form a single series through trial and error, and 5 points for the ability to form a single series using a systematic approach.

**Ordering a Matrix (Adapted From Experiments by Bruner and Kenny)**   Bruner and Kenny designed this task to find out at what age

Table 13.   Scoring form for manipulative tasks (ability to order a series
and to conserve)

---

D.  Ordering a series (based on experiments by Piaget, 1970, p. 29)[a]

Present the series of ten sticks in a pile and ask the child to put them
in order from the shortest to the longest (the longest is 4 inches, the
shortest is 2 inches).

1.____places three or more correctly but does not form a single series

3.____forms a single series through trial and error

5.____forms a single series using a systematic approach

E.  Ordering a matrix (based on experiments by Bruner and Kenny, p. 156)[b]

Present the nine cylinders on a matrix as shown. Then remove one,
two, and three cylinders at a time and ask child to replace them.

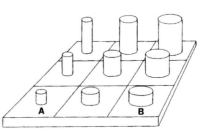

Next, scramble the cylinders
and ask him to "build something
like what was there before."

Again scramble the cylinders
but this time place cylinder A in
grid B and ask if he can make
something like what was there
before, without moving A.

1.____can replace cylinders

3.____can reproduce matrix

5.____can transpose matrix

F.  Conserving (based on experiments by Piaget cited by Bruner, p. 184)[b]

Present the two identical, clear jars filled with lentils and ask the child
to give them the same amount. When he says they are the same, ask
him to pour the lentils in one jar into the third, wider, taller jar and ask,
"Is there still the same amount here (pointing to the larger) as here
(pointing to the smaller)?"

0.____says the amounts are different

5.____says the amounts are the same

---

[a] Piaget, J. 1970. Genetic Epistemology. Columbia University Press, New York.
[b] Bruner, J. S. 1966a. Studies in Cognitive Growth. John Wiley and Sons, New York.

children are able to deal with an array of objects in terms of their
features, rather than with each object individually. They were particularly interested in finding out at what age children are able to deal with
two variables at a time, that is, double classification. In their experiments they found that only the older group of children, age seven,
were able to perform a matrix transposition task at all well. None of the
five-year-olds and only a small fraction of the six-year-olds succeeded
at transposition, although most of the children were able to reproduce a
matrix (Bruner, 1966a, p. 160).

This test presents a set of nine cylinders on a matrix, as indicated
in Figure 113. The cylinders differ sequentially in height and diameter.

Figure 113.   Matrix ordering test

First, one, two, and then three cylinders at a time are removed, and the child is asked to replace them. Next the cylinders are scrambled and the child is asked to reproduce the arrangement by building "something like what was there before." And finally the cylinders are again scrambled, but this time the cylinder that was formerly in the southwest corner of the grid is placed in the southeast corner. The child is again asked whether or not he can make something like what was there before, leaving the one cylinder where it was placed (cf. Bruner, 1966a, p. 157).

Responses are scored 1 point for the ability to replace a matrix, 3 points for the ability to reproduce a matrix, and 5 points for the ability to transpose a matrix (as indicated in Table 13).

*Conservation*   This task is adapted from the classic experiment done by Piaget and described by Bruner (Bruner, 1966a, p. 184).

The child is shown two identical, small, clear plastic jars filled to the brim with lentils, and asked if there is the same quantity of lentils in one jar as there is in the other (Figure 114). If he says no, he is asked to make them the same by taking a few lentils from one jar and adding them to the other.

When he is satisfied that the quantities are the same, the contents of one of the jars is poured into a third jar, which is wider and taller than the identical jars, and again the child is asked if there is the same quantity of lentils in the larger jar as there is in the smaller one (Figure 115). If he answers yes, his score is 5 points. If he says the quantities are different, his score is zero.

Figure 114.   Conservation test, part one

Figure 115.   Conservation test, part two

## REMEDIATION

### Painting

Each child is presented with a series of cards in one color and four progressively lighter tints, then asked if the colors are the same or different. After he has given some thought to similarities and differences, the cards are scrambled and the child is asked to put them back in order.

Next the child is given a paper palette and palette knife and asked to choose one color of paint, either red, blue or yellow, and to put a dab of his color on the upper right corner of his palette. Then he is asked to put a dab of white on the upper left corner, and, after a brief demonstration, to mix a series of tints between the two colors by adding more and more white to the color selected.

Then the child chooses a second primary color for the lower right corner of his palette and is asked to see how many colors he can invent by adding more and more of one color to the other. Finally he is asked to put a dab of black in the lower left corner and to complete the circle by mixing a series of shades between the second color and black, and then a series of greys between the black and the white.

The painting materials are shown in Figure 116. The palette on the left in Figure 117 shows the response of a child who could do the task; the palette on the right shows the response of a child who could not.

Figure 116.  Painting equipment

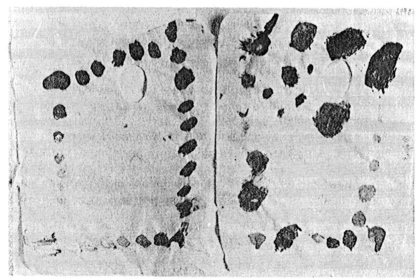

Figure 117.  Series ordering with paint

The task is presented as a game rather than as a test, watching for signs that it may be causing anxiety rather than pleasure. Regardless of whether or not a child can produce a series of colors, we limit the task to ten minutes at most. The rest of the time is devoted to free-choice activity. Some children continue to mix colors, making nonrepresentational paintings, while other children start to paint representational pictures.

## Modeling Clay

Modeling people, animals, and objects from imagination can be a useful remediation technique. Taking some clay away from here and adding it there seems to trigger ideas of conservation. The "slab" technique can also be useful: the child rolls out the clay like dough, cuts it into shapes, and pinches the shapes together into three-dimensional forms.

With children who are unable to conserve, a technique developed by Sonstroem is followed (see Bruner, 1966a, p. 215). The child is presented with two balls of Plasticine and asked if they contain the same amounts of clay. If he says they are not the same, he is asked to make them the same by pinching off some clay from one ball and adding it to the other. When he is satisfied that they are the same, he is asked to roll one ball into a "hot dog." He is then asked whether they still have the same amounts, or whether there is more in the ball than in the "hot dog."

In the Sonstroem experiment, the children who gave nonconserving answers like "the hot dog has more because it is longer" were then given training trials, in which they were asked to change one ball into another shape, such as a "pencil," and back into a ball again. After each alteration they were asked to judge the amounts of clay, and to explain their answers. Each such trial was duplicated with the other ball, and each child had five duplicated trials. The posttest was the same as the pretest, except that the experimenter made a "snake," much longer than the "hot dog." Sonstroem found that eight of the ten (normal) children learned to conserve. Apparently the combination of labeling and manipulating enabled the children to recognize that the amount of clay does not change with the change in its shape.

In working with handicapped children we made minor changes in the Sonstroem technique in order to compensate for a minimum of talk. We asked the children to hold one of the amounts of clay in each hand after each duplicated trial, and, with closed eyes, to compare the weights.

## Manipulating Objects Followed by Painting

With a child who scored 3 points or less in the predictive drawing task, it has been found useful to invite him to test out his predictions with a

Figure 118.  Testing out predictions

straight-sided bottle half filled with tinted water, a plumbline of string weighted with a lump of clay and suspended from a stick, and toy mountains and houses, as illustrated in Figure 118.

The bottle is presented at eye level on a table, so that the parallels between the bottom of the bottle and the surface of the table are clearly visible as the bottle is slowly tilted. The plumbline, tied to a stick ("fishing pole"), is suspended next to windowframes or doors so that the vertical parallels are clearly visible as the stick is slowly tilted. When toy houses topple off the mountain, wedges of clay are offered to prop them up.

After about five minutes the children are asked to draw or paint pictures of someone fishing with a mountain nearby, in the hope that the children will reflect on the learning experiences while they paint.

## RESULTS[1]

### Horizontal and Vertical Orientation

In the State Urban Education Project, the thirty-four children with language and hearing impairments who participated in the art program showed significant improvement. Comparing mean scores before and after the program, improvement was found at the $p < 0.01$ level. The thirty-four children in the control group, who did not attend art classes, did not improve.

---

[1] Statistical analyses are presented in detail in Chapter 12.

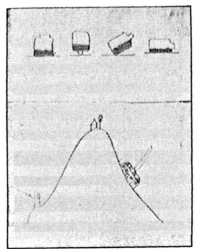

Figure 119.   David's first predictive drawing

To illustrate, Figure 119 is the first response by David, a nine-year-old with language and hearing impairments. It was scored 1 point in horizontal orientation because he represented the water with a line parallel to the side of the tilted bottle, and 1 point in vertical orientation because he drew the house perpendicular to the slope.

After manipulating the plumbline and other objects, he painted a picture of someone fishing from a boat (Figure 120).

Figure 120.   David's painting of someone fishing

When he had finished painting, David was again asked to do the predictive drawing task. In this second attempt he represented the water with an oblique line in the tilted bottle (3 points). Then, spontaneously, he drew another bottle on the test form, and represented the water with a line that was almost horizontal (4 points). In drawing the house on the slope he produced a vertical house suspended above a platform (3 points for questionable support) (as shown in Figure 121).

One month later the task was presented again. David drew horizontal lines in all the bottles and a vertical house resting on a platform, scoring 5 points in each category (Figure 122). He seems to have developed the concepts of horizontal and vertical orientation.

When comparing the sixty-eight language- and hearing-impaired children with the sixty-eight normal children (all of them completed this portion of the whole test) the normal children had significantly higher scores in horizontal orientation on the pretest. On the posttest, however, there was no significant difference between the scores of the handicapped children who had participated in the art program, and the scores of the normal children.

In vertical orientation the normal children also had significantly higher scores than the handicapped children on the pretest. On the posttest, however, the handicapped children who had participated in the art program had significantly higher scores than the normal children.

In the study in which eleven graduate students worked under supervision with eleven children who had visuo-motor disabilities, five

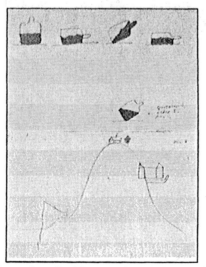

Figure 121.   David's second predictive drawing

Figure 122.   David's last predictive drawing

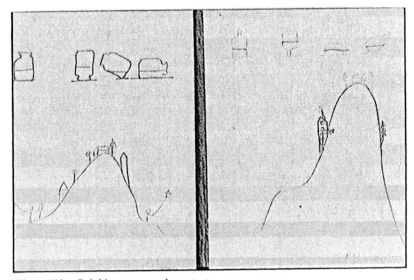

Figure 123.   Ralph's pretest and posttest

children showed improvement after the art program, five showed no improvement, and one child was able to perform the tasks before the art program began.

It is interesting that the results suggest that the abilities under consideration are independent of analytical and verbal skills. Ralph, the child with learning disabilities and an IQ score of 77, who produced Figures 1 (Chapter 1), and Figures 70 through 73 (Chapter 4), had no difficulty with the predictive drawing tasks, scoring 5 points on the

Figure 124.  Ralph's painting of someone fishing

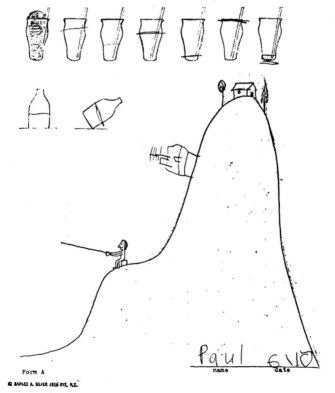

Figure 125.  Paul's predictive drawing

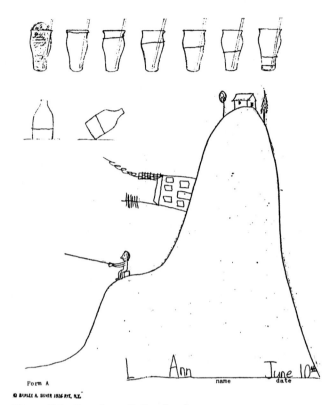

Figure 126.   Lucy's predictive drawing

pretest and posttest (Figure 123). His painting of someone fishing near a mountain is additional evidence of his spontaneous use of horizontal and vertical frames of reference (Figure 124).

More surprising is the finding that normal children with high intelligence, and even highly educated adults, have considerable difficulty with the predictive drawing tasks. Figure 125 is the response of Paul, age eight, one of the normal children in the suburban public school. It was scored 1 point for the ability to order a series (two or more series of lines in the soda glass), 3 points for horizontal orientation (an oblique line), and 1 point for vertical orientation (house perpendicular to the slope).

Paul's classroom teacher described him as one of the two brightest children in her class, rating him 5 points each for intelligence, language skill, and reading skill. In drawing from imagination and from observation his scores averaged 3 points.

The other child who shared the teacher's highest rating for intelligence and academic skill was an eight-year-old girl who produced Figure 126. It was scored 5 points for the ability to order a series, and 1 point

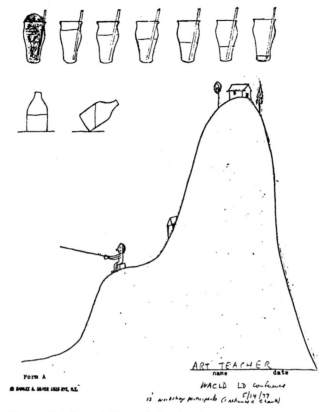

Figure 127.   One adult's predictive drawing

each for horizontal and vertical orientation. Her score in drawing from observation was also low, but in drawing from imagination she averaged 4.3 points out of a possible 5.

A professional adult at a conference for children with learning disabilities produced Figure 127.

Another adult at another conference, who identified herself as a student, wife, and mother, produced Figure 128.

### Sequential Ability

Before the State Urban Education Project, seven of the eighteen handicapped children in the Fall art program were unable to put a series of sticks into a single sequence systematically. Of the seven, four were able to sequence through trial and error, while three were unable to sequence at all. After the art program two of the eighteen children were unable to sequence systematically, suggesting that five children had developed the ability. In the control group eleven children were unable to sequence systematically. Of these, six were able to sequence

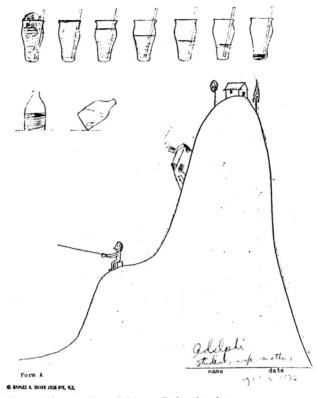

Form A

© STANLEY A. SILVER 1976 RYE, N.Y.

Figure 128.    Another adult's predictive drawing

through trial and error and five were unable to sequence at all. In the posttest thirteen children were able to sequence systematically, while five were unable to sequence at all.

In the ability to order a matrix, eight of the eighteen children in the experimental group were unable to transpose the matrix, four were unable to reconstruct the matrix, and one was unable to replace the cylinders. After the art program five were unable to transpose, and one was unable to reconstruct. All were able to replace the cylinders. In the control group there was very little change between pretest and posttest: ten children remained unable to transpose and all remained able to replace, while six were unable to reconstruct on the pretest, and five on the posttest.

In the study involving eleven graduate students and eleven learning-disabled children, improvement in ability to order a matrix was significant at the $p < 0.01$ level. On the pretest six of the eleven children were unable to transpose, and four of the six were unable to reconstruct the matrix. On the posttest three of the six children were able to transpose, and the remaining three were able to reconstruct, as indicated in Table 28 (Chapter 12).

## Conservation

In the pilot study none of the ten children were initially able to conserve, but after the Sonstroem training trials eight of the ten apparently became conservers.

In the study of children with language and hearing impairments, three of the eighteen children in the Fall program were initially able to conserve. After the training trials seven were apparently able to conserve.

In the study of children with learning disabilities, three of the eleven children were initially able to conserve. After the training trials five were apparently able to conserve.

# Chapter 10

# Ability to Perceive and Represent Concepts of Space Through Drawing From Observation

## RATIONALE

Concepts of space are the third of the three basic structures of mathematics cited by Piaget, and the third of Bannatyne's three categories of WISC subtests (see Chapter VII).

In tracing the development of concepts of space, Piaget and Inhelder observed that a young child starts out regarding each object in isolation, its various features taken in turn. Gradually he begins to regard objects in relation to neighboring objects, linking them into a single system by coordinating different points of view. At the same time he begins to coordinate objects as such, developing ideas of straight lines, parallels, and angles. This coordination assumes the conservation of distance—relations of order applied simultaneously to all three dimensions. Eventually he arrives at a coordinated system embracing objects in three directions—left-right, before-behind, and above-below (Piaget and Inhelder, 1967, p. 375).

In the study of children with language and hearing impairments, it was found that asking them to draw from observation produced some interesting responses. First they were asked to draw an arrangement of three cylinders and a toy bug, then a week later a toy landscape, and finally the cylinder arrangement again.

Ralph, age twelve, with an IQ of 77, had clearly arrived at a coordinated system embracing objects in the three directions. His drawings (Figures 129 and 130) are accurate representations of the two arrangements, except for the omission of a second tree to the right of the large house in Figure 130.

Ben, fourteen, with an IQ of 70, had clearly not arrived at a coordinated system. He represented the cylinders as circular forms with

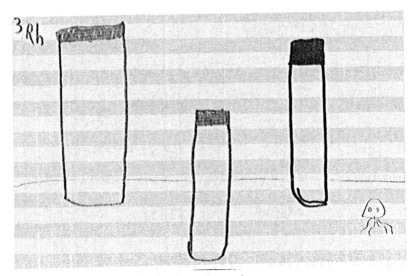

Figure 129.    Ralph's first drawing from observation

Figure 130.    Ralph's second drawing from observation

circular scribbles inside them. He perceived their depth relationships, but represented them not as they appeared from where he was sitting, but as they would appear when viewed from above. He perceived that the widest cylinder was farthest to the left, and the toy bug farthest to the right, but only the bug rests squarely on the table, and one cylinder seems to float above it (Figure 131).

In his landscape drawing (Figure 132), Ben noticed that the dinosaur on the left was in front of the tree. The large empty space between them and the other objects suggests, however, that he still related objects on a one-to-one basis, or perhaps was just beginning to regard objects in relation to neighboring objects.

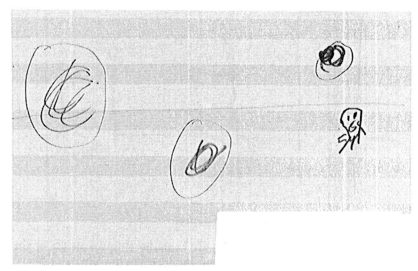

Figure 131.    Ben's first drawing from observation

Figure 132.    Ben's second drawing from observation

Surprisingly, when the cylinder arrangement was presented again, Ben produced Figure 133. He drew recognizable cylinders, their heights and widths fairly accurately, all resting on the table. Dotted lines below the central cylinder suggest that Ben was aware that it was in the forefront, and was well on his way to representing it accurately. (Ben, at age seven, showed a motor age of approximately three years, perseveration, and severe motor perceptual organization on the

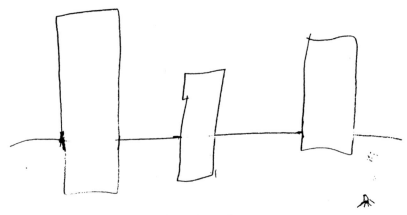

Figure 133.    Ben's third drawing from observation

Bender-Gestalt scale. On the Peabody scale he showed an IQ of 104 and a mental age of six years and four months. On the Vineland Social Maturity Scale, his SQ was 62, and his SA, 3.9 years.)

Dan, age fifteen, with an IQ of 65, unable to read, and having the diagnosis of "congenital expressive aphasia," produced Figure 134. His representation of cylinders seems to be in a transitional stage between circular forms and perceiving the tops of the cylinders as circles. His drawing is fragmented: two cylinders are vertical, and the third cylinder and the bug are horizontal.

Dan's second drawing from observation, the landscape, was much better than his first, and his third attempt, drawing the cylinder arrangement from the opposite side of the room, was better than his second (Figures 135 and 136).

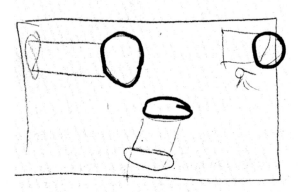

Figure 134.    Dan's first drawing from observation

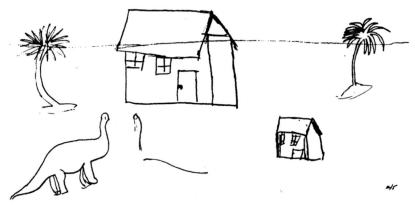

Figure 135.   Dan's second drawing from observation

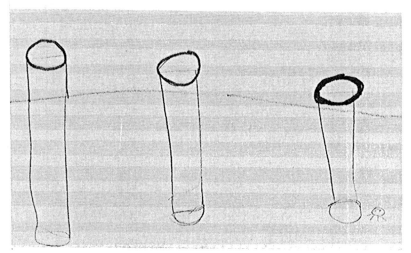

Figure 136.   Dan's third drawing from observation

Other children also showed improvements within a short period of time. David, age nine, used a baseline as his frame of reference in the landscape drawing, as might be expected from a child of his age (Figure 137). He broke away from the baseline in Figure 138, and his second drawing of the cylinder arrangement (Figure 139) shows greater discrimination than his first.

Reuben, age eleven, with an IQ of 87, whose drawing from imagination ("The Babies Sitter," Figure 111, Chapter 9) showed confusion in spatial relationships, also seemed to take a giant step with each drawing from observation (Figures 140, 141, and 142).

These tasks were subsequently developed into the testing and remediation procedures that follow.

Figure 137.   David's landscape drawing

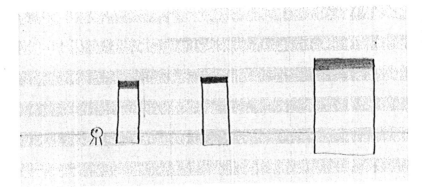

Figure 138.   David's first drawing

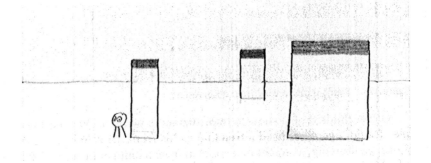

Figure 139.   David's third drawing

## TESTING PROCEDURES

Children, individually or in groups, are asked to draw an arrangement of a large pebble and three cylinders, which differ in height, width, and color. The pebble and cylinders are placed on a cardboard base, and their outlines are traced so that they can be replaced in the same positions (as indicated in Figure 143). The arrangement is placed in the

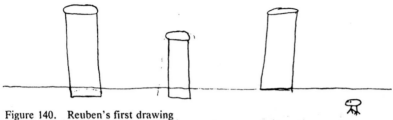

Figure 140.   Reuben's first drawing

Figure 141.   Reuben's second drawing

Figure 142.   Reuben's third drawing

front of the room against a wall, so that the back of the base plane touches the wall.

To clarify the task, a quick sketch of the arrangement (taking no more than twenty seconds) is made by the therapist, then removed from sight. Responses are scored on a scale of 0 to 5 points for the ability to represent spatial relationships (as indicated in Table 14).

Figure 143.   Photograph of the arrangement

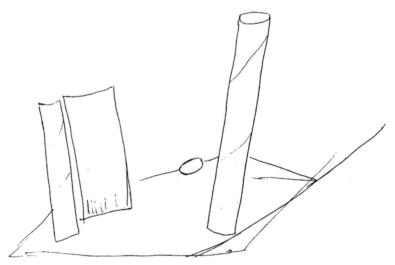

Figure 144.   Drawing scored for the ability to represent spatial concepts

## Left-Right Orientation

A drawing is scored 1 point for the ability to represent horizontal relationships if only two adjacent objects are accurately related on the basis of width, as well as their positions to the left or right of one another. It is scored 3 points if three adjacent objects or two pairs are accurately related, and 5 points if all four objects are accurately related.

To illustrate, Figure 144 was scored 1 point because the left-right relationships of only two objects are represented accurately—the pebble and the cylinder to its right. The other two cylinders are reversed.

Table 14.  Scoring form for drawing from observation (ability to perceive and represent spatial relationships)

---

Materials: pen, 8½ × 11″ paper, and Set B (large pebble, three cylinders differ-
ing in height and width, and cardboard base)

Arrange objects as shown, placed against a wall so that the back of the base plane touches the wall.

Ask subject(s) to sketch the arrangement from observation. To clarify the task, demonstrate with a quick sketch (no more than 20 seconds) similar to front view, then remove your sketch.

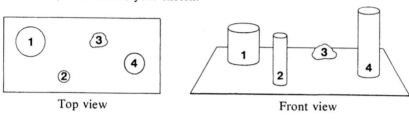

Top view                           Front view

---

name                    age    sex    diagnosis                        date

Score on the basis of 1, 3, or 5 points (using 0, 2, or 4 as needed)

A.  Left-right (horizontality)
  1. _____ two adjacent objects are correctly related in terms of left-right position and width
  3. _____ three adjacent objects or two pairs
  5. _____ all objects

B.  Above-Below (verticality)
  1. _____ two objects are correctly related in height
  3. _____ three adjacent objects, or two pairs
  5. _____ all objects

C.  Front-Back (depth)
  1. _____ two adjacent objects are correctly related in terms of fore-ground and background
  3. _____ three adjacent objects or two pairs
  5. _____ all objects

---

© Rawley A. Silver, 1976, Rye, N.Y.

## Above-Below Orientation

A drawing is scored 1 point for the ability to represent vertical relationships when only two objects are accurately related on the basis of
height. It is scored 3 points when three objects or two pairs are accurately related, and 5 points when all four objects are accurately related.

Figures 145–146. Drawings showing lack of the ability to represent depth

Figure 144 was scored 5 points because the above-below relationships of all four objects are represented accurately.

### Front-Back Orientation

A drawing is scored 1 point when only two adjacent objects are correctly related on the basis of foreground and background, 3 points when three adjacent objects or two pairs are accurately related, and 5 points when all four are accurately related in depth.

Figure 144 was scored 3 points for the ability to represent depth, because the front-back relationships of only two pairs of objects are

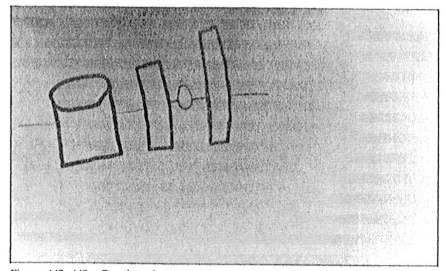

Figures 147–148.   Drawings showing lack of the ability to represent depth

represented accurately—the narrowest cylinder with the widest cylinder, and the pebble with the cylinder on the right. In this drawing the widest cylinder appears further forward than the pebble, but, actually, it is to the rear. (It may come as a surprise that Figure 144, scored a total of 9 points, was made by an adult in a workshop on art therapy. In such workshops there were always a few adults who had difficulty with the drawing tasks, as will be discussed later.)

The child who drew Figure 145 failed to represent any front-back relationship, scoring zero in this category.

The children who drew Figures 146, 147, and 148 were apparently aware of front-back relationships, but were unable to represent them accurately. In Figure 146 the objects seem to be standing on a hilly surface, and the two cylinders actually toward the front are perched on the hills, while the two objects actually in back are in the valleys. In the other two responses the cylinders are in a row in both, while the pebble is in the foreground in one, and in the background in the other.

The child who drew Figure 149 was able to discriminate and to represent the spatial relationships in all three dimensions, scoring 5 points in each of the categories under consideration.

## REMEDIATION

One goal of the remediation procedures is to improve discrimination of spatial relationships. Another goal is to improve recognition of differences between objects that are the same, and similarities between ob-

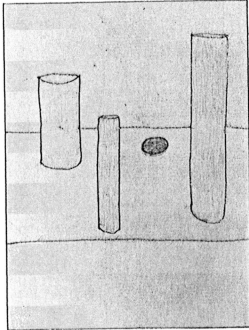

Figure 149.   Drawing showing the ability to represent accurately in all dimensions

jects that are different. These skills should be useful in science and geometry as well as art.

## Drawing Other Arrangements

Cylinders were again used because they are easy to draw and can be represented with just four lines, but for remediation they differed in size, color, and position from the cylinders in the pre/post test to assure that learning had been generalized.

The child is asked to set up an arrangement, and then the therapist draws it first, sitting beside the child so that the same point of view is shared. The therapist draws slowly, and talks as he draws, calling the child's attention to the differences in size, shape, or color, and to the line formed by the back of the table, which serves as a frame of reference. With a child who had difficulty with the pretest, the therapist starts with two cylinders, and, if it seems appropriate, places the child's hand on his as he draws.

Then it is the child's turn to draw from observation, and when he begins to draw, conversation stops. If he draws the red cylinder to the left of the blue one when it is actually to the right, the therapist might ask if the child is sure that is the way he wants it, but does not point out mistakes.

Since this task is highly structured, it is limited to about five minutes and followed by free-choice activity. Once the child begins to draw, talk is avoided and an attempt is made to prevent interruptions and distractions, hoping that he will reflect as he draws, integrating new information with what he has previously learned.

## Reversing the Arrangements

The task becomes more difficult, and assumes a higher level of skill, when the arrangement is placed in the center of the room and the child is asked to draw it from different points of view. Thus, from one side of the room the red cylinder is to the left of the blue one, while from the opposite side of the room it is to the right. Seen from another position, one cylinder may obscure another, and so forth.

## Drawing and Painting from Observation and Imagination

A toy landscape or other still-life is set up, and students are asked to draw or paint it, adding other subjects from imagination if they wish. In responding, some students are interested primarily in form, while others are more interested in content, as illustrated by Figures 150 and 151. The latter was painted by Dan.

We also include the drawing of human figures from observation. The children draw themselves while looking in a mirror, and take turns posing for one another.

Figure 150. Painting showing interest in form

Figure 151. Painting showing interest in content

## Manipulative Games

The following tasks are presented as games. They can also serve as tests for children and adults with severe neurological impairments or for children younger than seven years old.

*Matching the Positions of Objects*    The aim of this task is to sharpen awareness of spatial relationships by asking a child to observe, manipulate, and evaluate, using the edges of a sheet of paper as frames of reference.

The child is shown three rectangular blocks of different size placed within outline drawings on a sheet of paper. He is given identical blocks and asked to arrange them in the same way on his paper. When he has arranged them to his satisfaction, he is asked to trace their outlines. The two outline drawings are then superimposed and held up to the light so that they can be compared. Often this is all that is needed to enable a child to notice mistakes and correct them.

*Projective Straight Lines (Based on Experiments by Piaget and Inhelder, 1967, pp. 156–171)*    The child is presented with ten matchsticks held upright by bases of Plasticine, and asked to arrange them so that they form a straight line. The first and last matchsticks are placed in position .equidistant from the edge of a straight-sided table. If the child can form a straight line between them, the first and last matchsticks are placed below and to one side of a corner of the table so that a straight line between them forms a triangle with the corner edges of the table. If the child can again form a straight line between them, the first and last matchsticks are placed on the floor (with no frame of reference) and again the child is asked to form a straight line between them.

In their experiments, Piaget and Inhelder found that children younger than four were unable to form a straight line even though they were able to distinguish between a straight line and a curve. Children between four and seven years of age were able to form a straight line, but only if the end poles were parallel to the edge of the table. After the age of seven, the children were able to form a straight line in any location (Piaget and Inhelder, 1967, pp. 156–160).

*Reversing a Toy Landscape (Based on Experiments by Piaget and Inhelder, 1967, pp. 421–426)*    Two identical toy landscapes are built on cafeteria trays—mountains, rivers, paths, trees, and houses made from plaster, cardboard, matchsticks, and clay. On one of the landscapes seventeen positions are marked by number.

The child is asked to place his doll on the unmarked landscape in the same position as the doll on the other landscape (placed by the teacher or another child). After a few trials the child's landscape is turned 180 degrees, requiring him to locate his doll by relating it to parts of the landscape rather than his own position. The game proceeds as the therapist places her doll from positions 1 to 17, each increasingly difficult to locate (Piaget and Inhelder, 1967, pp. 421–426).

The scoring form used for these tests is shown in Table 15.


## RESULTS

Since the final form of pre/post test was developed in the Fall program of the State Urban Education Project, it was used for the first time in

Table 15.   Scoring form for manipulative games

---

| Name | Age | Diagnosis | Date |

A.   Placing Blocks in Given Positions
   1. _____ Outlines overlap 25% or less
   3. _____ Outlines overlap about 50%
   5. _____ Outlines overlap 75% or more

B.   Projective Straight Line[a]
   0. _____ Matchsticks are clustered at ends or form a curve
   1. _____ Matchsticks form a straight line parallel to edge of table
   3. _____ Matchsticks form a straight line at oblique angle to table edge
   5. _____ Matchsticks form a straight line on the floor (no parallels near)

C.   Reversing Toy Landscape[a]
   1. _____ Can reverse one position
   3. _____ Can reverse seven positions
   5. _____ Can reverse fourteen positions

---

[a] Based on experiments by Piaget and Inhelder in The Child's Conception of Space, W. W. Norton and Co., New York, 1967.

the Spring program. The sixteen children with language and hearing impairments showed significant improvement in the ability to represent left-right, above-below, and front-back relationships. Before the art program their mean score was 9.37. After the program it was 11.43, a gain significant at the $p < 0.05$ level. The sixteen impaired children who did not attend art classes (controls) showed no significant improvement.

The sixty-three normal children, who were tested only once, had slightly higher scores when compared with the pretest scores of both groups of impaired children. On the posttests, although the impaired experimental children had slightly higher scores than the normal children, these differences were not significant. What was significant was the improvement of the experimental group.

In the study of children with learning disabilities, significant improvements were also found in spatial orientation (at the $p < 0.05$ level, $t = 2.42$). The statistical analyses of these studies are presented in Chapter 12.

## OBSERVATIONS

The results are surprising when we consider the children who did well and the children who did poorly on the test in the 1973 study. At that time the maximum possible score for representing spatial relationships

Table 16.   Children scoring in the top and bottom 10% in test of spatial concepts

**Language- and Hearing-Impaired Children**

| | Score Pre- | Post | Group | Age | Sex | IQ | Diagnosis (Receptive/Expressive) |
|---|---|---|---|---|---|---|---|
| Top 10%: | 10 | 15 | Experimental | 8 | F | 97 (Merrill-Palmer) | R |
| | 15 | 15 | Experimental | 12 | M | 50 (Stanford-Binet) [no score Peabody] | R/E, mild CP |
| Bottom 10%: | 0 | 4 | Control | 7.5 | F | 3 years below CA (Peabody) | E/R, grapho-motor impairment |
| | 9 | 4 | Control | 8 | M | did not respond (Stanford-Binet) | R/E, hyperlexia |
| | 0 | 4 | Control | 8 | M | 106 (WISC) | R/E |
| | 4 | 4 | Control | 13 | F | 73 (Leiter) [26 (Peabody)] | R, perceptive and motor impairment |

**Normal Children**

| | Score | Age | Sex | Math | Reading | Art | Other |
|---|---|---|---|---|---|---|---|
| | | | | | Levels of Ability (av = average) | | |
| Top 10%: | 16 | 8 | M | −av | −av | +av | "highly verbal" |
| | 16 | 10 | F | av | +av | +av | amblyopia |
| | 16 | 12 | M | +av | +av | | +av in science |
| | 16 | 14 | M | −av | −av | | −av in science |
| Bottom 10%: | 4 | 8 | F | +av (comp) av (prob) | av | +av | |
| | 4 | 9 | M | av | av | av | potentially above average student |
| | 4 | 10 | M | −av | av | +av | |
| | 4 | 10 | M | −av | −av | av | |
| | 4 | 13 | M | av | av | av | |

accurately was 16 points. (Presently the maximum score is 15 points, due to changes in scoring.)

Of the normal and handicapped children (a total of 95), only four scored 16 points. Although all four were "normal," they were not the oldest or brightest children, as might be expected. They ranged in age from eight to fourteen years, and ranged widely in academic ability. The youngest, an eight-year-old boy, was rated by his teacher as below average in reading, above average in mathematics (both computation and problem solving), highly verbal, and above average in art (as indicated in Table 16).

The second child with the maximum score of 16 points was a ten-year-old girl who was average in mathematics and above average in reading and art. She also had a visual impairment (amblyopia, or "lazy eye") and wore corrective glasses which provided depth perception. The third child was a twelve-year-old boy, described as well above average in mathematics, reading, and science. The fourth child, a fourteen-year-old boy, was below average in mathematics, reading, and science.

Five of the ninety-five children scored 15 points. Among them two were language- and hearing-impaired children who had participated in the art program. They were an eight-year-old girl (with an IQ of 97 on the Merrill-Palmer scale) who had scored only 10 points on the pretest, and a twelve-year-old boy (with an IQ of 50 on the Stanford-Binet scale) who had scored 15 points on both pretest and posttest.

There was also a wide range in age and academic ability among the children who scored 4 points or less (the lowest 10%). They included five normal children, ages eight to thirteen, and four impaired children from the control group, ages eight to thirteen (as indicated in Table 16).

# Chapter 11

# Case Studies

## BURT

Burt, age thirteen, had many handicaps—receptive and expressive language impairments, as well as severe hearing loss (75 dB) in his better ear. His IQ was estimated at 43 (Stanford-Binet). (When Burt was seven, several IQ tests were administered. His scores were: Vineland, MA 4.4, SQ 59; Merrill-Palmer, MA 4.2, PQ 56; Stanford-Binet, IQ 40, MA 3.1.)

Before the art program began, his classroom teacher evaluated his abilities and disabilities using a rating scale of 1 to 5 points (Table 17). She gave him the lowest score, "almost never," for the ability to select named objects or to combine words into sentences. She also gave him the lowest score for the ability to group objects on the basis of class, or to associate new information with what he knows. She repeated the evaluation when the art program ended three months later, and again after six months, at the end of the school year. His average score in these categories improved from 1 point to 3.2 points out of a possible 5. This was, of course, a subjective evaluation, and it is not claimed that art experience alone could take credit for his gains, but they are mentioned because they seem to parallel his gains as measured by the project's pretests and posttests.

Burt was present at nine of the eleven art periods. In the first period the children were shown an arrangement of four toy animals on a sheet of paper. They were then asked to select the same animals from a pile and to arrange them in the same way on their own sheets of paper. Burt selected three of the four animals, placed only two correctly in relation to one another, and placed none correctly in relation to the edges of his paper. This task was adapted from an experiment by Piaget and Inhelder, and Burt's response corresponded to their Stage 2, typical children younger than seven who have not yet developed the ability to relate objects according to a system of reference (Piaget and Inhelder, 1967, p. 428).

After this brief task the children were free to draw or paint whatever they liked. Burt drew a faceless man with a knife in his stomach,

Table 17.  Profile evaluation of Burt[a]

|  | October | January | June |
|---|---|---|---|
| **Is (s)he able to:** | | | |
| 1. Select named objects | 1 | 4 | 4 |
| 2. Comprehend words and phrases | 4 | 4 | 4 |
| 3. Follow instructions | 4 | 4 | 4 |
| 4. Find the right word | 4 | 1 | 2 |
| 5. Use nouns, synonyms, antonyms | 2 | 1 | 3 |
| 6. Combine words into sentences | 1 | 1 | 3 |
| 7. Use connective words, pronouns, adjectives, adverbs | 3 | 1 | 2 |
| 8. Sequence events, tell stories | 4 | 3 | 3 |
| 9. Explain his thoughts or ideas | 4 | 2 | 3 |
| 10. Discuss hypothetical questions | 2 | 2 | 1 |
| **In non-verbal activities, does (s)he:** | | | |
| 11. Detect similarities between objects | 3 | 3 | 3 |
| 12. Group objects on the basis of invisible attributes, such as class or function | 1 | 2 | 2 |
| 13. Put objects in sequence such as size or weight | 3 | 3 | 3 |
| 14. Recognize that appearances may be deceiving (knows that spreading out a row of pebbles does not increase the number, for example) | 1 | 3 | 2 |
| 15. Associate new information with what he knows, incorporate and make use of it | 1 | 4 | 3 |
| 16. Concentrate for more than five minutes | 3 | 3 | 4 |
| 17. Retain information and carry a task through to completion | 3 | 1 | 2 |
| 18. Solve problems | 1 | 1 | 2 |
| 19. Engage in imaginary play | 5 | 4 | 2 |
| 20. Originate ideas or forms | 1 | 2 | 2 |
| **Does (s)he tend to:** | | | |
| 21. Work independently without asking for help or direction | 1 | 1 | 3 |
| 22. Control emotions (does not cry easily or hit, shove, fight) | 2 | 1 | 4 |
| 23. Tolerate frustration | 4 | 2 | 3 |
| 24. Join readily in group activities | 4 | 5 | 4 |
| 25. Cooperate with adults | | | 4 |
| 26. Cooperate with other children | 3 | 3 | 3 |
| 27. Be interested in learning language | 4 | 2 | 3 |
| 28. Be interested in learning generally | 4 | 2 | 3 |
| 29. Be playful, humorous (Oct)[b] | 5 | 2 | 2 |
| 30. Have self-confidence, self-esteem | 3 | 2 | 3 |

[a] Rated on the basis of 1 to 5 points: 1 = almost never, 2 = on rare occasions, 3 = sometimes, 4 = fairly often, 5 = very often.
[b] Wording of item 29 was changed in the January and June rating scale to "have a sense of humor".

then stopped. I asked if he would like to give the man a face. He said no, then asked me how to draw a face. I started to demonstrate on the blackboard, but this was not what he wanted. He asked me to draw his own likeness, and I did. Burt then added the face to his drawing (Figure 152), and proceeded with the house and car. When the period ended, he was so engrossed in drawing that his classroom teacher offered to let him stay on.

In the second art period the children were presented with the stimulus cards. Burt chose the boy and the knife, but did not draw them. Instead, he drew airplanes dropping bombs on ships and buildings (Figure 153). He connected bombers and targets with scribbled or dotted lines, accompanying each strike with sound effects.

There is a difference between his two drawings in the way he related his subjects. Although both drawings are fragmentary, with a jumble of points of view, the subjects in his first drawing are related in the most elementary way, through proximity and distance. The man, for example, is larger than the car and the house. In his second drawing, his subjects are related with conventional symbols—dotted lines and scribbles, perhaps intended to be smoke.

In the third period the children were introduced to painting. Burt worked hard, but his hands trembled and his attempts to retrieve drops of paint with the palette knife usually made matters worse.

Clay was introduced in the fourth period, which started with the Sonstroem technique designed to help children learn to conserve (see Chapter 9). Although language could play only a minimal role with

Figure 152a.   Burt's first drawing, man with knife in his stomach

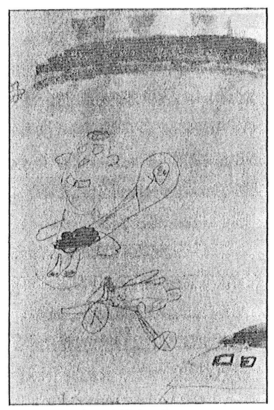

Figure 152b.   Closeup, Figure 152a

Burt, he apparently learned to conserve. He was one of eleven children in the experimental group who were unable to conserve on the pretest. In the posttest, some months later, four of these children were able to conserve amounts of liquid, and Burt was among them. Some studies have found normal adults unable to conserve when presented with the same task.

Burt went on to model the clay, and made a box with a slit on top—a bank. He was so delighted with it that he couldn't wait a week to let it dry, and brought it back to his classroom with him.

In the fifth art period the stimulus cards were again presented. Burt chose the sketch of a nurse showing only her head and shoulders. In his painting, he drew the nurse full length, combined with an object of his own invention—crutches (Figure 154). This painting is organized in both form and content. There is no fragmentation. The forms are placed on the paper as though its edges served as frames of reference, and the functional relationship between nurse and crutches suggests that Burt had a story in mind.

Figure 153.    Burt's drawing of airplanes dropping bombs

With time to spare, Burt painted Figure 155, using black paint and a few touches of red and blue. When he had finished he began to talk about his painting, and I wrote his words on the blackboard. He copied them, spontaneously, on his painting, "No cars, no people, rain all over, can't walk, get a boat, swim."

The sixth art period was similar to the first, placing objects in given positions. Burt showed decided improvement over his performance in the first period, scoring 16 points out of a possible 18. He then painted a nonrepresentational design in flat color planes and dotted line. His hands no longer trembled, as they had in the third period, and there was no suggestion of frustration in the painting or in his classroom behavior.

The next three periods (the seventh, eighth, and ninth) were spent drawing from observation. In the last two periods the children were free to draw, paint, or model clay, as they wished.

Burt's progress in drawing from observation is evident in Figure 156. In his first attempt (Figure 156a) he missed the depth relationships. In his second attempt (Figure 156b) he related the cylinders correctly but omitted the toy bug. In his third attempt (Figure 156c) he was asked to change places with a classmate on the opposite side of the arrangement, and the reversed positions of the objects apparently confused him. His lateral relationships are wrong and the two cylinders

Figure 154.   Burt's nurse on crutches

appear to float above the table. These drawings suggest that Burt had reached Piaget's Stage 2, typical of normal children four to seven years old.

Burt's last drawing (the landscape, Figure 156d), however, is an accurate representation of the seven objects presented only one week later. His distances and proportions are accurate, as well as the lateral and depth relationships. His only mistake was drawing the trees on the top edge of the base plane rather than standing within it. Burt's earlier mistakes had not been pointed out to him; therefore his gains reflect his own observations and corrections.

This drawing suggests that he was at Stage 3, typical of children age nine to eleven, or possibly Stage 4, typical of children his own chronological age, but there was no way to be sure. Piaget's experiments had depended on verbal exchanges and abstract terms. Because verbal exchange with Burt was limited, Piaget's experiment with dia-

Figure 155. "No cars, no people, rain all over," etc.

grammatic layouts could not be carried out (Piaget and Inhelder, 1967, p. 432).

In the ninth art period the children were presented with the predictive drawing task. Burt's score on the pretest was 2 points in horizontal orientation and 4 points in vertical orientation (Figure 157). He explained his painting from imagination (Figure 158) as follows: "The house [suspended above the landscape] will not fall down. The baby fish is eating its mother. The red lines on her body are his bites. A boy sitting on the dock is watching. Another boy [behind the crosshatching] is in jail. They can't fish because the sign says no. Between them is a fish graveyard."

On the posttest he received the highest score (5 points) in both horizontal and vertical orientation (Figure 159). Since studies have found college students who have not learned that water remains horizontal regardless of the tilt of its container, Burt seems to have done very well on his own.

The raw data of the posttests were broken down into fourteen key items. The median score of the experimental group was 11.75, and that

Figure 156.  Burt's drawings from observation

of the control group, 8.5. Burt's score was 12 points, slightly above the median of the experimental group and well above the median of the control group.

Table 18.   Burt's performance on project tests

| Cognitive skills | Pretest October | Posttest January | Changes |
|---|---|---|---|
| 1.  Conserving liquid | 0 | 5 | +5 |
| 2.  Conserving solids | 0 | 5 | +5 |
| 3.  Conserving numbers | 5 | 5 | 0 |
| 4.  Ordering a series | 5 | 5 | 0 |
| 5.  Ordering a matrix | 3 | 5 | +2 |
| 6.  Ordering colors | 1 | 5 | +4 |
| 7.  Placing objects in given positions | 3 | 5 | +2 |
| 8.  Horizontal orientation | 3 | 5 | +2 |
| 9.  Vertical orientation | 5 | 5 | 0 |
| 10.  Grouping three objects | 3 | 3 | 0 |
| 11.  Grouping from an array | 5 | 3 | −2 |
| 12.  Selecting | 1 | 5 | +4 |
| 13.  Combining | 1 | 5 | +4 |
| 14.  Representing | 1 | 5 | +4 |
| mean | 2.57 | 4.71 | 2.17 |

Figure 157.   Burt's predictive drawing pretest

Figure 158.   Burt's drawing from imagination

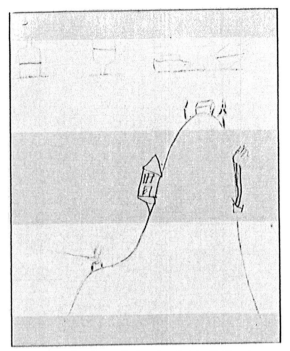

Figure 159.   Burt's predictive drawing posttest

Burt's score on the pretests totaled 36 points out of a possible 70. On the posttests his score was 66 points. His mean score on the pretests was 2.57 out of a possible 5, and on the posttests his score was 4.17 (as indicated in Table 18).

VITO

Vito, age eight, had receptive language impairment and severe sensorineural hearing loss secondary to maternal rubella. With a hearing level of 76–75 dB in his better ear, he had profound speech and language delay secondary to his hearing loss, as well as central language problems. His intelligence was thought to be above average.

In his first drawing (Figure 160) there is little relationship between barely recognizable objects. It was scored 2 points for the ability to select, 2 points for the ability to combine, and 2 points for the ability to represent.

For his second drawing Vito selected the mouse, the bug, and the man from the stimulus cards, and drew them all very small, near the

Figure 160.   Vito's first drawing

Figure 161.   "Mouse, bug"

bottom of his paper. The man at one end is calling to the mouse and the bug at the other end (Figure 161). With most of his paper left blank, Vito seems to have made a collection of the small and weak, including himself, by name, at the end of the line. This drawing was scored 3 points for the ability to select, 3 points for the ability to combine, and 3 points for the ability to represent.

Figure 162. "Vito me"

The third week, when he was introduced to painting, Vito had loudly exclaimed "Green!" when he saw yellow and blue paints mixed on the palette, but he did not try to mix colors of his own. He produced Figure 162, titled "Vito me," using blue for the ground, and yellow for his shoes and face. The absence of hands on his self-portrait may reflect a feeling of inadequacy, but even though the figure still occupies a small part of his paper, it is now at center stage.

The following week Vito selected the cat, the dog, and the tree. Once again he seems to have selected and combined at the lowest levels, and this time his name is spelled backward (Figure 163).

Figure 163. "Otiv"

Figure 164.   Vito's magician

Next he painted a magician (Figure 164). He said the magician was holding an egg, which had been inside the hat on the table beside him. This may reflect a feeling of achievement, since, for the first time, Vito mixed colors on his palette, producing (with a little magic?) green for the ground.

Figure 165 is Vito's drawing of the toy landscape. He mixed red, yellow, and black, producing brown for the ground.

Figure 166 is his response to the request to paint a picture of someone fishing with a mountain nearby. It began in imitation of his classmate, David, who sat beside him. In David's painting (see Figure 120, Chapter 9), the boy says, "I love fishing," while the girl echoes,

Figure 165.   Vito's landscape

Figure 166. "Vito, Vito, Vito"

"me too." In Vito's painting, it is the girl (with green hair) who dominates. She is saying, "I got fish." The boy says nothing.

I intervened with the comment, "Vito, you don't have to copy David. You have very good ideas of your own." With that he wrote his name three times in the sky in formations of flying birds. This painting was scored 5 points for each of the abilities to select, to combine, and to represent.

Vito also showed improvement in sequential ability and in predictive drawing. He had been unable to put a series of colors in order on the pretest, but did so on the posttest. He improved in horizontal orientation from 3 points to 5, and in vertical orientation from 3 points to 4.

During the Fall semester Vito showed progress academically, and in the Spring semester he was placed for part of each day in a class of normal children in a regular public school. I would not say that Vito's improvement was caused by his experience with art, but his participation in the art program may well have helped. Certainly his growing self-confidence is reflected in the series of pictures. Comparing his signatures alone, we have a record of positive change.

Even though he had left the art program in the second term, Vito made one last painting when he dropped in one day for a visit. In Figure 167 the tiny figure at the lower right is firing an arrow into the dinosaur's flank, suggesting that Vito may have gained courage in dealing with "dinosaurs" of his own.

Figure 167.  Vito's dinosaur

## STROKE PATIENTS

The testing and remediation procedures were presented to eight stroke patients who had suffered language impairments in varying degrees. One was a patient in a day hospital, a young man (age fifteen) paralyzed on both sides of his body, with movement limited to two fingers of his left hand. Five patients were paralyzed on the right side, and were confined to a hospital in a rehabilitation center. The other two were outpatients who had recovered, except for residual language impairments.

The young man, who will be called Gary, seemed the most severely impaired, yet he was the only patient able to perform the tasks presented. He could not sit unsupported and could not prevent saliva escaping from his mouth. He seemed to understand everything I said, however, and although he did not speak he communicated by spelling, pointing to the letters of the alphabet printed on a board on his lap. To signal the end of a word he tapped the bottom of the board, as though it were the space bar of a typewriter.

I presented Gary with three tasks: drawing from imagination, drawing from observation, and the Kinetic Family Drawing technique discussed in Chapter 6 (see Figure 90). For his drawing from imagination, Gary chose the stimulus drawing of the car. Then, with a felt-tipped pen between his two functioning fingers, he drew two cars, one above the other. He used the cartoon device of a balloon around the upper car and the moon, indicating that it was the lower car's dream (Figure 168). Then he spelled out a title: "Dreaming about a Dune Buggy."

Figure 168.  "Dreaming about a Dune Buggy"

The idea of a car dreaming about another car suggests that Gary was not only alert, but had a lively imagination. The dreaming car, headlights and taillights turned on, is green. The dream car is the complementary color, red. The green car, asleep and dreaming about its opposite, could represent Gary's immobilized self dreaming about romance. This drawing seems to indicate that Gary's abilities to select, to combine, and to represent were intact.

In drawing from observation, Gary was so enthusiastic that he included not only the cylinder arrangement, but also the table where it was placed and a nearby chair (Figure 169). Thus his ability to perceive and represent spatial relationships, in three dimensions, also seemed intact.

Unlike Gary, four of the five hospitalized patients were unable to perform most of the tasks presented (as indicated in Table 19).

Mrs. Verne, unable to speak, performed only one of eleven tasks. She placed a series of colors in order through trial and error, but was unable to order a series of sticks. Reluctant to end the testing, I drew the figure of a man, omitting the face, and offered her the pencil. She responded by scribbling over the face. I then drew other incomplete human figures and each time, she scribbled faces and attempted to retrace some lines (Figure 170).

I then began a portrait sketch of Mrs. Verne. She held quite still, watching the movement of my pencil on the table between us. When the sketch was finished, I offered her the pencil and a sheet of paper,

Table 19. Cognitive skills of stroke patients[a]

| Level of Ability to | Gary | Mrs. Verne | Mrs. Brown | Mrs. Jones | Mr. Long | Mrs. Moore | Mrs. Jensen (first) | Mrs. Jensen (second) | Mrs. Quinn (first) | Mrs. Quinn (second) |
|---|---|---|---|---|---|---|---|---|---|---|
| **Associate and represent** | | | | | | | | | | |
| 1. Select | 5 | 0 | 1 | 1 | 3 | 3 | 1 | 3 | 3 | 3 |
| 2. Combine | 5 | 0 | 0 | 1 | 5 | 1 | 1 | 5 | 1 | 1 |
| 3. Represent subjects | 5 | 0 | 1 | 1 | 3 | 1 | 1 | 3 | 3 | 3 |
| 4. Action or interaction | 5 | 0 | 0 | 1 | 4 | 3 | 1 | 5 | 1 | 4 |
| 5. Verbal association, if any | 5 | 0 | 0 | 1 | 0 | 0 | 0 | 1 | 1 | 1 |
| 6. Skill or sensitivity | 1 | 0 | 1 | 1 | 1 | 1 | 1 | 2 | 1 | 1 |
| **Represent spatial relationships[b]** | | | | | | | | | | |
| 7. Left-right | 5 | 0 | 0 | 0 | 0 | 5 | 5 | | 5 | |
| 8. Above-below | 5 | 0 | 0 | 0 | 0 | 5 | 5 | | 5 | |
| 9. Front-back | 5 | 0 | 0 | 0 | 0 | 5 | 5 | | 5 | |
| **Predict spatial relationships[b]** | | | | | | | | | | |
| 10. Horizontal | 0 | 0 | 0 | 0 | | 5 | 1 | | 3 | |
| 11. Vertical | 0 | 0 | 0 | 0 | | 5 | 3 | | | |
| 12. Diagonal | 0 | 0 | 0 | 0 | | 4 | 4 | | 3 | |
| **Order and conserve[b]** | | | | | | | | | | |
| 13. Order a series | 3 | 3 | 0 | 3 | 5 | 3 | 5 | | 5 | |
| 14. Order a matrix | 0 | 0 | 0 | 0 | | 2 | 3 | | 5 | |
| 15. Conserve quantity | 0 | 0 | 0 | 5 | | 5 | | | 5 | |
| **For severely impaired[b]** | | | | | | | | | | |
| 16. Copy geometric figures | 0 | 0 | 3 | 3 | | 5 | 3 | | 5 | |
| 17. Project a straight line | 0 | 0 | 5 | 5 | | | 5 | | | |
| 18. Match toy animals | 0 | 0 | 2 | 3 | | | | | | |

[a] Scored on the basis of 0 to 5 points, 5 indicating normal ability.
[b] The author was unable to complete testing of some patients in these areas.

Figure 169.   Gary's drawing from observation

Figure 170.   Mrs. Verne's first attempts to draw

Figure 171.    Mrs. Verne's second attempt to draw

and this time she drew a face, smiling (Figure 171). Did she progress from scribbles to drawing because her attention was caught and held by her own likeness? Or was it because she had ample time to associate and integrate the moving pencil and the lines produced?

Three of the hospitalized patients were able to perform some of the other tasks. Mrs. Brown, speaking with the incoherence and fluency characteristic of Warnicke's aphasia, was able to put matchsticks (on Plasticine bases) into a straight line, copy some geometric figures, and match some toy animals. She showed no response to a sketch of herself. Mrs. Jones, who did not speak, was able to do these tasks and in addition was able to conserve, and to order a series through trial and error. Mr. Long, who uttered a single word ("yes") repeatedly and expressively, was able to do most of the tasks, except drawing from observation and predictive drawing, which he was unable to do at all (Table 19).

One of the hospitalized patients, Mrs. Moore, performed most of the tasks with ease (Figures 172, 173). Where she failed was in combining subjects in her drawings from imagination. This difficulty seemed to parallel her inability to talk, just as the ease with which she selected subjects seemed to parallel her ability to understand what was said.

As noted in Chapter 8, the ability to select and the ability to combine are regarded as the two fundamental operations underlying verbal behavior. Disturbance of the ability to select words is associated with receptive language disorders, and disturbance of the ability to combine words into sentences is associated with expressive language disorders. In aphasia, selecting is said to remain intact, while combining is impaired.

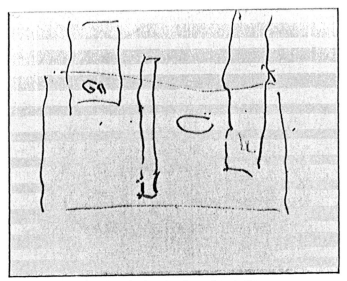

Figure 172.   Mrs. Moore's drawing from observation

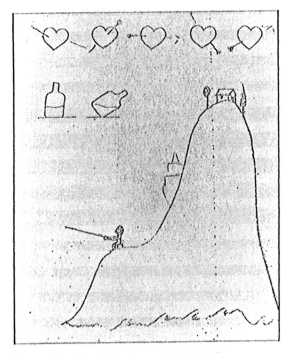

Figure 173.   Mrs. Moore's predictive drawing

Figure 174.    Mrs. Moore's first drawing from imagination

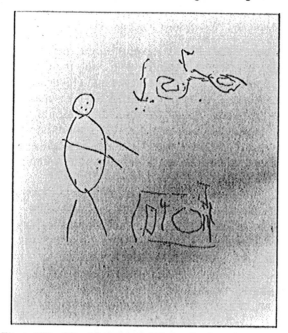

Figure 175.    Mrs. Moore's second drawing from imagination

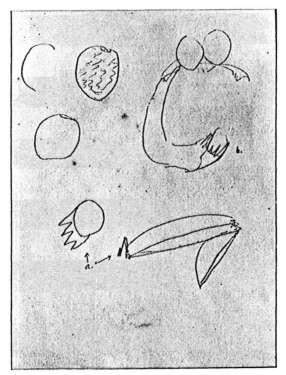

Figure 176.   Mrs. Jensen's first drawing from imagination

The first time Mrs. Moore was offered the stimulus cards she chose the man, the car, and the hammer. She then drew them as isolated objects, unrelated in size or placement (Figure 174).

To suggest a way of relating them, I drew a man breaking a car window with a hammer. Then I offered Mrs. Moore the cards again. This time she chose the man, the motorcycle, and the tray of food, but drew them in isolation as before. I asked if she could show how they might be related, and she responded by giving the man arms, reaching toward the tray (Figure 175).

The third time she was offered the stimulus cards Mrs. Moore chose the man and the dog and drew them side by side. Since she did not respond when I asked if she could show how they might be related, I gave the dog a leash, drawing a line from the man's hand to the dog's collar. She spontaneously reinforced the line with her pencil. Offered the stimulus cards again, she chose the drawing of the banana and drew it in the man's other hand.

Mrs. Moore's receptive language seemed intact, like her ability to select subjects to draw. Her impaired ability to combine seemed to extend beyond language to nonverbal expression in drawing, to the

Figure 177.   Mrs. Jensen's second drawing from imagination

inability to synthesize the parts of her drawing into an integrated whole.

This raises the question of whether or not improvement in the ability to combine in a drawing would carry over to improvement in expressive language. Attempts at remediation were possible only with the two outpatients. The first, Mrs. Jensen, had recovered from her stroke, except for difficulty in using verbs. Like the verbs missing from her sentences, action and interaction were missing from her drawings. Offered the stimulus cards, she chose the incomplete drawing of two people with their arms around each other, and the drawings of an apple and a banana. She then drew them as isolated objects (Figure 176). I asked if she could draw the apple the way it would look if it were held in the hand, then placed in her hand the large pebble from the drawing from observation task. First she added the jagged lines to her sketch of the banana and one of the apples (Figure 176a), then she added the hand holding the apple (Figure 176b).

Given another sheet of paper, Mrs. Jensen was asked if she could draw her subjects acting out a verb. She drew Figure 177, completing both human figures from imagination and adding scenery, then wrote, "Adam is touching a apple."

Her first drawing was scored 1 point for the abilities to select, to combine, and to represent. Her second drawing was scored 3 points for selecting at the functional level, 5 points for combining into a unified whole, 3 points for representing at the level of restructuring, and 1 point for verbal association at the level of description. Thus, Mrs. Jensen showed some improvement in the ability to associate and represent graphically.

Mrs. Quinn had suffered a stroke eighteen months earlier. After leaving the hospital, she returned three times a week for speech therapy. According to the speech therapist, her receptive language was superior to her expressive language, and again there seemed to be a parallel between verbal and graphic expression. In the ten drawings she produced in three meetings with me, her average score for the ability to select was 3.2, while her average score for the ability to combine was 1.7. She made some gains between her first and last drawings, as measured by her scores—the first drawing averaged 1.6 points and the last, 2.1 points.

# Chapter 12

# Statistical Analyses

.

STATE URBAN EDUCATION PROJECT FOR
LANGUAGE- AND HEARING-IMPAIRED CHILDREN

The question asked in the initial project was whether or not an experimental group of thirty-four children could acquire concepts of space, order, and class by means of art procedures. Eighteen children attended experimental art classes in a Fall program from September 1972 to January 1973; sixteen children, in a Spring program from February to June 1973. The first objective of the project was to help the children develop the concepts. The second objective was to develop procedures for teaching the concepts. The third objective was to develop procedures for evaluating cognitive abilities and disabilities (Silver, 1973, 1976, 1977).

The children who took part in the program suffered from impairments caused by brain damage. Some had difficulty producing language—that is, talking or writing. Others had difficulty comprehending language—interpreting what is said or written. Many had both kinds of impairment and were hearing impaired as well, and, as might be expected, some were emotionally disturbed.

Sixty-eight such children participated in the study, half attending experimental art classes while the other half, who did not attend art classes, served as controls. Intelligence tests had previously been given to twenty-six of the thirty-four children in the experimental group. Their mean IQ score was 85.4. Their ages ranged from seven to fifteen.

The handicapped children included the total available population in one school for language- and hearing-impaired children and three classes in another school. The children in the experimental group were a randomly selected 50% sample of twelve classes. In each group there were twenty-one boys and thirteen girls. Since all classes in the schools were limited to eight children, there was a maximum of four children in each of the experimental art classes.

Subsequently some of the tests were administered to sixty-eight unimpaired children in a suburban public school in order to compare handicapped children with normal children. The unimpaired children included thirteen eight-year-olds (half the number of children in one class, who had previously been selected at random by their teacher for other school activities), twenty-five children ages nine to eleven selected at random by their school principal, and thirty children ages eleven to fourteen in an elective science class. The three tests given (selected because they did not require individual administration) were drawing from imagination, drawing from observation, and predictive drawing. They were administered in November 1973.

The tests were administered over a period of several days to children in various classes. Since some of the children were absent from school occasionally during this period, the drawing from observation test was administered to sixty-three children, the drawing from imagination test was administered to sixty-three children, and the predictive drawing test was administered to sixty-eight children.

## Fall Program

There were thirty-six children in the Fall program, eighteen experimental and eighteen control. The experimental children attended one forty-minute art class once a week for eleven weeks, while the control children remained with their classroom teachers, doing academic work.

A cognition test was developed and administered to both groups, in October and in January. This test originally consisted of six items, Items A through F in Table 20. During the Fall program additional tests were developed, and they were included in the Fall program posttest as well as in the Spring program pre- and posttests. These are Items G through J in Table 20, together with the first three items of the drawing from imagination test (selecting, combining, and representing) described in Chapter 8.

## Spring Program

There were thirty-two children in the Spring program, sixteen experimental and sixteen control. The experimental children attended only nine art classes because, after the first two weeks, I became ill and the program was suspended. Teaching was resumed in May, with an education aide working with some of the experimental children under supervision of a licensed teacher in the school, while I worked with another group of children. For this reason some of the results of the Fall and Spring programs have been analyzed separately.

## Results

The statistical analyses comparing the experimental and control groups were performed by John L. Kleinhans, Ph.D., Assistant Professor of

Psychology at Manhattanville College, Purchase, New York. The analyses comparing the impaired and unimpaired children were performed by Claire Lavin, Ph.D., Director of Graduate Programs in Special Education, College of New Rochelle, New Rochelle, New York.

The pre- and posttests were administered and scored by Ms. Andrea Stein, and evaluated by Ms. Ruth Weissmann and Ms. Marilyn Slapikas, teachers of Special Education.

The drawings and paintings were evaluated for art skills and expressiveness by Mildred Fairchild, Ed.D., Professor of Art, Teachers College, Columbia University, and by Ms. Jane Field, registered art therapist and painter.

### Test of Cognitive Skills (Ability to Conserve, Group, Order Sequentially, and Predict Spatial Relationships)

*Fall Program, Pre- and Posttests (Six Items)*    Pre- and posttest performances of the experimental group on the first six critical items were evaluated by a sign test. The improvement was significant at the $p < 0.01$ level (exact probability was less than .006). The control group had a net decline.

*Fall Program Posttest Together With Posttest of Drawing From Imagination (Fourteen Items)*    Although the posttest scoring form included forty-eight possible responses, only eleven affirmative responses indicated cognitive ability. The others indicated lack of ability or lower levels of ability. The eleven key items (as indicated in Table 20) are as follows: the ability to conserve an amount of liquid (A3), the ability to conserve numbers (B5), the ability to group on the basis of class (C13), the ability to group on the basis of function (D18), the ability to order a series of sticks systematically (E22), the ability to transpose a matrix (F25), the ability to conserve an amount of clay (G32), horizontal orientation (H37), vertical orientation (H42), the ability to order a series of color cards systematically (I45), and the ability to place objects in given positions (J48). Three items (the abilities to select, combine, and represent) were taken from the drawing from imagination test, and used with these eleven items in scoring the test of cognitive skills.

Comparing experimental and control groups, a highly significant difference was found at the $p < 0.001$ level in favor of the experimental group. Dr. Kleinhans' analysis may be found in the Chapter Appendix.

### Drawing from Imagination Test (the Ability to Select, Combine, and Represent)

*Fall and Spring Programs Combined*    Comparing scores of the thrity-four language- and hearing-impaired children in the experimental groups before and after the art programs, improvement was found at the $p < .01$ level in the combined abilities of selecting, combining, and representing. Their pretest mean was 8.0; their posttest mean was

Table 20.    Scoring form, Fall program posttest of cognition

| Name | Class | Age | Date |
|------|-------|-----|------|

A.  Conservation of liquid
  1. _____ says amounts are different when they appear different and are different
  2. _____ says amounts are different when they appear the same but are different
  3.[a]_____ says amounts are the same when they appear different but are, in fact, the same

comment

B.  Conservation of number
  4. _____ makes line about as long but disregards number
  5.[a]_____ puts out eight black discs
  6. _____ says they are the same when they are, in fact, different
  7. _____ says there are eight discs in black row
  8. _____ says the rows are the same
  9. _____ says the rows are different
  10. _____ says there are more discs in black row

comment

C.  Grouping three objects
  11. _____ selects clock and banana
  12. _____ selects clock and apple
  13.[a]_____ selects apple and banana
  14. _____ uses concrete language, such as "yellow" or "round"
  15. _____ uses functional language, such as "to eat"
  16. _____ uses abstract language, such as "food"

comment

D.  Grouping objects from an array
  17. _____ selects _____ pictures on the basis of perceptual attributes
  18.[a]_____ selects _____ pictures on the basis of functional attributes
  19. _____ verbal response is based on perceptual attributes
  20. _____ verbal response is based on functional attributes

comment

E.  Ordering a series
  21. _____ forms single series through trial and error
  22.[a]_____ forms single series using systematic approach, such as starting with smallest, next smallest, etc.

comment

F.  Ordering a matrix
    23. _____ can replace objects
    24. _____ can reproduce matrix in its original position
    25.[a]_____ can transpose matrix
    26. _____ verbal response is based on differences
    27. _____ verbal response is based on similarities
    28. _____ uses global language, such as "big" and "little"
    29. _____ uses dimensional language, such as "tall" and "short"
    30. _____ uses confounded language, such as "tall" and "little"

---

comment

G.  Conservation of clay
    31. _____ says the ball has more clay, or the hotdog has more clay
    32.[a]_____ says the ball and the hotdog have the same amounts

---

comment

H.  Horizontal and vertical orientation
    33. _____ represents water with scribbles or round blot
    34. _____ represents water with line parallel to base of bottle
    35. _____ represents water with oblique line in tilted bottle
    36. _____ represents water with almost horizontal line in tilted bottle
        (while water in other bottles appears horizontal)
    37.[a]_____ represents water in all bottles as horizontal
    38. _____ draws house or tree within or parallel to mountain
    39. _____ draws house or tree perpendicular to mountain slope
    40. _____ draws house or tree between perpendicular and vertical
    41. _____ draws house or tree vertical but without apparent support
    42.[a]_____ draws house or tree vertical with apparent support

---

comment

I.  Ordering color cards
    43. _____ places three or more cards in series but does not form correct
        single series
    44. _____ forms single series correctly through trial and error
    45.[a]_____ forms single series correctly systematically, starting with one
        card and working up or down from it

---

comment

J.  Placing objects in given positions
    (in order to evaluate, superimpose outlines and hold them up to light)
    46. _____ block outlines overlap 25% or less
    47. _____ block outlines overlap about 50%
    48.[a]_____ block outlines overlap 75% or more

---

[a] Key items indicating cognitive ability.

Table 21: Comparing Mean Performance Scores in Drawing from Imagination by Handicapped Experimental and Control Children, and by Normal Children[a]

| Experimental (N = 34) | | | | Control[b] (N = 34) | | | |
|---|---|---|---|---|---|---|---|
| Age | Name | Pre | Post | Age | Name | Pre | Post |
| 8 | Vi | 15 | 15 | 7 | Ba | 9 | 4 |
|  | Je | 9 | 8 |  | Ch |  | 5 |
|  | We | 3 | 9 | 8 | Ke | 5 | 4 |
|  | Ca | 3 | 15 |  | An | 9 | 10 |
|  | Fe | 3 | 10 |  | Jo | 13 | 14 |
|  | Ro | 3 | 14 |  | Mi | 9 | 9 |
|  | Ev | 3 | 11 |  | Ki | 5 | 5 |
|  | Do | 5 | 7 | 9 | Mi |  | 6 |
|  | Li | 5 | 4 |  | Di |  | 6 |
| 9 | Da | 11 | 11 |  | Ro | 3 | 4 |
|  | Ra | 8 | 9 |  | Sa | 7 | 14 |
| 10 | Al | 3 | 12 |  | Ca | 3 | 8 |
|  | Ca | 5 | 11 |  | El | 7 | 6 |
|  | Ke | 15 | 9 | 10 | Ja |  | 15 |
| 11 | Ja | 9 | 3 |  | Jo | 11 | 9 |
|  | Ru | 7 | 15 |  | Be | 3 | 6 |
|  | Je | 3 | 13 | 11 | Pa |  | 9 |
| 12 | Ep | 10 | 15 |  | He |  | 3 |
|  | Ba | 3 | 11 |  | Mi |  | 5 |
|  | Ru | 5 | 7 |  | An | 12 | 13 |
|  | El | 15 | 13 |  | De |  | 11 |
|  | Ra | 15 | 11 |  | Al |  | 7 |
|  | Ja | 11 | 14 | 12 | Ma |  | 9 |
|  | Ma | 13 | 14 |  | Fe |  | 5 |
| 13 | Do | 9 | 13 |  | Ga | 13 | 8 |
|  | Sh | 3 | 15 |  | Ev | 13 | 14 |
|  | Bi | 3 | 15 |  | Ro | 9 | 8 |
|  | Ei | 14 | 15 | 13 | Gl |  | 11 |
|  | An | 7 | 7 |  | El |  | 15 |
| 14 | Ca | 13 | 13 |  | Ma |  | 6 |
|  | To | 13 | 15 |  | Jo |  | 15 |
|  | Ja | 11 | 12 | 14 | An |  | 3 |
| 15 | Da | 6 | 13 |  | An |  | 15 |
|  | Ed | 11 | 11 | 15 | De |  | 5 |
|  | Mean | 8.0 | 11.47 |  |  | 8.18[c] | 8.44 |

| Normal children $(N = 63)^d$ | | | Normal children $(N = 63)^d$ | | |
|---|---|---|---|---|---|
| Age | Name | Prepost | Age | Name | Prepost |
| 8 | Ni | 11 | | Da | 11 |
| | Pa | 10 | | Ji | 13 |
| | An | 4 | | To | 6 |
| | St | 12 | | Ma | 9 |
| | Da | 9 | | Jo | 11 |
| | Ca | 7 | | Al | 10 |
| | Mi | 13 | 12 | La | 11 |
| | El | 14 | 13 | Ch | 7 |
| | Ja | 8 | | Ka | 12 |
| | Ja | 6 | | Ro | 13 |
| | Da | 12 | | Le | 13 |
| | Ch | 5 | | Je | 11 |
| | Bo | 8 | | Mi | 8 |
| 9 | Jo | 7 | | | |
| | Li | 9 | | Mi | |
| | Ho | 8 | | El | 7 |
| | Ka | 9 | | Te | 8 |
| | Di | 10 | | Er | 14 |
| | To | 4 | | Ly | 8 |
| | Lo | 9 | | Jo | 8 |
| | Al | 9 | | Jo | 9 |
| 10 | Da | | | We | 12 |
| | De | 8 | | An | 8 |
| | Ja | 8 | | An | 7 |
| | Hu | 13 | | St | |
| | An | 9 | | Cl | 8 |
| | Ma | 11 | | Ju | 12 |
| | An | 7 | | Ch | 15 |
| 11 | Th | 7 | 14 | Ju | 12 |
| | Li | 12 | | An | 8 |
| | An | 9 | | Ol | 8 |
| | Ma | 11 | | Lo | 10 |
| | | | | Mean | 9.47 |

[a] Scored on basis of 1 to 5 points for level of development; 5 = highest level.

[b] Control children who participated in the Fall program did not have pretests, since teaching and evaluating procedures were developed during the term. Their only test for the ability to select, combine, and represent was the Fall program posttest.

[c] For the Spring program only.

[d] Five children were absent when the test was given.

11.47; $t = 3.62$, significant at the $p < 0.01$ level with df $= 33$ (two-tailed test) (as indicated in Table 21).

The mean posttest score for the thirty-four impaired children in the control groups was 8.44. Since this test was devised and introduced into the study after it had started, and included in the Fall program posttest and the Spring program pre- and posttests, the test was given to only a portion of the total group. There were no pretest scores of these abilities for the control group children in the Fall program. Mean pretest score for the control group children in the Spring program was 8.18 (as indicated in Table 21).

*Fall Program Only*   Mean differences evaluated by $t$ test.

1. Select: Experimental mean $= 4.5$; Control mean $= 3.28$; $t = 2.63, p < 0.05$ with df $= 34$ (two-tailed test).
2. Combine: Experimental mean $= 4.17$; Control mean $= 2.33$; $t = 3.78$, $p < 0.01$ with df $= 34$ (two-tailed test).
3. Represent: Experimental mean $= 4.11$; Control mean $= 2.78$; $t = 3.08$, $p < 0.01$ with df $= 34$ (two-tailed test).

In each of the three areas, children in the experimental group performed significantly better than those in the control group.

*Spring Program Only*   The data are analyzed twice: first, all data are analyzed by a $t$ test (a); second, only data from Dr. Silver's groups are analyzed by $t$ tests (b).

1a. Select (all students): Experimental mean $= 3.75$; Control mean $= 3.06$; $t = 1.92, p > 0.05$. Not significant.
1b. Select (Dr. Silver's students): Experimental mean $= 4.25$; Control mean $= 2.87$; $t = 2.29, p < 0.05$. Significant.
2a. Combine (all students): Experimental mean $= 3.06$; Control mean $= 2.44$; $t = 1.30, p > 0.05$. Not significant.
2b. Combine (Dr. Silver's students): Experimental mean $= 3.5$; Control mean $= 1.75$; $t = 2.82, p < 0.05$. Significant.
3a. Represent (all students): Experimental mean $= 3.19$; Control mean $= 2.38$; $t = 1.93, p > 0.05$. Not significant.
3b. Represent (Dr. Silver's students): Experimental mean $= 3.5$; Control mean $= 2.0$; $t = 3.0, p < 0.01$. Significant.

*Comparing Combined Scores of Impaired Experimental Children With Those of Unimpaired Children*   The unimpaired group ($N = 63$) was superior on the pretest, but not quite significantly better ($t = 2.05$). On the posttest, however, the impaired experimental children ($N = 34$) were significantly superior to the unimpaired children (who did not participate in the art program and were tested only once). Mean score of the unimpaired group was 9.47. Mean score of the experimental group was 11.47; $t = 3.31$, significant at the $p < .05$ level with df $= 92$ (two-tailed test).

*Predictive Drawing Test of Horizontal and Vertical Orientation (Fall and Spring Programs Combined)*    Comparing mean scores of the impaired experimental children before and after the art program, significant improvement was found after the art program in both horizontal and vertical orientation. The control group, which did not participate in the art program, did not improve (see Tables 22 and 23).

For the thirty-four experimental children who attended the art classes, a significant difference was found between their pre- and posttest scores. Their pretest mean in horizontal orientation was 2.88; their posttest mean was 3.76; $t = 5.50$, significant at the $p < 0.01$ level with 67 df (as indicated in Table 24). In vertical orientation, their pretest mean score was 2.91; their posttest mean was 4.11; $t = 8.57$, significant at the $p < 0.01$ level. Thus, there was highly significant improvement in mean horizontal and vertical scores after the art program.

There was no significant difference between the experimental and control groups on the pretests (as indicated in Table 25). Both groups had the same mean scores on the horizontal pretest (2.88); on the vertical pretest, the experimental group mean was 2.91, the control group mean was 2.82.

On the posttest, however, there seemed to be significant improvement in the vertical test score of the Spring program control group, which had both pre- and posttests (see Table 26). This is confusing, since improvement would not normally be expected. It is also confusing to see some children switch from scores of 5 on the pretest to less than 5 on the posttest. The marked inconsistency of these children in test performance, and in other behavior, has been noted by many observers.

The difference between the experimental group after the art program and the control group, which did not participate in the art program, was highly significant, in favor of the experimental group (see Table 27). Comparing the mean scores of the experimental group posttests with those of the control group pretests, difference of means was 0.88 ($t = 5.18$) in horizontal orientation, and 1.06 ($t = 9.21$) in vertical orientation, with df = 67.

The Fall program experimental and control groups were also evaluated by $t$ test for differences in horizontal and vertical orientation. Significant difference was found in horizontal, but not in vertical, orientation. The horizontal mean for the experimental children was 4.22; for the control children, 3.19; $t = 2.19$, $p < 0.05$, with df = 34 (two-tailed test). The vertical mean for the experimental children was 4.17; for the control children, 3.56; $t = 1.59$, $p > 0.05$, with df = 34 (two-tailed test).

Comparing the unimpaired children with both groups of impaired children, it was found that the unimpaired children performed signifi-

Table 22.  Results, predictive drawing test, by experimental and control children[a]

| | | | | | Experimental group | | | |
| --- | --- | --- | --- | --- | --- | --- | --- | --- |
| | | | | Fall program (N = 18) | | | | |
| | | | | | Horizontal | | Vertical | |
| Name | Sex | Age | Diagnosis | IQ | Pre | Post | Pre | Post |
| Do | F | 13 | ER | Av | 3 | 5 | 2 | 3 |
| Sh | F | 13 | ER | Av | 3 | 5 | 3 | 5 |
| Ca | F | 14 | R | 95 | 4 | 5 | 3 | 4 |
| To | M | 14 | ER | 97 | 3 | 4 | 5 | 5 |
| Bu | M | 13 | ER | 56 | 2 | 5 | 4 | 5 |
| Da | M | 15 | E | 100 | 4 | 5 | 4 | 5 |
| Ed | M | 15 | E | 65 | 3 | 4 | 2 | 5 |
| Ep | M | 12 | E | 85 | 3 | 4 | 4 | 5 |
| Ev | F | 13 | ER | 90 | 2 | 2 | 2 | 5 |
| Ba | F | 12 | R | 86 | 4 | 3 | 3 | 4 |
| Je | F | 11 | ER | 72 | 3 | 5 | 3 | 5 |
| El | F | 12 | ER | 140 | 5 | 5 | 5 | 5 |
| Ro | M | 12 | E | DN | 2 | 3 | 5 | 2 |
| Ri | M | 12 | ER | 77 | 5 | 5 | 5 | 5 |
| Ru | M | 11 | R | 87 | 5 | 3 | 2 | 5 |
| Vi | M | 8 | R | ab Av | 3 | 5 | 3 | 4 |
| Da | M | 9 | ER | DN | 2 | 5 | 2 | 5 |
| Ru | F | 9 | ER | 75 | 1 | 1 | 2 | 3 |

| | | | | Spring program (N=16) | | | | |
| --- | --- | --- | --- | --- | --- | --- | --- | --- |
| | | | | | Horizontal | | Vertical | |
| Name | Sex | Age | Diagnosis | IQ | Pre | Post | Pre | Post |
| Je | M | 8 | ER | 68 | 2 | 2 | 1 | 5 |
| We | M | 8 | E | 94 | 1 | 2 | 2 | 5 |
| Ca | M | 8 | ER | 94 | 2 | 4 | 3 | 5 |
| Fe | M | 8 | E | 104 | 2 | 2 | 2 | 4 |
| Al | M | 10 | E | Av | 3 | 5 | 1 | 3 |
| Ro | F | 8 | R | 66 | 2 | 4 | 3 | 3 |
| Ca | M | 10 | R | 87 | 5 | 5 | 5 | 5 |
| Ev | M | 8 | R | 96 | 5 | 5 | 2 | 5 |
| An | M | 13 | R | 72 | 2 | 2 | 2 | 3 |
| Ja | F | 12 | E | 83 | 2 | 2 | 2 | 3 |
| Je | F | 14 | E | 100 | 2 | 2 | 3 | 3 |
| Ma | M | 12 | ER | 50 | 5 | 5 | 5 | 5 |
| Ja | M | 11 | ER | | 3 | 4 | 2 | 2 |
| Ke | M | 10 | ER | DN | 1 | 2 | 2 | 3 |
| Do | F | 8 | ER | 97 | 2 | 3 | 3 | 3 |
| Li | F | 8 | ER | 86 | 2 | 5 | 2 | 3 |
| | | | Combined mean: | | 2.88 | 3.76 | 2.91 | 4.11 |
| | | | Combined (sd)$^2$: | | 1.55 | 1.76 | 1.47 | 1.08 |

| | | | | | Control group | | | |
|---|---|---|---|---|---|---|---|---|

**Control group**

**Fall program (N = 18)**

| Name | Sex | Age | Diagnosis | IQ | Horizontal Prepost | Vertical Prepost |
|---|---|---|---|---|---|---|
| Gl | F | 13 | ER | 99 | 2 | 1 |
| El | F | 13 | ER | Av | 2 | 2 |
| De | F | 15 | ER | 65 | 5 | 4 |
| An | M | 14 | ER | 79 | 3 | 2 |
| Pa | M | 11 | ER | 94 | 5 | 5 |
| Ma | M | 13 | E | 74 | 2 | 2 |
| Jo | M | 13 | E | 70 | 5 | 5 |
| Mi | M | 11 | E | 75 | 5 | 4 |
| He | F | 11 | ER | | 2 | 4 |
| Ma | F | 12 | E | | 1 | 2 |
| An | F | 11 | ER | Av | 2 | 2 |
| De | F | 11 | ER | 73 | 2 | 2 |
| Al | M | 11 | E | Def | 2 | 3 |
| Fe | M | 12 | E | 87 | 5 | 5 |
| Mi | M | 9 | E | 92 | 2 | 4 |
| Di | M | 9 | ER | 77 | 2 | 4 |
| Ja | M | 10 | E | 83 | 5 | 2 |
| Ch | F | 7 | E | 57 | 2 | 4 |

**Spring program (N = 16)**

| Name | Sex | Age | Diagnosis | IQ | Horizontal Pre | Horizontal Post | Vertical Pre | Vertical Post |
|---|---|---|---|---|---|---|---|---|
| Ro | M | 9 | ER | 65 | 2 | 2 | 1 | 3 |
| Ke | M | 8 | ER | Av | 2 | 2 | 2 | 4 |
| An | M | 8 | ER | 106 | 5 | 5 | 2 | 3 |
| Jo | M | 8 | ER | 94 | 3 | 4 | 2 | 5 |
| Sa | M | 9 | ER | 77 | 2 | 2 | 3 | 3 |
| Ba | F | 7 | R | | 1 | 2 | 3 | 3 |
| Ca | M | 9 | R | 99 | 5 | 3 | 2 | 5 |
| Ki | M | 8 | R | Av | 2 | 4 | 2 | 5 |
| Ga | M | 12 | ER | 110 | 5 | 5 | 5 | 5 |
| Ev | F | 12 | E | 65 | 2 | 2 | 3 | 5 |
| An | F | 14 | ER | 89 | 2 | 2 | 5 | 2 |
| Mi | M | 8 | E | | 5 | 3 | 2 | 2 |
| Ro | M | 12 | ER | 72 | 2 | 2 | 2 | 3 |
| Jo | M | 10 | ER | bd | 2 | 2 | 2 | 3 |
| El | F | 9 | R | 73 | 2 | 2 | 1 | 1 |
| Be | F | 10 | ER | | 2 | 2 | 2 | 5 |
| | | | Combined mean: | | 2.88 | 2.75 | 2.82 | 3.44 |
| | | | Combined (sd)$^2$: | | 2.05 | 1.27 | 1.60 | 1.75 |

$^a$ Scored on the basis of 1 to 5 points for level of development;
1 = Piagetian Stage 1, 5 = Piagetian Stage 3b.

Table 23.  Raw data, predictive drawing test by experimental and control groups

|  | Horizontal | | Vertical | |
|---|---|---|---|---|
|  | Pretest | Posttest | Pretest | Posttest |
| Experimental group ($N=36$)[a] | | | | |
| mean | 2.88 | 3.76 | 2.91 | 4.11 |
| (sd)$^2$ | 1.55 | 1.76 | 1.47 | 1.08 |
| Control group ($N=36$)[b] | | | | |
| mean | 2.88 | | 2.82 | |
| (sd)$^2$ | 2.05 | | 1.60 | |
| Control group ($N=16$) | | | | |
| mean | 2.75 | 2.75 | 2.38 | 3.44 |
| (sd)$^2$ | 1.93 | 1.27 | 1.33 | 1.75 |

[a] Combined scores.
[b] Combined scores for pretest only (Fall group had only one test).

Table 24.  Raw data analysis, predictive drawing test—comparison of experimental group pre- and posttest scores, indicating highly significant improvement in mean horizontal and vertical scores after art program

|  | Horizontal | Vertical |
|---|---|---|
| Difference of means | .88 | 1.20 |
| pooled estimate (sd)$^2$ | 1.65 | 1.27 |
| estimate of standard error | 0.16 | 0.14 |
| $t$ | 5.50 | 8.57 |
| $p$ (df = 67) | <0.01 | <0.01 |

Table 25.  Raw data analysis, predictive drawing test. Comparison of experimental to control group on pretest, indicating no significant difference between experimental and control group mean scores on pretest

|  | Horizontal | Vertical |
|---|---|---|
| Difference of means | 0.00 | 0.09 |
| pooled estimate (sd)$^2$ | 1.80 | 1.59 |
| estimate of standard error | 0.16 | 0.15 |
| $t$ | 0.00 | 0.60 |
| $p$ (df = 67) | >0.05 | <0.05 |

cantly better than the impaired children in horizontal orientation before the art program. After the art program, however, no significant difference was found (see Table 28).

For the sixty-eight unimpaired children the mean score was 4.059 on the pretest. Since the mean for the impaired children was 2.88, $t$

Table 26.   Raw data analysis, predictive drawing test. Comparison of Spring program control group on pre- and posttest, indicating highly significant improvement in mean score in vertical orientation, no significant improvement in horizontal orientation

|  | Horizontal | Vertical |
|---|---|---|
| Difference of means | 0 | 1.06 |
| pooled estimate (sd)$^2$ | 1.60 | 1.54 |
| estimate of standard error | 0.23 | 0.22 |
| $t$ | 0 | 4.82 |
| $p$ (df = 31) | <0.05 | >0.01 |

Table 27.   Raw data analysis, predictive drawing test. Comparison of experimental group posttest to control group pretest, indicating highly significant difference in both horizontal and vertical orientation between experimental group after art program and control group, in favor of experimental group

|  | Horizontal | Vertical |
|---|---|---|
| Difference of means | 0.88 | 1.06 |
| pooled estimate (sd)$^2$ | 1.60 | 1.54 |
| estimate of standard error | .17 | .14 |
| $t$ | 5.18 | 9.21 |
| $p$ (df = 67) | >0.01 | >0.01 |

value was 5.695, significant at the $p < 0.01$ level, with df = 146 (as indicated in Tables 23 and 28).

Following the art program the experimental children were no longer significantly inferior to the unimpaired children, although they had slightly lower scores. The posttest mean for the impaired experimental children was 3.55; $t = 1.1278$, not significant.

In vertical orientation it was found that the unimpaired children performed significantly better than the impaired children before the art program. After the art program, however, significant difference was found in favor of the impaired experimental group.

Comparing the same impaired and unimpaired children, the mean for the impaired children was 2.87; for the unimpaired children, 3.485; $t = 2.543$, significant at the $p < 0.05$ level, with df = 146.

Following the art program the mean score of the experimental impaired children was significantly higher than that of the unimpaired children, who did not attend the art classes. The posttest mean for the impaired experimental children was 4.11; $t = 2.358$, significant at the $p < 0.05$ level, with df = 112. In other words, the impaired experimental children had improved to a point at which they were significantly superior to the normal children.

Table 28.   Results, predictive drawing test by normal children ($N = 68$)

| Age | Name | Horizontal | Vertical | Age | Name | Horizontal | Vertical |
|-----|------|-----------|----------|-----|------|-----------|----------|
| 8 | Ni | 4 | 0 | | Ma | 1 | 2 |
| | Pa | 5 | 0 | | Jo | 5 | 5 |
| | An | 4 | 5 | | Al | 1 | 4 |
| | St | 5 | 4 | | El | 5 | 4 |
| | Da | 4 | 1 | | Su | 3 | 2 |
| | Ca | 1 | 0 | | Jo | 3 | 1 |
| | Mi | 1 | 2 | | Di | 5 | 1 |
| | El | 4 | 0 | | Je | 4 | 2 |
| | Ja | 4 | 1 | | Jo | 1 | 1 |
| | Ja | 4 | 0 | | Da | 3 | 1 |
| | Da | 1 | 0 | | Am | 4 | 1 |
| | Ch | 5 | 4 | 12 | La | 5 | 5 |
| | Bo | 4 | 1 | | Pa | 4 | 4 |
| 9 | Jo | 3 | 1 | | Ti | 3 | 2 |
| | Li | 4 | 4 | | Da | 3 | 4 |
| | Ho | 5 | 5 | | To | 4 | 1 |
| | Ka | 5 | 0 | | Ma | 2 | 4 |
| | Di | 4 | 3 | | Ga | 4 | 5 |
| | To | 5 | 0 | 13 | Ch | 5 | 5 |
| | Lo | 5 | 0 | | Jo | 5 | 5 |
| | Al | 4 | 0 | | Mi | 3 | 5 |
| 10 | Da | 1 | 1 | | Pa | 5 | 5 |
| | De | 4 | 4 | | Bo | 5 | 4 |
| | Ja | 4 | 1 | | Th | 4 | 4 |
| | Hu | 1 | 5 | | Ma | 5 | 1 |
| | An | 4 | 3 | | Ro | 4 | 5 |
| | Ma | 5 | 3 | | Ka | 5 | 2 |
| | An | 5 | 2 | | Le | 3 | 3 |
| 11 | Th | 1 | 3 | | Je | 5 | 5 |
| | Li | 4 | 4 | 14 | Ju | 1 | 1 |
| | An | 3 | 3 | | An | 5 | 5 |
| | Ma | 5 | 1 | | Ol | 5 | 5 |
| | Da | 1 | 1 | | Lu | 5 | 5 |
| | Ja | 5 | 0 | | | | |
| | To | 1 | 3 | Mean scores | | 3.68 | 2.56 |

Comparing the impaired children with the unimpaired children, significant difference was found on the pretest, in favor of the unimpaired children ($N = 68$). The pretest mean of the impaired experimental and control children combined ($N = 68$) was 2.88 in horizontal orientation. The mean for the unimpaired children was 4.059; $t = 5.695$, significant at the $p < 0.01$ level, with df = 146. In vertical orientation, the pretest mean for the impaired children was 2.87; for the unimpaired children, 3.485; $t = 2.543$, significant at the $p < 0.05$ level, with df = 146.

On the posttest, however, no significant difference was found between the unimpaired children and the impaired experimental children in horizontal orientation. The posttest mean for the impaired experimental children was 3.55 ($t = 1.1278$), not significant.

In vertical orientation significant difference was found in favor of the impaired experimental children. Their posttest mean was 4.11; $t = 2.358$, significant at the $p < 0.05$ level, with df = 112.

About 13% of the total population of sixty-eight impaired and sixty-eight unimpaired children had previously developed both horizontal and vertical concepts, as measured by scoring 5 points on the pretest. Of these eighteen children, eight were impaired and ten were unimpaired; four were girls, fourteen were boys, and all but two were age twelve or older (as indicated in Tables 22 and 28).

There seemed to be no correlation between these two spatial abilities and intelligence as measured by intelligence tests administered to the impaired children. Of the eight impaired children who had previously developed both concepts, IQ scores ranged between 50 (Stanford-Binet) and 140 (Goodenough) (see Table 23).

Of the twenty-six impaired experimental children who had not previously developed either horizontal or vertical concepts, sixteen (61%) subsequently developed either or both concepts, as measured by scoring 5 points on the posttest. Of the eleven children in the control group, for whom there were prepost results and who had not previously developed the concepts, only four (36%) developed either or both concepts, as measured by scoring 5 points on the posttest.

Five experimental children apparently developed horizontal but not vertical concepts, while five apparently developed vertical but not horizontal concepts. Eve, for example, scored 2 points in each category on the pretest (Figure 44). This was surprising in view of her age (thirteen), and her IQ (90). Her drawing and posttest (Figures 45 and 46, Chapter 2) suggest that she learned something about horizontals in the particular instance of the tilted bottle, but failed to generalize the learning, since she continued to draw the water parallel to the base of the bottle on its side.

One child, age eight, with an IQ of 68, progressed from the lowest score in vertical orientation to the highest, as indicated in Figure 47 (Chapter 2). In other words, Jeb's pretest response was typical of four- or five-year-old children, while his posttest response, four months later, was typical of children age nine or older (see Piaget and Inhelder, 1967, p. 384).

Of the ten children who failed to score 5 points in either category, eight progressed at least one stage of development. Of the two remaining children who failed to progress, one was Jenny, age fourteen, with an IQ of 100 (Goodenough). Her responses are shown in Figure 48 (Chapter 2). The other was Ruth, age eight, with an IQ of 75. Her confusion seems reflected in her painting (Figures 49 and 50, Chapter 2), which she described as a boy fishing.

To summarize, six of the thirty-four children in the experimental groups had developed horizontal orientation before the art program began, compared to ten of thirty-four children in the control groups or four of the sixteen control children for whom pre- and posttests are available. Of the remaining twenty-eight experimental children who failed to draw horizontal lines in all bottles on the pretest, eleven did so on the posttest, compared to none of twelve control children, suggesting that art procedures and experiences had helped them learn that the surface of water remains horizontal regardless of the tilt of its container. Eight of the eleven experimental children progressed through two Piagetian stages of development. One child progressed through three stages. Of the seventeen children who had not developed concepts of horizontal orientation (as determined by scoring 5 points on the test) nine improved, compared to three of twelve control group children (as indicated in Table 22).

In vertical orientation, six of the thirty-four experimental children had previously developed the concept compared to five of thirty-four children in the control group or two of the sixteen control children for whom prepost test results are available. Of the remaining twenty-eight experimental children who failed to draw vertical and supported houses on the pretest, thirteen did so on the posttest, compared to five of sixteen control children. Six of the thirteen children progressed through three Piagetian levels of development, four progressed through two levels of development, two progressed through one level, and one child progressed through four levels. Of the sixteen children who did not develop this concept, eleven improved.

*Drawing from Observation (Test of Ability to Perceive and Represent Left-Right, Front-Back, and Above-Below Spatial Relationships)* Since the testing and remediation procedures were developed in the Fall program, the pre- and posttests were administered to only the experimental and control children in the Spring program, and the results discussed here reflect those scores, and the scores of the unimpaired children.

For the sixteen experimental children who attended the art classes, significant difference was found in their pre- and posttest scores. Their pretest mean was 9.37; their posttest mean was 11.43; $t = 3.03$, significant at the $p < 0.05$ level, with df = 15 (two-tailed test). Thus, the experimental group improved significantly after the art program (as indicated in Table 29).

Table 29: Comparing Mean Performance Scores in Drawing from Observation by Handicapped Experimental and Control Children, and by Normal Children[a]

| Experimental group (N = 16) | | | | Control group (N = 16) | | | |
|---|---|---|---|---|---|---|---|
| Age | Name | Pre | Post | Age | Name | Pre | Post |
| 8 | Je | 7 | 11 | 7 | Ba | 0 | 4 |
| | We | 6 | 12 | 8 | Ke | 9 | 4 |
| | Ca | 8 | 11 | | An | 6 | 4 |
| | Fe | 8 | 7 | | Jo | 6 | 6 |
| | Ro | 10 | 15 | | Mi | 13 | 14 |
| | Ev | 12 | 12 | | Ki | 7 | 8 |
| | Do | 10 | 14 | 9 | Ro | 3 | 7 |
| | Li | 10 | 7 | | Sa | 6 | 10 |
| 10 | Al | 3 | 10 | | Ca | 13 | 10 |
| | Ca | 10 | 12 | 10 | Jo | 11 | 13 |
| | Ke | 9 | 12 | | Be | 13 | 9 |
| 11 | Ja | 12 | 10 | 12 | Ga | 14 | 13 |
| 12 | Ja | 12 | 14 | | Ev | 13 | 8 |
| | Ma | 15 | 15 | | Ro | 5 | 9 |
| 13 | An | 6 | 12 | 13 | El | 4 | 4 |
| 14 | Ja | 12 | 9 | | An | 14 | 13 |
| | Mean: | 9.37 | 11.43 | | | 8.56 | 8.50 |

| Unimpaired children (N = 63)[b] | | | Unimpaired children (N = 63)[b] | | |
|---|---|---|---|---|---|
| Age | Name | Prepost | Age | Name | Prepost |
| 8 | Ni | 13 | | Da | 5 |
| | Pa | 8 | | Ji | 8 |
| | An | 7 | | To | 10 |
| | St | 11 | | Ma | 9 |
| | Da | 7 | | Jo | 7 |
| | Ca | 6 | | Al | 7 |
| | Mi | 10 | 12 | La | 16 |
| | El | 12 | 13 | Ch | 11 |
| | Ja | 6 | | Ka | 13 |
| | Ja | 16 | | Ro | 15 |
| | Da | 10 | | Le | 9 |
| | Ch | 4 | | Je | 13 |
| | Bo | 5 | | Mi | 8 |
| 9 | Jo | 12 | | Mi | 8 |
| | Li | 12 | | El | 15 |
| | Ho | 5 | | Te | 10 |
| | Ka | 14 | | Er | 12 |
| | Di | 10 | | Ly | 10 |
| | To | 4 | | Jo | 13 |
| | Lo | 8 | | Jo | 10 |
| | Al | 4 | | We | 14 |

(continued)

Table 29 (Continued)

| Unimpaired children ($N = 63$)[b] | | | Unimpaired children ($N = 63$)[b] | | |
|---|---|---|---|---|---|
| Age | Name | Prepost | Age | Name | Prepost |
| 10 | Da | 4 | | An | 4 |
| | De | 16 | | An | 8 |
| | Ja | 13 | | St | 5 |
| | Hu | 4 | | Ci | 13 |
| | An | 13 | | Ju | 10 |
| | Ma | 15 | | Ch | 5 |
| | An | 10 | 14 | Ju | 8 |
| 11 | Th | 11 | | An | 5 |
| | Li | 8 | | Ol | 7 |
| | Ar | 12 | | Lo | 16 |
| | Ma | 13 | | Mean: | 9.63 |

[a] Scored on the basis of 1 to 4 points for number of correct representations of left-right, above-below, front-back and proportional relationships, in drawing from observation.

[b] Five children were absent when the test was given.

For the sixteen control children, who did not attend the art classes, no significant difference was found in their pre- and posttest scores. Their pretest mean was 8.56; their posttest mean was 8.50. Thus, they did not improve.

For the sixty-three unimpaired children the mean was 9.63. They were tested only once, since they did not attend the art classes, and it was assumed that their test scores would not have changed without art classes, as was the case for the control group of impaired children.

For the thirty-two impaired children (experimental and control groups combined) the mean score on the pretest was 8.96. Since the mean score for the unimpaired children was 9.63 ($t = .5877$), there was no significant difference between the impaired and the unimpaired children before the art classes.

The mean score on the posttest for the impaired experimental children was 11.43. Compared with the mean score of the unimpaired children (9.63), $t$ value was 1.1642, not significant.

In other words, although the unimpaired children had higher scores on the pretest, and the impaired experimental children had higher scores on the posttest, the differences were not significant. What was significant was the improvement of the experimental children in the ability to perceive and represent spatial relationships, as compared with a slight decline in that ability for the control group, which did not attend art classes.

***Test of Artistic Expressiveness and Skill***    As discussed in Chapter 5, a university professor of art and an art therapist-painter

Table 30. Scoring form used by university professor of art and art therapist-painter

|  | To be filled in after evaluation: |
|---|---|
|  | Child's name |
| Identifying number          Date | Subject matter, if any |
| In this drawing or painting, the child seems to have organized his experiences by: | Structuring, if any |

A. Selecting images on the basis of
   1. _____ perceptible attributes (appearance, colors, shape, etc.)
   2. _____ functional attributes (what subjects do, what can be done to them)
   3. _____ an idea (logical or illogical, story telling or abstract)

B. Combining images on the basis of
   1. _____ proximity, distance, enclosure (fragmentary)
   3. _____ baseline or bottom of paper
   5. _____ over-all coordination, attention given to whole paper

C. Combining language with images on the basis of
   1. _____ description
   3. _____ amplification
   5. _____ transformation (abstract or symbolic meaning)

D. Representing objects or events on the basis of
   1. _____ description (imitative, learned, impersonal)
   3. _____ restructuring (goes beyond description, elaborates or edits)
   5. _____ transformation (beyond restructuring, highly personal, imaginative)

E. Representing attitudes on the basis of
   1. _____ solitary or isolated people or animals
   2. _____ villains, victims, weapons, danger, injury or threat of injury
   3. _____ heroes, heroines, romance, escape or happy occasion
   4. _____ omissions or distortions (size, placement, reality)
   5. _____ line or brush quality (vague, stabbing, heavy, etc.)
   6. _____ fine expression of a central idea

F. Representing thoughts and fellings through art forms
   1. _____ commonplace form or content
   3. _____ moderately skillful, exploratory, or sensitive to art qualities
   5. _____ highly skillful, exploratory, or sensitive, suggests much care or enjoyment

Table 31. Results, evaluation of art works by university professor of art

| Evaluation[a] number | Name | Work[b] | Selecting A | Combining B | Language C | Representing D | Attitudes E | Sensitivity and Skills F |
|---|---|---|---|---|---|---|---|---|
| 33 | Da | 1 | 1 | 5 | 3 | 3 | 1 | 1 |
| 56 |    | 2 | 4 | 5 | 3 | 3 | 0 | 2 |
| 50 |    | 3 | 1 | 5 | 0 | 2 | 0 | 2 |
| 51 | Su | 1 | 4 | 5 | 3 | 3 | 4 | 2 |
| 49 |    | 2 | 3 |   | 3 | 3 | 3 | 2 |
| 26 |    | 3 | 1 | 5 | 0 | 1 | 1 | 1 |
| 52 | Ca | 1 | 1 | 4 | 0 | 1 | 0 | 1 |
| 24 |    | 2 | 5 | 5 | 3 | 5 | 3 | 2 |
| 60 |    | 3 | 1 | 5 | 0 | 5 | 0 | 5 |
| 16 | Bu | 1 | 1 | 1 | 0 | 1 | 4 | 1 |
| 36 |    | 2 | 5 | 5 | 3 | 3 | 0 | 2 |
| 18 |    | 3 | 1 | 5 | 3 | 5 | 2 | 2 |
| 28 | To | 1 | 1 | 1 | 0 | 1 | 1 | 2 |
| 54 |    | 2 |   |   |   |   |   |   |
| 42 |    | 3 |   |   |   |   |   |   |
| 34 | Da | 1 | 5 | 5 | 3 | 3 | 0 | 1 |
| 15 |    | 2 | 5 | 4 | 3 | 3 | 0 | 2 |
| 9  |    | 3 | 5 | 5 | 0 | 1 | 0 | 3 |
| 1  | Do | 1 | 1 | 1 | 3 | 1 | 1 | 1 |
| 27 |    | 2 | 3 | 5 | 3 | 3 | 0 | 2 |
| 38 |    | 3 | 5 | 5 | 3 | 3 | 0 | 1 |
| 12 | El | 1 | 1 | 3 | 0 | 1 | 0 | 1 |
| 53 |    | 2 | 3 | 5 | 3 | 5 | 0 |   |
| 59 |    | 3 | 3 | 4 | 3 | 3 | 0 |   |
| 47 | Ev | 1 | 5 | 5 | 3 | 3 | 3 | 3 |
| 11 |    | 2 | 3 | 5 | 1 | 2 | 0 | 2 |

| ID | Student | No. of work | | | | | | |
|----|---------|-------------|---|---|---|---|---|---|
| 19 |  | 3 | 5 | 5 | 0 | 4 | 6 | 4 |
| 57 | Be | 1 | 1 | 1 | 1 | 1 | 1 | 1 |
| 5 |  | 2 | 5 | 5 | 0 | 3 | 6 | 5 |
| 46 |  | 3 | 5 | 5 | 0 | 3 | 0 | 4 |
| 48 | Ja | 1 | 3 | 4 | 3 | 2 | 3 | 2 |
| 44 |  | 2 | 1 | 4 | 0 | 1 | 0 | 0 |
| 14 |  | 3 | 1 | 5 | 0 | 2 | 0 | 1 |
| 32 | El | 1 | 5 | 5 | 3 | 4 | 0 | 1 |
| 8 |  | 2 | 5 | 5 | 0 | 4 | 3 | 4 |
| 55 |  | 3 | 2 | 5 | 0 | 2 | 0 | 2 |
| 3 | Ro | 1 | 1 | 4 | 0 | 1 | 0 | 1 |
| 23 |  | 2 | 5 | 5 | 3 | 5 | 2 | 3 |
| 30 |  | 3 | 5 | 5 | 0 | 4 | 4 | 5 |
| 39 | Ri | 1 | 5 | 5 | 0 | 4 | 0 | 5 |
| 2 |  | 2 | 1 | 5 | 1 | 3 | 3 | 3 |
| 4 |  | 3 | 5 | 5 | 0 | 5 | 6 | 5 |
| 22 | Ru | 1 | 5 | 5 | 3 | 3 | 0 | 1 |
| 29 |  | 2 | 3 | 5 | 3 | 3 | 0 | 2 |
| 20 |  | 3 | 3 | 5 | 0 | 3 | 0 | 2 |
| 41 | Da | 1 | 1 | 4 | 0 | 3 | 0 | 3 |
| 58 |  | 2 | 1 | 3 | 0 | 2 | 1 | 2 |
| 7 |  | 3 | 5 | 5 | 3 | 3 | 6 | 5 |
| 45 | Ru | 1 | 1 | 1 | 0 | 1 | 4 | 1 |
| 37 |  | 2 | 5 | 5 | 5 | 5 | 4 | 3 |
| 17 |  | 3 | 5 | 5 | 5 | 5 | 6 | 5 |
| 31 | Vi | 1 | 1 | 1 | 0 | 1 | 1 | 1 |
| 67 |  | 2 | 2 | 3 | 1 | 2 | 1 | 1 |
| 6 |  | 3 | 5 | 5 | 0 | 5 | 6 | 5 |

[a] Used instead of students' names to identify art works for evaluation purposes

[b] Number of work: 1 = first, 2 = middle, 3 = last

Table 32.  Results, evaluation of art works by art therapist-painter

| Evaluation number[a] | Name | Work[b] | Representation | Attitudes | Sensitivity and skill |
|---|---|---|---|---|---|
| 33 | Da | 1 | 2 | 4 | 1 |
| 56 |    | 2 | 1 | 0 | 1 |
| 50 |    | 3 | 1 | 0 | 1 |
| 51 | Su | 1 | 3 | 3 | 1 |
| 49 |    | 2 | 1 | 2 | 1 |
| 26 |    | 3 | 1 | 0 | 1 |
| 52 | Ca | 1 | 3 | 0 | 3 |
| 24 |    | 2 | 4 | 0 | 3 |
| 60 |    | 3 | 5 | 0 | 5 |
| 54 | To | 1 | 4 | 0 | 4 |
| 28 |    | 2 | 4 | 4 | 5 |
| 42 |    | 3 | 5 | 6 | 5 |
| 16 | Bu | 1 | 1 | 2 | 1 |
| 36 |    | 2 | 3 | 4 | 2 |
| 18 |    | 3 | 5 | 4 | 5 |
| 34 | Do | 1 | 5 | 4 | 3 |
| 15 |    | 2 | 2 | 0 | 3 |
| 9 |    | 3 | 5 | 6 | 5 |
| 1 | Da | 1 | 1 | 0 | 1 |
| 27 |    | 2 | 1 | 0 | 1 |
| 38 |    | 3 | 3 | 6 | 3 |
| 12 | El | 1 | 1 | 0 | 1 |
| 53 |    | 2 | 1 | 0 | 1 |
| 59 |    | 3 | 1 | 0 | 2 |
| 57 | Be | 1 | 2 | 0 | 1 |
| 5 |    | 2 | 5 | 0 | 5 |
| 46 |    | 3 | 5 | 5 | 5 |
| 47 | Ev | 1 | 2 | 0 | 2 |
| 11 |    | 2 | 1 | 0 | 3 |
| 19 |    | 3 | 2 | 0 | 1 |
| 48 | Ja | 1 | 1 | 0 | 2 |
| 44 |    | 2 | 1 | 0 | 1 |
| 14 |    | 3 | 2 | 0 | 1 |
| 32 | El | 1 | 3 | 0 | 3 |
| 8 |    | 2 | 4 | 0 | 3 |
| 55 |    | 3 | 1 | 0 | 2 |
| 3 | Ro | 1 | 2 | 0 | 1 |
| 23 |    | 2 | 5 | 4 | 5 |
| 30 |    | 3 | 5 | 4 | 5 |
| 39 | Ri | 1 | 5 | 2 | 5 |
| 2 |    | 2 | 4 | 2 | 3 |
| 4 |    | 3 | 5 | 3 | 5 |
| 22 | Ru | 1 | 1 | 0 | 1 |
| 29 |    | 2 | 5 | 0 | 3 |
| 20 |    | 3 | 4 | 0 | 5 |

(Continued)

| Evaluation number[a] | Name | Work[b] | Representation | Attitudes | Sensitivity and skill |
|---|---|---|---|---|---|
| 41 | Da | 1 | 5 | 3 | 5 |
| 58 | | 2 | 5 | 0 | 5 |
| 7 | | 3 | 5 | 6 | 5 |
| 45 | Ru | 1 | 1 | 0 | 1 |
| 37 | | 2 | 5 | 3 | 5 |
| 17 | | 3 | 5 | 6 | 5 |
| 31 | Vi | 1 | 1 | 0 | 1 |
| 61 | | 2 | 1 | 0 | 1 |
| 6 | | 3 | 5 | 6 | 5 |

[a] Used instead of students' names to identify art works for evaluation purposes.
[b] Number of work: 1 = first, 2 = middle, 3 = last.

evaluated three drawings or paintings by each of the eighteen children in the Fall program experimental group. The three pieces of artwork were: each child's first work, his last work, and a work produced midway in the program. The fifty-four works were identified only by numbers, and shown in random order. The judges, working independently, used the scoring form presented in Table 30.

Both judges found improvements that were significant at the $p <$ 0.01 level. As rated by the art therapist-painter, the mean score of artwork produced in the first class was 4.44; the mean score for artwork produced in the last class was 7.27; $t = 3.13$, significant at the $p < 0.01$ level. As rated by the university professor of art, the mean score for artwork produced in the first class was 3.66; in the last class, 6.33; $t = 3.29$, significant at the $p < 0.01$ level.

In the category of sensitivity and skill, the university professor of art gave four children the lowest score on their first works, and the highest score on their last works (as indicated in Table 31).

The art therapist-painter found the same improvements in six children, as indicated in Table 32.

## ART PROGRAM FOR CHILDREN WITH LEARNING DISABILITIES

This project was concerned with two questions: would the testing and teaching procedures developed in the State Urban Education Project be useful with children who have learning disabilities rather than language and hearing impairments; and could the procedures be used effectively by teachers or art therapists other than the one who developed them? (Silver and Lavin, 1977).

Eleven graduate students worked under supervision with eleven children. The students had registered for an elective course in Therapeutic Techniques in Art Education, taught from September to December 1974 in the master's degree program at the College of New

Rochelle. Their skills and backgrounds were varied. Most had provisional certification to teach art. Some had not received provisional certification and others had permanent certification. They worked individually with the children.

The children were not systematically selected, but were enrolled as their applications were received. Announcements were sent to newspapers and to members of the Westchester Association for Children with Learning Disabilities, stating that art classes were being offered to children with learning problems or other disabilities. The first fifteen children who applied were enrolled.

One child had been diagnosed as hyperkinetic. Another was severely disturbed and attended a day school program in a psychiatric hospital. The others attended private schools or special classes in public schools. All but two had disabilities of a visuo-spatial or visuo-motor nature, and these two were eliminated from the statistical analysis (one was deaf and the other was emotionally disturbed, and both were able to perform the pre- and posttest tasks). Also eliminated from the analysis were a child who withdrew from the program, and a child whose teacher became ill and withdrew from the course.

Eleven children were included in the study—seven boys and four girls, ages seven to eleven. Eleven graduate students worked with them.

The children attended ten one-hour classes. The classes were held on Saturday mornings, and all participants worked together in one large studio under the supervision of the course instructor, who had developed the teaching and testing procedures. The graduate students attended three preliminary lectures. Thereafter, each week for half an hour before the children arrived, they prepared for the day's activities. They stayed on for another half hour after the children left, to organize their notes and evaluate results.

When the classes ended, six of the graduate students scored the forty-four pre- and posttest drawings, which were identified only by numbers and presented in random order. The results were analyzed for reliability, and for changes in the ability to group and to represent spatial concepts. Scores for the ability to order were obtained from each of the graduate students, who tested their students individually. In addition, parents were asked for anonymous evaluations of the program.

**Results**    The children improved significantly in the three areas of cognitive development, as indicated in Table 33. In ability to form groups, the obtained $t$ value (4.79) was significant at the $p < 0.01$ level. In spatial orientation, the obtained $t$ value (2.42) was significant at the $p < 0.05$ level. In sequential ordering, the obtained $t$ value (6.54) was significant at the $p < 0.01$ level.

Table 33.   Results of art program for children with learning disabilities taught by graduate students at College of New Rochelle, Fall 1974

| | | | Ability to form groups[a] | | | Spatial orientation[b] | | | Ability to order a matrix[c] | | |
|---|---|---|---|---|---|---|---|---|---|---|---|
| Child | Age | Sex | Pre | Post | Change | Pre | Post | Change | Pre | Post | Change |
| Da | 7 | F | 1.16 | 2.66 | +1.50 | 2.16 | 2.16 | 0 | 1 | 5 | +4 |
| Ro | 11½ | M | 1.50 | 3.33 | +1.83 | 2.91 | 7.33 | +4.42 | 5 | | |
| Do | 9 | M | 1.00 | 2.50 | +1.50 | 0.91 | 5.00 | +4.09 | 3 | 5 | +2 |
| Ra | 9 | M | 1.16 | 1.83 | +0.67 | 2.08 | 1.25 | −0.83 | 5 | | |
| Ca | 11 | M | 1.66 | 1.16 | −0.50 | 0.75 | 1.58 | +0.83 | 5 | | |
| Ma | 7 | M | 1.08 | 3.41 | +2.33 | 0.00 | 1.66 | +1.66 | 1 | 3 | +2 |
| Ma | 7¼ | F | 2.91 | 2.41 | − .50 | 4.50 | 2.16 | −2.34 | 5 | | |
| Ca | 7 | F | 1.83 | 1.16 | − .67 | 0.83 | 2.58 | +1.75 | 2 | 3 | +1 |
| Ma | 11½ | F | 2.75 | 3.50 | + .75 | 3.66 | 5.16 | +1.50 | 5 | | |
| Pa | 8½ | M | 2.58 | 2.83 | + .25 | 3.58 | 2.50 | −1.08 | 4 | 5 | +1 |
| To | 8 | M | 3.00 | 2.00 | −1.00 | 2.16 | 2.58 | + .40 | 2 | 3 | +1 |

[a] Average scores of two tests scored on the bases of 1 to 5 points with 5 = highest score. As measured by test of ability to form groups (select and combine), improvement was significant at the $p < 0.01$ level ($t = 4.79$).
[b] As measured by test of spatial orientation (left-right, above-below, front-back), improvement was significant at the $p < 0.05$ level ($t = 2.42$).
[c] As measured by test of ability to order the matrix, improvement was significant at the $p < 0.01$ level ($t = 6.54$)

The judges displayed a high degree of agreement in scoring the tests. The obtained reliability coefficient was 0.852 for ability to form groups and 0.944 for spatial orientation.

The statistical analysis, performed by Claire Lavin, Ph.D., Director of Graduate Programs in Special Education at the College of New Rochelle, is reprinted here.[1]

The reliability of judges' ratings of the test results was determined by using an analysis of variance to estimate reliability of measurements as described by Winer (1962, p. 128). The obtained reliability quotient was based upon the scoring of tests by six judges. Separate analyses were performed for scores both on the tests of the ability to form groups and on the tests of spatial orientation.

For the ability to form groups, the obtained reliability coefficient was .852. The reliability coefficient for spatial orientation was .944. The obtained coefficients reveal that the six judges, based upon their training, had a similar frame of reference and displayed a high degree of agreement in scoring the tests.

The effectiveness of the training program was evaluated by using a $t$ test ($N = 11$) for correlated means to determine the significance of differences in mean pre- and post-test scores. Separate analyses were performed for scores on the tests of the three separate areas of cognition—the ability to form groups (select and combine), spatial orientation, and the ability to order a matrix.

All the obtained $t$ values were statistically significant. The improvement in the ability to form groups ($t = 4.79$) and in ordering a matrix ($t = 6.54$) was significant at the .01 level. The improvement in spatial orientation was significant at the .05 level ($t = 2.42$). The impaired children who engaged in the therapeutic art program, therefore, improved significantly in the three areas of cognitive development that were the focus of the study.

Of the 15 parents, 14 returned the questionnaires. In response to the question, "Did your child enjoy coming to the class?" 12 checked the highest rating, and 13 indicated that they would like to be informed about future classes. These results are indicated in Table 34.

The statistical analyses and the questionnaire responses support the hypothesis that children with learning disabilities would show improvement in the three areas of cognitive development under consideration when taught by graduate students trained in using the art procedures developed in the project for children with communication disorders.

The success of this training program reveals that art techniques can be used to assist learning disabled children in expressing concepts nonverbally through visual-motor channels in spite of impaired functioning in this area. Through the use of cognitively oriented experiences with drawing, modeling, and painting, learning disabled children were able to develop the skills needed to bring order to their perceptually disoriented world. The variety of media provided tactile and kinesthetic feedback while the

Table 34.   Results, questionnaire sent to parents of fifteen children who attended art classes (with total of responses indicated)

Dear Parent:
    Now that our experimental art class is coming to an end, we would like to know if it was worthwhile for the children who participated. It would be most helpful in planning future classes if you would answer the following questions with checkmarks in the appropriate boxes.

1. Was the art class beneficial for your child in:

|  | Not at all | Very little | Sometimes | Much | Very much |
|---|---|---|---|---|---|
| Visual-motor development |  |  | 3 | 1 | 2 |
| Cognitive development |  |  | 3 | 1 | 2 |
| Artistic development |  | 1 | 2 | 1 | 3 |
| Emotional development |  |  | 2 | 1 | 5 |
| Social development | 1 |  | 1 | 2 | 2 |
| Other_____ |  |  |  |  |  |

2. Did you child enjoy
   coming to the class? 1  1  12

3. Would you like to be informed about
   future classes?          Yes 13          No 1

    There are no plans for continuing the class next term. Arrangements made directly with student teachers for continuing would not be under the auspices of the College of New Rochelle, and accordingly the College would have no responsibility for supervision.

COMMENTS:

nature of the art activities provided practice in the cognitive visual skills of analysis, integration, and synthesis. The instructional activities were conducted in a success oriented, nonthreatening atmosphere in conjunction with enjoyable art activities far removed from those specifically academic tasks that to many learning disabled children simply mean failure. As a result of these factors, the children made significant progress in the cognitive skills that were the focus of the study.

The present study revealed that visual-motor weaknesses can be attacked successfully through the use of art experiences. Since the tested abilities, forming groups, perceiving and representing spatial relationships, ordering and conserving, are also fundamental in the development of language as well as mathematics and reading ability, future investigations into the effect upon these more complex behaviors might also be fruitful.

## APPENDIX

Statistical Analysis of Test of Cognition Based on Piagetian Principles of Conservation, Grouping and Seriation: and Test of Ability to Select, Combine and Represent. (Analysis performed by John L. Kleinhans, Ph.D. Assistant Professor of Psychology, Manhattanville College, Purchase, New York.)

The raw data for the first term posttest of cognition were broken down into fourteen key items. A positive response (marked by an x in the data table) constituted one score point. Thus, an individual student's composite score is

Table.    Data used in performing median test.

| Score | Frequency (Experimental group) | Frequency (Control group) |
|-------|-------------------------------|---------------------------|
| 1 | 0 | 0 |
| 2 | 0 | 1 |
| 3 | 0 | 0 |
| 4 | 0 | 1 |
| 5 | 2 | 2 |
| 6 | 0 | 2 |
| 7 | 0 | 2 |
| 8 | 0 | 1 |
| 9 | 2 | 6 |
| 10 | 3 | 1 |
| 11 | 1 | 0 |
| 12 | 4 | 1 |
| 13 | 5 | 0 |
| 14 | 1 | 1 |
| | $N = 18$ | $N = 18$ |

Combined median = 9.37

| | Experimental group | Control group |
|---|---|---|
| Above combined median | 14 | 3 |
| Below combined median | 4 | 15 |

simply the total number of positive responses on the key items; the potential range is 0 to 14. The composite scores cannot be assumed to form an interval scale; therefore, distribution-free (non-parametric) descriptive and inferential methods are appropriate to this data. A median test generating a chi square statistic was used to evaluate the significance of any difference between control and experimental groups.

## Descriptive Summary Statistics

The median score for experimental and control groups combined was 9.37. The median of the experimental group was 11.75, and of the control group, 8.5. Of the eighteen experimental students, fourteen had scores exceeding the combined median and four fell below. Of the eighteen control students, three were above, and fifteen below the combined median. The chi square value derived from the resulting $2 \times 2$ contingency table was 11.15. With one degree of freedom, the observed chi square exceeds the criterion value of 10.83 required for the rejection of the null hypothesis of no difference between groups at the $p < 0.001$ level of confidence. Thus the observed difference between groups, in favor of the experimental group, is shown to be highly significant.

# Chapter 13

# Discussion
# and Conclusions

## COGNITIVE ABILITIES

There is a recognized need for greater precision in identifying the abilities and disabilities of handicapped children. The need is becoming critical—free public education must be made available to all handicapped children by September 1978, and for each handicapped child there must be an individualized educational program based on nondiscriminatory testing and evaluation.[1]

A recent survey has found much confusion in the count of learning-disabled children. Although New York claimed to be serving 35,093 such children as of February 1, 1977, a clear definition of "learning-disabled" had not been provided, and, when local school officials were asked how they had recognized the children and made the count, the answers were found to be varied and confusing.[2]

The deaf child's ability to conceptualize is of major concern, and educators have been looking for nonverbal instruments to help them assess the cognitive and affective potentials of deaf children. The findings of the studies presented here indicate that drawing procedures can serve as instruments for assessing and developing cognitive abilities of children or adults who cannot communicate well verbally. These cognitive abilities include the ability to associate and represent concepts, the ability to order sequentially, and the ability to perceive and represent spatial relationships.

It is surprising that these abilities appear relatively independent of language impairment and verbal-analytical thinking, and to some extent even independent of age. The studies described in Chapters 5 and 12 found a wide range of ability regardless of whether the tasks were presented to handicapped or unimpaired children or adults. Some children like Ralph, with an IQ of 77, had high scores in all the drawing tests. In predictive drawing only eighteen of the 136 handicapped and

---

[1] Public Law 94–142, The Education for All Handicapped Children Act.
[2] New York Association for the Learning Disabled News. 15(2):Mar/Apr, 1977.

normal children scored 5 points in the pretest, indicating that they had previously developed horizontal and vertical concepts. Of these eighteen, ten were normal children, ranging in age between nine and fourteen. The remaining eight children were handicapped, with IQs ranging between 50 (Stanford-Binet) and 140 (Goodenough). They ranged in age between ten and thirteen.

When the tests were presented to audiences of teachers and other professionals, without fail some drew houses perpendicular to the slope, or lines parallel to the sides or bottom of the tilted bottle, or confused spatial relationships in drawing from observation. (For examples, see Figures 127 and 128 in Chapter 9.)

In the drawing from observation test, only six of the ninety-five children had high scores of 15 or 16 points (the maximum score was 16). They ranged in age between eight and fourteen years. Four were unimpaired, and two were impaired children from the experimental group. Among low scorers, nine of the ninety-five children scored 4 points or less. They also ranged between eight and thirteen years. Five were unimpaired and four were impaired children, all from the control group (See Table 16, Chapter 10).

How can these findings be explained? The obvious answer, lack of experience in drawing, seems inadequate, because the drawing tasks call for more than art skills. It may be, instead, that children, and adults, who like to say they cannot draw a straight line actually have difficulty processing spatial information. They may have subtle cognitive dysfunctions, easily overlooked because our school systems emphasize verbal-analytical skills—it does not matter much if students cannot draw.

By the same token, subtle cognitive skills may also be escaping detection. It may well be important to identify and evaluate strengths in visuo-spatial thinking if the strengths can enable children with language dysfunctions to learn concepts that are normally associated with language. The children in our experimental groups improved significantly on several tests measuring concepts of space, order, and class.

Although educators usually distinguish between children identified as learning disabled and children whose learning problems are primarily the result of hearing impairment, the distinctions seemed unimportant in the findings reported here. Some children from each group had high scores, while others had low scores. For some purposes it may be better to group children on the basis of visuo-spatial ability rather than on the basis of whether their handicaps are related to learning disability or to hearing impairment.

It may also be useful to ask whether or not the teaching methods employed here were responsible for the development of cognitive skills seen in the children who had received art classes. It had been hypothesized that an effective approach in working with handicapped children and adults would be to emphasize communication, adjustment, enjoyment, and exploratory learning. The classroom atmosphere was deliberately supportive and encouraging. The art tasks were intended to arouse curiosity and provide opportunities to manipulate, observe, and reflect, as in tilting the half-filled bottle at eye level on a table.

The fact that experimental groups improved after relatively few art periods is also of interest. The children were confronted with problems involving facts about the world, and their attention was guided toward ways of solving them. In the past they may have been puzzled by similar problems, but could not ask questions or understand explanations. In the art classes they were able to solve the problems for themselves, with a little help, much encouragement, and time for the reveries that seem essential in art experience.

The responses of stroke patients suggest that the drawing tests can help in evaluating the perceptual and cognitive abilities of stroke patients with language impairments. It will be important to see whether or not art therapy can be useful in their rehabilitation.

Why has art been overlooked? Perhaps because teachers have low expectations regarding the helpfulness of art procedures. Perhaps because the problems of teaching handicapped children are so urgent that art activities may seem an uneconomical use of school time. Perhaps because specialists and educators in various fields are often unaware of objectives and achievements in other fields, such as art education and art therapy. Certainly misconceptions about art education abound. Some educators see art only as a vaguely enriching form of entertainment, possibly because they had little experience with art in their own educational backgrounds.

The role art can play in helping language-impaired children and adults make maximum use of their cognitive abilities seems to merit further study. Like reading and mathematics, art activities involve discriminating, recalling, and processing spatial information. Whether or not identifying and building on these aptitudes or skills will lead to improvements in reading or mathematics is another question worth exploring.

## CREATIVE ABILITY

The question of whether or not emphasizing cognitive growth would interfere with creativity in art was of much concern. It was hypothesized that art experience could be educational and therapeutic concurrently, and this hypothesis was supported by the findings of the

1966 and 1973 projects. In the 1966 project the twenty art educators found evidence of sensitivity to art values and technical skill in the same artwork in which psychologists and other specialists found evidence of adjustment and cognition. The 1973 project found statistically significant improvements in expressiveness and art skills, even though the main purpose of the project was to develop cognitive skills. Thus we do not have to sacrifice one developmental need for another. Art teachers can try to stimulate cognition and adjustment without abandoning traditional goals of teaching art, and art therapists can try to develop art skills and cognitive skills without sacrificing spontaneity. We can stimulate many kinds of growth that reinforce one another.

Art therapy and art education can be viewed as a continuum rather than as two distinct fields. At one end of the continuum are art educators concerned mainly with aesthetics and instruction. At the opposite end are art therapists concerned mainly with diagnosis and treatment of mental illness, functioning usually as part of a team of psychiatrists, psychologists, social workers, and other therapists. Between them are art teachers concerned with more than instruction, and art therapists concerned with more than mental illness.

It might be worthwhile to consider expanding master's degree programs: in art education, programs might include courses in art therapy and special education; in art therapy, programs might include courses in studio art and special education; and in special education programs, courses in studio art and art therapy might be included. Each field may benefit from expanded services and broader contributions to the development of all children, handicapped and unimpaired.

The approach in working with handicapped students was essentially the same as in working with normal students—to encourage inquiry, not just to transmit information. It was believed that art techniques and skills are means, not ends—means of helping students become aware of aesthetic qualities, and articulate in expressing ideas and experiences through visual forms.

This approach to teaching is not new, nor is it limited to the visual arts. It has been formulated by many writers in different fields of education. Different ideas and practices can make decisive differences in the evidence of aptitude for art. This is not to say that art teachers can take credit for the talents of their students. They can take credit for evidence of their influence on student work, and should take the blame as well for evidence of destructive influence—paintings that are trite and imitative or have strong resemblances to one another and to the teacher's own preferences.

The value of an art program depends on more than the instructor's knowledge of art. If his goals are restricted to transmitting techniques, if his procedures are imitative and his expectations low, then a student who has high potential may show little evidence of what he is capable of achieving.

Handicapped students can be expected to develop qualities that are associated with talent, such as originality and sensitivity. Sensitivity seems to grow out of the need to solve problems or to adjust. Handicapped children and adults are faced with many problems and must adjust to many obstacles and pressures. Their handicaps are likely to mobilize their resources and to enhance their sensitivity to the people, objects, and events in their lives.

The deaf child or adult must often guess at the meaning of events and be attuned to whatever clues he can find. Deafness intensifies the importance of vision. While the hearing child learns about the world through vision and hearing both, the deaf child may have to rely on vision alone. With his perceptions already concentrated on what he sees, it would seem natural for him to express his reactions visually, through the same channel from which he receives most of his impressions.

The behavior of deaf students in the 1967 project classes, and their responses to the questionnaires, suggest that the deaf may have, potentially, more interest in the visual arts than students with normal hearing. It may be that the frustrations of deafness produce a desire for expressing thoughts and feelings which a hearing person does not have in the same way or to the same degree. If this interest is not readily apparent, it may be because the deaf usually receive so little education in art, and because the innate rewards in art experience are so easily destroyed.

The visual arts can compensate for deafness in many ways. The enjoyment of works of art can be profound, and there can be joy as well in creating art forms. The visual arts can provide the deaf with a major source of enjoyment throughout life if they receive adequate introduction to studio experiences and to the offerings of museums. The project findings indicate that some deaf students, like some hearing students, are truly gifted, and that all are capable of enjoying art activities and appreciating works of art. If deaf young people could leave schools with portfolios of artwork showing what they are capable of accomplishing in industrial design, commercial art, the crafts, and fine arts, much would be accomplished.

The findings of the studies reported here suggest that the potentials of art in the education of hearing-impaired or language-impaired children and adults not only go unrecognized, but also meet with resistance when they are demonstrated. There is still an urgent need to reexamine expectations about the artistic and intellectual capabilities of the handicapped, and to take a further look at the role art can play in their lives.

## CONCLUSIONS

The statistical analyses, evaluations by educational and other specialists, and classroom observation all support the following conclusions:

1.  Drawings can serve as instruments for identifying and evaluating cognitive skills that are usually associated with language: the ability to associate and to represent concepts, the ability to order sequentially, and the ability to perceive, to predict, and to represent spatial relationships.
2.  Art procedures that emphasize communication, adjustment, enjoyment, and exploratory learning can help children with communication disorders and children with learning disabilities develop concepts of space, order, and class.
3.  The same kind of art experience can serve aesthetic and therapeutic goals; cognitive growth can be stimulated without neglecting creative and affective growth, and art experiences can be structured without sacrificing spontaneity.
4.  Children and adults who are deaf, or who are deficient in language, can be expected to have as much aptitude, interest, and creative ability in the visual arts as their normal peers.

# Epilogue, 1986

During the years since this book was published in 1978, the studies it describes have continued. I will summarize the work in the following pages, and suggest areas where future research may be worthwhile.

## Stimulus Drawings

The stimulus drawing technique discussed on pages 138-9 was expanded and published (Silver, 1979, 1982). It now includes 50 drawings of people, animals, places and things, some of which are shown in Figure 1.

To summarize the technique, we ask an individual to choose two stimulus drawings, imagine something happening between them, then draw a picture that shows what is happening. When drawings are finished , they are given titles and discussed, then rated on a scale for evaluating sense of well-being (or distress).

Vilstrup has written a review of the technique (1983). Sandburg, Silver, and Vilstrup have reported on the use of stimulus drawings with various populations (1984). Sandburg used them to stimulate change and to encourage socialization among adult psychiatric patients. Vilstrup used them to develop insight into the problems of disturbed adolescents. Silver used them to evaluate cognitive skills of adult stroke patients who had lost the power of speech.

## A Drawing Test

The findings described in chapters 7 to 10 led to the development and publication of the Silver Drawing Test of Cognitive and Creative Skills (1983a). The test consists of three tasks: Predictive Drawing to assess understanding of sequential concepts, Drawing from Observation to assess concepts of space, and Drawing from Imagination to assess creativity and ability to select, combine and represent.

In the test, drawing responses are scored on scales of 0 to 5 points, as indicated on pages 124-133, 143-5, 166-169. When appropriate, drawings are also score for Projection, ranging from representations of distress (1 point) to representations of pleasure (5 points), with 3 points for ambivalent or unclear representations.

To determine the reliability of the scales, sample test booklets were scored independently by various therapists in four studies, and the results correlated. A high degree of reliability was found, as reported in the test manual.

Figure 1. Stimulus Drawings

Test-retest reliability was also examined, and scores on the Silver Test were correlated with scores on traditional tests of intelligence and achievement. Significant correlations were found with ten such tests, including the WISC, WAIS, Bender and Metropolitan Achievement tests.

To develop norms, the Silver test was administered to 513 children ages 7 to 16, in nine schools, in low, middle and high income areas in New York, New Jersey, Pennsylvania, California, and Canada. Their scores showed gradual improvement through the school years. Where reversals occurred, they were well within chance limits. In addition, 250 adults took the test. Percentile ranks were then developed so that individual scores can be compared with typical scores.

The test was also administered to more than 700 handicapped and gifted children and adults in 32 schools, hospitals, and other institutions in various parts of the United States, Canada, the Netherlands and Scotland.

Hayes (1978) used the Silver test to examine the correlation with reading achievement as measured by the SRA Reading Achievement tests. Administering both tests to 75 normal first, second, and third grade children, she found significant correlations between Drawing from Imagination subtest scores and reading achievement in all three grades. Correlations between Drawing from Observation and reading achievement were significant for the third-graders only; while Predictive Drawing correlated significantly with reading for the first grade only.

Horovitz (1985) reviewed the Silver Test. She also reported on its use in screening cognitive skills nonverbally, and in measuring gains over time, in a presentation at the 1984 National Conference on Mental Health and Deafness (in press).

## National Institute of Education Project
A 1979-80 project, supported by a grant from NIE, attempted to build upon previous studies by using a more controlled research design, a more diverse population, and a wider variety of settings (Silver, Lavin, Boeve, Hayes, Itzler, O'Brien, Terner, and Wohlberg (1980): 84 children, ages 7 to 11, at least one year below grade level in reading or mathematics, were nominated by administrators in five schools: one school for learning disabled children and four schools for both normal children and children with special needs.

Five art therapists, one in each school, worked with two groups of five children once a week for 12 weeks. During the first six weeks, the therapists used the same procedures (pages 138-9, 148-51, 173). During the second six weeks, they adapted the procedures to meet individual needs, and devised procedures of their own. They administered the Silver Test before and after the art program to the experimental group and to a matched control group.

Although the experimental group gained more than the control group, there was no significant difference between the posttest scores of the two groups, as shown in Figure 2.

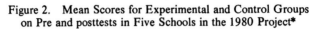

Figure 2.   Mean Scores for Experimental and Control Groups
on Pre and posttests in Five Schools in the 1980 Project*

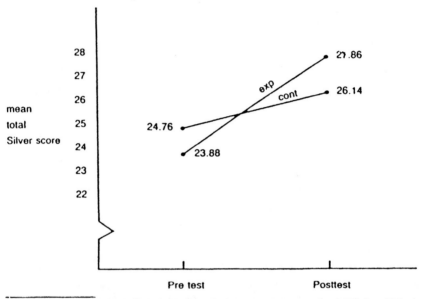

Pre test                    Posttest

* Both posttest scores differed significantly from pretest scores (p. < .05). In addition, the experimental group's posttest scores differed significantly from the combination of the other three groups of scores. Analysis and Figure 9 prepared by John Kleinhans. PhD

After the project ended, a school-by-school analysis of net change scores was undertaken. This time, in one of the schools, the school for learning disabled children, the posttest scores of the experimental group were significantly higher than the posttest scores of the control group. The art therapist who worked with these children was Judith Itzler, ATR.

Why was the school for learning disabled children the only school with significant differences between posttest scores of experimental and control groups? Did it reflect superior skills of a particular art therapist? Was it because she was the only therapist who worked with learning disabled children? Was it combination of both?

There is evidence that learning disabled children have been confused with gifted children whose major deficits were feelings of inadequacy (Whitmore, 1980). Were the learning disabled children in the NIE project gifted children with feelings of inadequacy who had been helped by the art therapy program?

There were no opportunities to explore this question during the NIE project, but the behavior of "Joey" suggests that he may have been such a child. Joey did not attend one of the five schools in the project. In his school, the remediation teacher had asked if she might participate. Since she lived elsewhere, in Canada, we arranged that she would work with one child once a week for 12 weeks using our procedures, supervised via phone and correspondence.

The child she worked with, Joey, age 8, was in the second grade in a school for normal children. As measured by the Canadian Cognitive Abilities Test (CCAT), his IQ score was 91. Only two of the 24 children in his class has lower scores. As measured by the Silver test, Joey had the highest score in his class in Drawing from Imagination, and the lowest score in Drawing from Observation.

To clarify the relationship between the two tests, the scores of the 24 children on both tests were correlated. Significant correlations were found between the CCAT and Drawing from Imagination at the .01 level ($r = .50$). No significant correlations were found between the CCAT and Drawing from Observation.

Joey was described as "lashing out at his peers, sometimes justified but often uncalled for". He had difficulty learning to read and had been placed in a behavior modification program. In Drawing from Imagination, he ranked in the 99th percentile as compared with the mean score of the 103 second graders in the test's normative sample. His score even exceeded the mean score of the adult sample.

Except for Joey, most of his classmates were about as successful in Drawing from Imagination as they were in the CCAT. To illustrate, the three children with the next highest scores in Drawing from Imagination, had CCAT scores ranging between 123 and 150.

Joey's pretest Drawing from Imagination is shown in Figure 3. It seems to represent a doctor operating on a patient who calls for help even though anaesthetized. Joey's title for this drawing was, "The Killier" (sic).

Although we do not have Joey's explanation, his drawing provides information. It indicates that he selected the stimulus drawings in the test booklet at the abstract rather than concrete level, on the basis of an imaginative, well-organized idea that implies more than is visible: His drawing goes beyond simply showing what his subjects do — the functional level typical of 8-year olds (see pages 122-130). In ability to combine, his drawing goes beyond the base line level, also typical of children his age (someone is upstairs in bed snoring). In ability to represent, it goes beyond imitating or restructuring the test booklet drawings — it is both original and expressive. In Projection, this drawing scored 1 point, for representing feelings of distress.

Figure 3.   "The Killier" (sic) by Joey, age 8, Pretest Drawing from Imagination

In the Drawing from Observation subtest, Joey had a very low score, ranking in the 14th percentile, Figure 4. The task is to draw an arrangement of three cylinders and a stone (see pages 166-172). In Joey's drawing in the pretest, only one of the four objects is in the correct position — the tallest cylinder on the right. He confused all the other horizontal and vertical relationships, and failed to show any depth although two objects in the arrangement were, in fact, in the foreground. This drawing suggests that Joey may be suffering from deficits in visual perception or memory.

Joey's responses to the various sessions of the art program are reported in detail elsewhere (Silver, 1983b). His responses to the posttests however, are presented here. In Drawing from Observation, the spatial relationships of all four objects are correct — horizontally, vertically, and in depth — even though his discriminations are crude (Figure 5). This drawing scored in the 85th percentile, up from the 14th percentile of his pretest drawing.

In his posttest Drawing from Imagination, Figure 6, the distress reflected in his pretest drawing is absent. His posttest drawing scored 2 points in Projection (moderate discomfort). Although the cat is being chased, it does not appear unhappy compared with the man on the operating table.

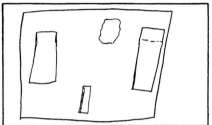

Figure 5. Posttest Drawing from Observation, by Joey.

Figure 4. Pretest Drawing from Observation by Joey.

Figure 6. "The Dog Chasing the Cat," by Joey, Posttest Drawing from Imagination.

While the art program was in progress, the CCAT was again administered. Joey's IQ score increased from 91 to 99 while the mean score of his 25 classmates decreased from 113 to 108.

Joey appears to be gifted as well as learning disabled, as evaluated by the Silver test. Like his pretest drawing from Imagination, his "lashing out" may reflect his frustration at being unable to keep up with his classmates academically. The question whether there was any carry over of his gains in adjustment and spatial concepts, remains unexplored. After the summer recess two letters addressed to his remediation teacher went unanswered. Then, on learning that her telephone number had been reassigned, I wrote to the school's principal who replied that she had died. Since, then, inquiries about Joey's progress in school have produced meager information. When the CCAT was again administered the following year, Joey's score dropped back to 90.

## Subsequent Research

In an attempt to provide greater precision in evaluating the sense of well-being or distress expressed through response drawings, the Projection scale was expanded from 5 to 7 points.

As indicated in the Scoring Guidelines below, the scale ranges from strongly negative content, such as drawings about suicide (1 point) to

# 7-Point Projection Scale

## Guidelines for Scoring Responses to the Stimulus Drawings and Drawing from Imagination Subtest

### Principal Subject (s)

| | |
|---|---|
| 1 point: | Strongly Negative, such as dead, dying, helpless, or in grave danger |
| 2 points: | Moderately Negative, such as frightened, frustrated, angry, remorseful, or suffering |
| 3 points: | Mildly Negative, such as sad, uncomfortable, wistful, foolish, struggling, isolated, disappointed, dissatisfied, or unfortunate |
| 4 points: | Intermediate Level, such as unclear, ambiguous, ambivalent, both negative and positive, or neither negative nor positive |
| 5 points: | Mildly Positive, such as smiling, safe, active, relaxed, or enjoying something |
| 6 points: | Moderately Positive, such as happy, strong, brave, big, effective, aggressive, or fortunate |
| 7 points: | Strongly Positive, such as loved, overcoming obstacles, escaping, or rescuing |

### Environment (including other people)

| | |
|---|---|
| 1 point: | Strongly Negative, such as life-threatening, dripping knives, smoking guns, tombstones, or prisons |
| 2 points: | Moderately Negative, such as hostile, dangerous, frustrating, stressful, rejecting, unhappy, or unfortunate |
| 3 points: | Mildly Negative, such as unpleasant activities or scenes, rain, snow, heat, dark clouds, bare trees, rocks, or storms |
| 4 points: | Intermediate Level, such as ambiguous, ambivalent, both negative and positive, or neither negative nor positive |
| 5 points: | Mildly Positive, such as pleasant activities or scenes, flowers, leafy trees, or fruits |
| *6 points: | Moderately Positive, such as tasty, friendly, helpful, pleasurable or fortunate |
| *7 points: | Strongly Positive, such as loving, protecting, or vulnerable |

*may represent wish fulfillment or other emotional needs

strongly positive content, such as drawings about honeymoons (7 points). The intermediate score (4 points) is used for drawings that are ambivalent, unclear, or neither negative nor positive. For each drawing, two scores are obtained, one for the principal subject and one for the environment depicted. Scoring examples are shown in Figures 7-12.

Figure 7.   "The Dying Bride"
by Caroline, 14
Subject 1, Environment 1

Figure 8.   "The Father is Yelling
at the Boy", by Omar, 7
Subject 2, Environment 2

Figure 9.   "Close but yet so far away"
by art therapy student, female
Subject 3, Environment 2

To determine the reliability of the 7-point Projection scale, a statistical analysis of interscorer agreement was prepared by Beatrice Krauss, PhD. Three registered art therapists independently scored 24 response drawings. These included four drawings selected at random from each of six populations of children and adults.

Figure 10.    "The Painter and his Son"
by Jim, 8
Subject 4 (unclear)
Environment 4 (both negative and positive)

Figure 11.    "Going to the Malt Shop"
by Sarah, 14
Subject 5, Environment 6

Figure 12.    "Midnight Break"
by art therapist (male)
Subject 7, Environment 7

We also asked whether the 7-point Projection scale could be used to assess responses to both the stimulus drawings and the Drawing from Imagination subtest. With this in mind, 12 of the 24 drawings were responses to the stimulus drawings and 12 were responses to the subtest.

Before scoring, the art therapists met for about one hour to discuss the new scale, and to score and discuss a group of practice drawings. Then the response drawing were presented individually at random, and scored without further discussion.

As shown in Table I, the agreement coefficients ranged between .924 and .549 as measured by Finn's r.* Thus the 7-point scale appears to be a dependable measure for evaluating sense of well-being (or distress) as projected into response drawings by children and adults.

Table I

| Stimuli | Finn's r |
|---|---|
| Subtest-Subject | .778 |
| Subtest-Environment | .924 |
| Stimulus Drawing-Subject | .806 |
| Stimulus Drawing-Environment | .549 |

In comparing responses to the stimulus drawings with responses to the Drawing from Imagination subtest, no significant difference in mean ratings was found, $t(22)=.8$, not significant. Thus there appears to be consistency of measurement in the 7-point Projection scale when it is used to rate response to either task, as shown in Table II:

Table II. The Means and Standard Deviations of the Ratings for Each Set of 12 Response Drawings

|  | M | SD |
|---|---|---|
| Test-subject | 3.75 | 1.90 |
| Test-Environment | 3.67 | 2.01 |
| STim Dr. Subject | 4.86 | 1.90 |
| St. Dr. Environment | 4.06 | 2.10 |

Further analysis found differences between the sexes. In a study involving 326 children and adults, the men and boys consistently expressed more negative views of the environments they depicted, and more positive views of their principal subjects, than did women and girls, as shown in Figure 13. These differences exceeded the .05 level of probability.

Another study found negative correlations between Projection scores and scores in Drawing from Imagination. In other words, the brightest children tended to have unhappy associations and negative fantasies while the children with low scores in cognitive and creative skills tended to represent a sense of well-being.

---

*Whitehurst, G. Interrater agreement for journal manuscript reviews, *American Psychologist*, (1984, 39, 22-28). A statistic readily interpretable as the proportion of the correspondence of observed ratings not due to chance. An r=.80, then denotes 80% agreement beyond chance agreement.

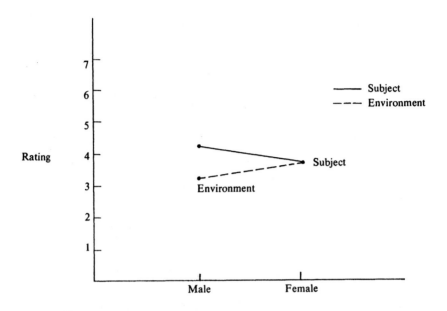

Figure 13.   Type of Score by Sex Interaction

These studies raise several questions that may be worth follow-up:

1. Can gifted children whose abilities are obscured by language deficits, learning disabilities or emotional problems, be identified by high scores in Drawing from Imagination?

2. Do new studies support the finding that men and boys tend to represent principal subjects more positively, and environments more negatively, than do women and girls?

3. Do new studies support the finding of negative correlation between high scores in Drawing from Imagination and low scores in Projection (negative subject matter)?

4. Can depression or potential suicide be determined by low scores in the Projection scale?
   A single such score may reflect nothing more than a passing mood. When such drawings occur, it is suggested that a second drawing be requested on another day. A second drawing scored 1 or 2 points would seem sufficient evidence for clinical follow-up.

5. Is there any correlation between Projection scores and measures of mood, such as the Moony checklist?

These questions are offered as the basis for, and encouragement of, further research.

# Epilogue, 1989

In the 1986 Epilogue, five questions were offered for further research. Since then, two questions have been explored: first, is there support for the finding of gender differences in response to the drawing task? and second, is a low score on the rating scale associated with depressive illness?

## 1. Gender Differences in the Emotional Content of Drawings

To verify the finding of differences between males and females in response to the Stimulus Drawing task, a Newman-Keuls Multiple Range Test was used to evaluate the responses by 326 girls, boys, women, and men. These subjects included groups of third graders, high school seniors, adults and the elderly (Silver, 1987a).

Results showed significant differences between males and females across the four age groups. Males tended to receive higher scores for their principal subjects than for their environments while female scores showed no significant differences. That is, as the score for one decreased, the score for the other also decreased. These differences exceeded the .05 level of probability. Although this finding of gender differences did not hold true for each respondent, female scores for subjects and environments were significantly correlated. Thus the preliminary findings (that males showed more negative views of environment and more positive views of principal subjects) were supported by the results of the Newman-Keuls Test.

Age differences approached but did not achieve significance ($p < .10$). The female groups tended to portray more negative subjects and environments, except for the high school girls and the elderly women who joined the elderly men in portraying their principal subjects positively. Of the four age groups, the high school girls received the highest scores for both categories while the third grade girls received the lowest scores. The most negative environments were portrayed by the group of elderly men. These results are shown in Figure 14.

Examples of gender differences in response to the drawing task are shown in Figures 15 and 16. "Man Escapes Danger", Figure 15, is a response by George, age 8, in the third grade who chose three Stimulus Drawings: the prince, the sword, and the horse. Although the environment of the horseback rider is life-threatening (1 point), he escapes (7 points).

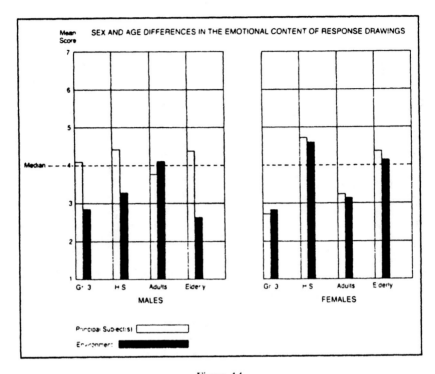

Figure 14.

"The tiger chases the chick to eat it" (dictated), Figure 16, is a response by Anna, age 8, also in the third grade. Like George, Anna drew a life-threatening environment (1 point), but unlike George, her chick does not escape (1 point).

To the extent that the Principal Subject of a response drawing reflects the self-image of the person who draws it, and the Environment reflects the way that person perceives the world, these findings suggest that men and boys tend to see themselves as fighting in a dangerous world, while women and girls tend to see themselves as part of the world rather than in conflict with it.

This study also found that many response drawings had strongly negative themes, receiving scores of 1 point. Did such negative fantasies reflect prevailing moods? If so, could the drawing task be useful in recognizing danger signs of depression? The search for answers led to additional studies.

Figure 15.   "Man Escapes Danger" by George, 8
Subject 7, Environment 1

## 2. Relationships Between Strongly Negative Responses and Depressive Illness

Two studies have examined relationships between depression and the score of 1 point (Silver, 1988a and b).

### Procedures

Because certain stimulus drawings seemed to have prompted negative fantasies, 14 of these drawings were selected to form a new instrument, Draw-a-Story. Although some changes were made in the drawing task and rating scale, they remain essentially the same (Silver, 1988b).

The Draw-a-Story task was presented to 350 children and adults, including groups of clinically depressed, normal, emotionally disturbed, learning

Figure 16.    "The tiger chases the chick to eat it" by Anna, 8
Subject 1, Environment 1

disabled, and hearing-impaired subjects. The task was presented by 24 art therapists, teachers, and counselors in Arizona, Georgia, Montana, Illinois, New Jersey, New York, Oregon, and Pennsylvania.*

Response drawings were then evaluated by means of the rating scale which ranges from strongly negative themes and fantasies, such as suicide (1 point), to strongly positive themes and fantasies, such as honeymoons (7 points).

To determine the inter-scorer reliability of the rating scale, 20 unidentified response drawings were scored blindly and independently by three registered art therapists. Correlations between judges were found significant at the .001 level.

To determine test-retest reliability, 24 third-graders were presented with the drawing task on two occasions. When 12 children who had previously

*Andrea Bianco-Riete, ATR; Kate Barker; Mariann De Masi; Fran Chapman; Linda Chilton, ATR; Bette Conley; Sylvia Corwin; Elisa Eisenman, ATR; Paula Fries; Cyrilla Foster; Robin Hanes, ATR; David Henley, ATR; Paula Jenkins; Nancy Malera; Eileen McCormick, ATR; Theresa McManus, RMT; Sally McKeever; JoAnn O'Brien, ATR; Ruth Obernbreit, ATR; Lillian Resnick, ATR; Andrea Seepo, ATR; Mary Towsley, SSJ, ATR; Christine Turner, ATR; Amy Vietze; and Katherine Weiss. Their assistance is gratefully acknowledged.

responded with negative fantasies were retested after an interval of approximately one month, 7 received the same scores. When 12 other children who
had previously responded with negative fantasies were retested after an interval of approximately two years, 11 received the same scores.

## Results

Approximately 63% of the depressed children and adolescents responded
with strongly negative themes or fantasies characterized by the score of 1
point. An example of this kind of response is shown in Figure 17.

In comparison, approximately 10% of the normal group scored 1 point,
7% of the elderly, 13% of the adult depressed, 19% of the emotionally
disturbed, 30% of the learning disabled, and none of the hearing-impaired
children and adolescents, as shown in Figure 18 and Table 3.

To determine whether these differences were significant, the chi-square
test was used. Results indicated that the proportion of depressed children
and adolescents scoring 1 point was significantly greater than the proportion
of any of the other groups scoring 1 point, at levels ranging between .001
and .0005.

These findings seem to indicate that strongly negative responses to the
Draw-a-Story task are associated with adolescent or childhood depression.

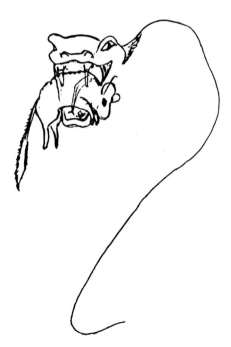

Figure 17.  "Prey" by Sam, 13, Depressed

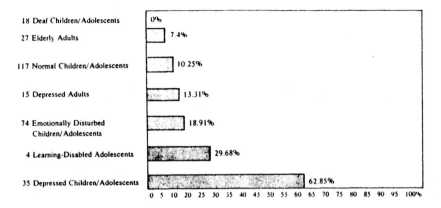

Figure 18.   Comparing Strongly Negative Responses to the Draw-a-Story Task
(Scored 1 Point)

By Depressed, Normal, Learning-Disabled, Emotionally Disturbed, and Deaf Children, Adolescents, and Adults

Although strongly negative responses do not necessarily indicate depression,
and conversely, positive responses do not exclude depression, the results
suggest that a child or adolescent who responds with a strongly negative
fantasy may be at risk, and that referral to a mental health professional for
thorough evaluation would be appropriate.

It is hoped that others will find the stimulus drawing tasks useful for
access to fantasies and opportunities for dialogue, as well as for early iden-
tification of children or adolescents who may be depressed.

Table III.   Comparing Responses to the Draw-a-Story Task By Depressed, Normal,
Emotionally Disturbed, Learning-Disabled and Deaf Children, Adolescents, and Adults

| Ages:<br>Scores* | 35 Depressed<br>Chil/Adols<br>6–17 | 117 Normal<br>Chil/Adols<br>5–19 | 74 Emotionally<br>Disturbed<br>Chi/Adols<br>8–21 | 64 Learning<br>Disabled<br>Adults<br>14–20 | 18 Deaf<br>Chil/Adols<br>9–18 | 27 Elderly<br>Adults | 15<br>Depressed<br>Adults<br>24–59 |
|---|---|---|---|---|---|---|---|
| 1 point | 22 (62.9%) | 12 (10.3%) | 14 (18.9%) | 19 (29.7%) | 0 | 2 (7.4%) | 2 (13.3%) |
| 2 points | 3 (8.56%) | 46 (39.3%) | 23 (31%) | 14 (21.8%) | 9 (50%) | 2 (7.4%) | 2 (13.3%) |
| 3 points | 1 | 12 | 6 | 3 | 0 | 2 | 0 |
| 4 points | 5 (14.3%) | 18 (15.3%) | 18 (24.3%) | 12 (18.8%) | 3 (16.7%) | 4 (14.8%) | 9 (60%) |
| 5 points | 2 | 7 | 10 | 4 | 3 | 11 | 0 |
| 6 points | 1 | 18 | 3 | 8 | 2 | 5 | 1 |
| 7 points | 1 | 4 | 0 | 4 | 1 | 1 | 1 |

* 1 point: strongly negative responses
2 points: moderately negative responses
3 points: mildly negative responses, self-disparaging humor
4 points: unemotional, ambivalent, or unclear responses

5 points: mildly positive responses, survivor humor
6 points: moderately positive responses, aggressive humor
7 points: strongly positive responses

# Epilogue, 2000

This epilogue will summarize studies of the cognitive and emotional content of responses to stimulus drawing tasks, published between 1989 and 1999.

## The Cognitive Content of Responses to Stimulus Drawing Tasks

### 1. Comparing Mean Scores of Deaf, Learning-Disabled, and Unimpaired Children
*Silver Drawing Test of Cognition and Emotion, 1996a*

This study compared the mean scores of 27 deaf, 28 learning disabled, and 28 unimpaired children, ages 9 to 11, on the Silver Drawing Test of Cognition and Emotion (SDT). The data were analyzed by using ANOVA and LSD tests to determine which groups differed on which measures.

In Predictive Drawing, the deaf children scored higher in concepts of Verticality than either the unimpaired or learning-disabled children at the .05 level of probability. No significant differences were found in Sequencing or Horizontality.

In Drawing from Observation, no significant differences were found between deaf and unimpaired children in representing spatial relationships in height, width, and depth. The deaf and unimpaired children scored higher than the learning-disabled children in representing Left-right Relationships.

In Drawing from Imagination, the unimpaired children scored higher than both deaf and learning-disabled children in Ability to Select, Ability to Combine, and Ability to Represent.

## 2. Gender Differences and Similarities in the Spatial Skills of Adolescents

*Silver, Art Therapy: Journal of the American Art Therapy Association, 13 (2), 1996c*

It is generally assumed that males are superior to females in spatial skills, based on the findings of many investigators. To test the assumption, this study examined responses to the *SDT Predictive Drawing and Drawing from Observation* subtests by 33 girls and 33 boys, ages 12 to 15, attending public schools in Nebraska, Pennsylvania, and New York. Their mean scores were analyzed using a computation of T-test scores.

No significant gender differences in spatial ability were found. The overall Manova indicated no gender differences in spatial measures. Although the girls' mean scores tended to be stronger than the boys in representing depth, the probability was less than .10 and not significant.

## 3 Gender Parity and Disparity in the Spatial Skills of Adolescents and Adults

*Silver, Art Therapy: Journal of the American Art Therapy Association, 15 (1) 1998a*

This study asked whether different scoring systems could explain why many studies have found female failures in performing tasks designed to assess concepts of horizontality and verticality. Subjects included 88 males and 88 females, ages 9 to 50 years. Their responses to the *SDT* Horizontality and Verticality tasks, previously scored on the 5-point scale, were rescored on the basis of success or failure. That is, respondents succeeded if they drew horizontal lines in the tilted bottle or vertical houses on the slope (5 points). They failed if they drew houses perpendicular to the slope, or drew lines parallel to the base or sides of the bottle (1 point).

No significant gender differences were found, as measured by T-tests. Although males performed more poorly on the verticality task, changing the form of assessment did not change the results.

## 4 The Brazilian Standardization of the Silver Drawing Test of Cognition and Emotion

*Allessandrini, C.D., Duarte, J.L., Dupas, M.A., Bianco, M.F., Art Therapy Journal of the American Art Therapy Association, 15 (2) 1998*

Allessandrini *et al* standardized the *SDT* on approximately 2,000 Brazilian children and adults. The trend in growth was similar in both cultures, increasing gradually with age and school level as found when the *SDT* was standardized in the United States. These findings confirmed the dependence of cognitive scores on educational level. Analyses of variance yielded differences in school grade and type of school at the .001 level of probability. Adults whose education had been limited to elementary or high schools had lower mean scores than most children. College graduates had higher scores than high school seniors; private school students, higher than public school students.

In emotional content, the authors found more negative than positive responses and a high rate of ambivalence.

## 5  Australian Study of Individual Differences in Information Processing, Personality, and Motivation in Responses to the Silver Drawing Test
*Hunter, G. An examination of individual differences in information processing, 1992*

Hunter administered the *SDT* to 193 college students in Australia, 128 women and 65 men, ages 15 to 53. Gender differences emerged. The performances of women appeared superior to the performances of men in drawing from Imaginaton and Drawing from Observation, based on a multivariate analysis of variance. Hunter found the results consistent with the *SDT* theory that cognitive skills evident in verbal conventions can be evident also in visual conventions. Hunter also suggested that gender differences be considered in developing course methodologies in order to facilitate learning.

## 6  Differences Among Aging and Young Adults in Cognition and Attitudes
*Silver, Art Therapy, Journal of the American Art Therapy Association, 16 (3) 1999b*

This study compared *SDT* performances of 57 aging and 51 young men and women. The young groups, mean age 29 years, attended colleges or participated in college audiences. The seniors, ages 64 to 95, lived independently in their homes or two retirement residences. Community A provided many services. Community B provided few services and amenities.

Gender and age groups were the variables of interest in an Analysis of Variance. They included Horizontality, Verticality, and Sequencing in responses to the Predictive Drawing task, and Cognitive Content, EmotionalContent, and Self-image scores in responses to the Drawing from Imagination task.

In cognitive skills, no significant age differences emerged, although the seniors had higher scores in Creativity. In Verticality, proportionally more young (54%) than old (15%)received the top 5-point score whereas more seniors scored 4-points (35% vs 19%), drawing vertical but unstable houses on the slope, perhaps a reflection of feeling unsteady on one's feet.

Men had significantly higher scores than women in both Horizontality and Verticality, prompting a closer look. The 13 women in community A (where residents remained more independent) had higher mean scores than the 13 women in Community B (where residents who became ill had to leave).

In Emotional Content and Self-Image scores, significant gender differences, not age differences emerged. Although the patterns of rising and falling scores were similar in both age groups, the men had significantly higher scores in Self-image, drawing more fantasies about powerful or effective principal subjects. The women had higher patterns of rising and falling scores in Emotional Content, drawing more fantasies about fortunate subjects and caring relationships.

The findings suggest that cognitive skills and emotions remain stable into old age, that fear of losing independence has adverse effects on both, and that being able to maintain independence may play a crucial role in successful aging.

# The Emotional Content of Responses to Stimulus Drawing Tasks

### 7  Gender Differences in Self-Images, Autonomous Subjects, and Relationships in Responses by Children
*Silver, Art Therapy: Journal of the American Art Therapy Association, 9 (2) 1992*

When children chose human rather than animal stimulus drawings, do they tend to draw fantasies about subjects the same gender as themselves? Do boys tend to represent autonomous subjects? Do girls tend to represent subjects interacting with others?

In this study, 145 boys and 116 girls, ages 7 to 10, in eight elementary schools, responded to the Drawing from Imagination task of the *Silver Drawing Test*.

A Chi-square test found that boys tended to draw pictures about males subjects; girls, about female subjects, to degrees that were significant at the .001 level of probability. This finding supported the theory that respondents tend to identify with the principal subjects they portray. Although boys (46%) outnumbered girls (37%) in drawing about autonomous subjects, and girls (63%) outnumbered boys (54%) in drawing about relationships, these differences were not significant.

## 8  Age and Gender Differences in Attitudes Toward Self and Others in Response Drawings by Children and Adults
*Silver, Art Therapy: Journal of the American Art Therapy Association, 10 (3) 1993b*

Expanding on the previous study, we asked whether male and female respondents tend to express characteristically different attitudes toward self and others, and if so, whether the attitudes change from youth to maturity to old age.

This study included 531 children, adolescents, and adults in five age groups - ages 7-10,13-16, 17-19, 20-50, 65 and older, who responded to the *SDT* Drawing from Imagination task. Their responses were divided into drawings about solitary subjects or about relationships, scored, then examined for gender differences and similarities.

Again, those who drew human subjects, drew subjects the same gender as themselves to a highly significant degree, degree ($X^2$=145.839, p < .001, phi =.657). Significantly more males than females expressed positive attitudes toward solitary subjects, negative attitudes toward relationships. Females expressed positive attitudes toward solitary subjects, but both positive and negative attitudes toward relationships.

More older men than any other age or gender group  drew fantasies about stressful relationships, but also used humor more often - self-deprecating humor. More males than females drew fantasies about assaultive relationships, whereas females showed significant age variability. More females males drew fantasies about caring relationships, whereas males showed significant age variability, like the men, ages 20 to 50, who drew caring relationships.

## 9  Identifying and Assessing Self-Images in Drawings by Delinquent Adolescents
*Silver and Ellison, J. The Arts in Psychotherapy, 22 (4) ,1995*

Part I of this study asked whether art therapists agree in identifying self-images in response drawings, whether they can identify self-images without knowing the individuals who drew them, and whether social workers agree in identifying self-images.

The *Draw a Story* array of stimulus drawings was presented by Ellison to 53 boys in a California residential detention facility. She asked them to identify characters in their drawings who might represent themselves, then sent only their drawings to Silver for blind evaluation. The level of agreement between the two art therapists and the 39 respondents who identified self-images, was viewed as an index of the validity of the Self-Image measure.

In addition, three other art therapists and five social workers were asked to identify self-images in 10 of the 53 drawings selected at random.

Ellison who knew the adolescents, accurately matched 76.8% in identifying their self-images. Silver, judging blindly, matched 71.8%. The inter-scorer agreement between Ellison and Silver across 53 respondents was 94.3%. These findings suggest that discussion is not essential for identifying the self-images in response drawings, although discussion is preferable, and the more discussion the more accurate interpretations are likely to be.

Among the five social workers, the average agreement was 54.0%; among the five art therapists, 78.2%; and among the sub-group of registered art therapists, 93.4%. This finding suggests that studio art experience, combined with training in psychotherapy, may be crucial in developing empathy as well as insight into the thoughts and feelings expressed through images.

In Part two of the study, Ellison presented six case studies and discussed tendencies that emerged, such as the tendency to draw isolated or aggressive, angry figures, and to portray themselves as heroes defending the weak. Wish-fulfilling drawings about successful love relationships were also common. Of the eight juveniles identified as alcoholic, four drew wish-fulfilling fantasies and four drew depressed, fearful, and sad principal subjects.

## 10  Sex Differences in the Solitary and Assaultive Fantasies of Delinquent and Non-Delinquent Adolescents
### *Silver, Adolescence, 31 (123) 1996b*

Building on the previous study, this study compared self-images expressed in response to the Draw a Story task by 64 adolescents in detention in California and 74 non-delinquent adolescents attending schools in Florida, Ohio, and New York. Their ages ranged from 13 to17; 82 were males, 56 were females.

The first analysis evaluated whether gender or delinquency was related to self-image scores. No significant differences were found. Significant differences appeared, however, in drawings about solitary subjects and drawings about assaultive relationships.

Proportionally more non-delinquent than delinquent boys drew fantasies about assaultive relationships. More than twice as many girls as boys drew sad, isolated, or endangered solitary subjects, regardless of delinquency. None of the delinquent girls expressed positive feelings toward their solitary subjects. More non-delinquent than delinquent adolescents drew positive self-images. For additional findings, statistical analyses, and implications, the reader is referred to the journal article.

## 11  Age and Gender Differences in Fantasies about Food and Eating

*Silver, Updating the Silver Drawing Test and Draw A Story Manuals, 1998b*

Chi-square analyses of responses to the *SDT* Drawing from Imagination task by 293 children, adolescents, and adults, indicated that females drew more fantasies about food than males. This difference reached borderline significance.

When the scores of adolescents and adults were combined, the gender differences also reached borderline significance (14% males, 33% females, Chi-square (1) = 4.25, p < .05). Among females, more adolescents (46.9%) drew fantasies about food or eating than girls(34.4%) and women (27.9%). Among males, more adolescents (29.4%), than boys (25%) and men (10.0%).

## 12  Sex and Age Differences in Attitudes toward the Opposite Sex

*Silver, Art Therapy: Journal of the American Art Therapy Association, (14 (4) 1997a*

This study examined fantasies about the opposite sex expressed by 116 children, adolescents, and adults responding to the *SDT* Drawing from Imagination task.

Although only 21% of the males and 27% of the females drew fantasies about subjects of the opposite sex, both genders expressed more negative than positive attitudes toward their opposite-sex subjects. The scores of both genders peaked at the moderately negative, 2-point level, portraying opposite-sex subjects as unfortunate, repulsive, or ridiculous. An analysis of variance found male responses significantly more negative than female responses.

It was suggested that this finding did not necessarily reflect male misogyny. It was also consistent with the previous finding that males draw more fantasies about assaultive relationships than females, and if it is typical to project positive self-images, then projecting negativity toward others might also be typical.

## 13  Correlations Between the SDT and DAS

*Silver, Updating the Silver Drawing Test and Draw A Story Manuals, 1998b*

The two drawing assessments use virtually the same rating scale and Drawing from Imagination task, but present different arrays of stimulus drawings. This raised the question whether different stimulus drawings affect the content of responses.

It was hypothesized that the *SDT* and *DAS* assess the same emotional and cognitive constructs. To test the hypothesis, both arrays were presented without a time interval to 38 children and adults, half of whom responded first to the *SDT* then the *DAS*, the other half responding first to the *DAS*.

Results indicated that the emotional content scores on both assessments had similar means and deviations and were correlated to a highly significant degree (r = 0.57, p <.0001). The correlations of cognitive scores were also significant (r = .66, p <.0001). Within test scores, no significant differences emerged.

The size of the correlations suggest that the two measures assess the same constructs, suggesting that the *SDT*, like *DAS* can be used to screen for depression, and that *DAS*, like the *SDT*, can be used to assess Ability to Select, Combine, and Represent.

## 14  Studies in Art Therapy, 1962-1998, Silver, 1999

This book includes 19 journal articles and 19 summaries of other publications by the author. Part 1 includes studies of children with auditory or language disorders; Part 2, studies of children, adolescents, and adults, with brain injury, learning disabilities, or mental illness; Part 3 studies of age or gender differences among unimpaired children, adolescents, and adults. Four of these studies received the annual research award from the American Art Therapy Association.

# References

Arnheim, R. 1969. Visual Thinking. University of California Press, Berkele.
Ca.

Bannatyne, A. 1971. Language, Reading and Learning Disabilities. Charles C.
Thomas, Springfield, Ill.

Barnett, S.A. 1967. Instinct and Intelligence. Prentice-Hall, Inc., Englewood
Cliffs, New Jersey.

Bell, C. 1958. The aesthetic hypothesis. In E. Vivas and M. Krieger (eds.), The
Problems of Aesthetics. Rinehard and Co., New York.

Boas, F. 1955. Primitive Art. Dover Publications, New York.

Brenner, C. A. 1974. Elementary Textbook of Psychoanalysis. Anchor Books,
New York.

Bruner, J. S., et al. 1966a. Studies in Cognitive Growth. John Wiley & Sons,
New York.

Bruner, J. S. 1966b. The perfectibility of intellect. In P.H. Oehser (ed.), Knowledge Among Men. Simon and Schuster, New York.

Buber, M. 1961. Between Man and Man. Beacon Press, Boston.

Burns, R. C., and Kaufman, S. H. 1972. Actions, Styles, and Symbols in
Kinetic Family Drawings. Brunner-Mazel, New York.

Deutch, B. Book review, New York Times. October 21, 1962.

Dubos, R. New York Times. October 17, 1971, p. 56.

Einstein, A. Quoted by Rudolf Arnheim. 1965. Visual thinking. In G. Kepes
(ed.), Education of Vision, p. 2. George Braziller, New York.

Elkind, D., and Flavell, J. H. 1969. Studies in Cognitive Development, Oxford
University Press, London.

Furth, H. 1966. Research with the deaf, Volta Rev. 68:34−56.

Hilgard, E. R. 1962. Introduction to Psychology. Harcourt, Brace, and World,
New York.

Hoben, T., Jamison, W. and Hummel, D. D. 1973. Observation is Insufficient
for Discovering That the Surface of Still Water is Invariantly Horizontal.
Science. 181: 193.

Howell, S. S. 1967. An Evaluation of the Arts and Crafts Programs Available
for Students Sixteen Years Old and Above in the Public Residential and Day
Schools for the Deaf in the United States. Unpublished master's thesis, University of Tennessee, Knoxville.

Jakobson, R. 1964. Linguistic typology of aphasic impairments. In A. V. S.
deReuck and Maeve O'Connor (eds), Disorders of Language. CIBA Founda-
tion Symposium. Little, Brown and Co., Boston.

Jersild, A. T. 1962. The Psychology of Adolescence. The Macmillan Company,
New York.

Jung, C. G. 1974. Man and His Symbols. Dell Publishing Co., New York.

Kepes, G. 1944. Language of Vision. Paul Theobald and Co., Chicago.

Kris, E. 1952. Psychoanalytic Explorations of Art. International Universities Press, New York.

Lampard, M. T. 1960. The art work of deaf children. Am. Ann. Deaf. 105:419–23.

Lowenfeld, V. 1961. Creative and Mental Growth. The Macmillan Company, New York.

Masland, R. L. 1969. Brain mechanisms underlying the language function. In Human Communication and Its Disorders. National Institutes of Health. Public Health Service, U.S. Department of Health, Education and Welfare, Washington, D.C.

Merryman, R. Interview with Ingmar Bergman. Life Magazine. October 15, 1971.

Myklebust, H. R. 1960. The Psychology of Deafness. Grune and Stratton, New York.

National Art Education Association. 1968. Position statement. The Essentials of a Quality School Art Program. Reston, Virginia.

National Institutes of Health. 1969. Human Communication and Its Disorders. Public Health Service, U.S. Department of Health, Education, and Welfare, Washington, D.C.

Olver, R. R., and Hornsby, J. R. 1966a. On equivalence. In J. S. Bruner, et al., Studies in Cognitive Growth. John Wiley & Sons, New York.

Piaget, J., and Inhelder, B. 1967. The Child's Conception of Space. W.W. Norton and Co., New York.

Piaget, J. 1970. Genetic Epistemology. Columbia University Press, New York.

Pintner, R. 1941. Artistic appreciation among deaf children. Am. Ann. Deaf. 86:218–223.

Rappaport, D., et al. 1972. Diagnostic Psychological Testing. International Universities Press, New York.

Rosenthal, R., and Jacobson, L. 1968. Pygmalion in the Classroom. Holt. Rinehart and Winston, New York.

Rugel, R. P. 1974. WISC Subtests Scores of Disabled Readers. A review in: J. Learn. Disabil. 7:57–64.

Sagan, C. 1977. Dragons of Eden. Random House, New York.

Silver, R. A. 1963. Art for the deaf child— its potentialities. Volta Rev. 65:8.

Silver, R. A. 1966. The Role of Art in the Conceptual Thinking, Adjustment, and Aptitudes of Deaf and Aphasic Children. Ed. D. project report. Columbia University, New York.

Silver, R. A. 1967. A demonstration project in art education for deaf and hard of hearing children and adults. U.S. Office of Education, Bureau of Research #BR 6-8598.

Silver, R. A. 1973. Cognitive skills development through art experiences. New York State Urban Education Project #147232101.

Silver, R. A. 1976. Using art to evaluate and develop cognitive skills. Am. J. Art Ther. 16(1):October.

Silver, R. A., and Lavin, C. 1977. The role of art in developing and evaluating cognitive skills. J. Learn. Disabil. 10(7):27–35.

Sinclair-de Zwart, H. 1969. Developmental psycholinguistics. In D. Elkind and J.H. Flavell (eds.), Studies in Cognitive Development. Oxford University Press, London.

Singer, D. G., and Lenahan, M. L. 1976. Imagination content in dreams of deaf children. Am. Ann. Deaf. 121:44–48.

Sinnott, E. W. 1961. Cell and Psyche: The Biology of Purpose. Harper and Brothers, New York.

Smith, M.D., et al. 1977. Intellectual characteristics of school labeled learning disabled children. Except. Child. 43:6. March 77 p. 352-357

Sonstroem, A. M. On the conservation of solids. In J. S. Bruner, et al., Studies In Cognitive Growth. John Wiley & Sons, New York.

Stratemeyer, F. B. 1957. Developing a Curriculum for Modern Living. Teachers College, Columbia University.

Strauss, A. A., and Kephart, N. C. 1955. Psychopathology and Education of the Brain Injured Child. Vol. 2. Grune and Stratton, New York.

Torrance, E. P. 1962. Guiding Creative Talent. Prentice-Hall, Inc., Englewood Cliffs, N.J.

Wilson, J. (ed.). 1971. Diagnosis of Learning Disabilities, McGraw-Hill Book Company, New York.

Witelson, S. F. 1976. Abnormal right hemisphere specialization in developmental dyslexia. In R.M. Knights and D.J. Bakker (eds.), The Neuropsychology of Learning Disorders. University Park Press, Baltimore.

Witkin, H. A., et al. 1962. Psychological Differentiation. John Wiley and Sons, Inc.

# Epilogue References

Hayes, K. 1978. The Relationship between Drawing Ability and Reading Scores. Unpublished Master's Thesis, College of New Rochelle, New York.

Horovitz, E. 1985. Review of Silver Drawing Test of Cognitive and Creative Skills. Art Therapy 2(1):44.

Sandburg, Silver, and Vilstrup. 1984. The Stimulus Drawing Technique. Art Therapy 1(3):132–140.

Silver, R. A. 1979, 1982, 1986. Stimulus Drawings and Techniques in Therapy, Development and Assessment. Ablin Press, New York.

Silver, R. A., Boeve, E., Hayes, K., Itzler, J., Lavin, C., O'Brien, J., Terner, N., and Wohlberg, P. 1980. Assessing and Developing Cognitive Skills in Handicapped Children Through Art. Report of National Institute of Education Project G 79 0081, College of New Rochelle, New York.

Silver, R. A. 1982. Developing Cognitive Skills Through Art in Current Topics in Early Childhood Education, 4, L. Katz, ed. ERIC Clearinghouse on Elementary and Early Childhood Education, University of Illinois, Ablex Publishing Co., New Jersey.

Silver, R. A., 1983a. Silver Drawing Test of Cognitive and Creative Skills, Special Child Publications, Seattle WA., distributed by Ablin Press, New York.

Silver, R. A., 1983b. Identifying Gifted Handicapped Children Through Their Drawings. Art Therapy. 1(1)40–46.

Silver, R.A. 1987a. Sex Differences in the Emotional Content of Drawings, Art Therapy, 4(2), 67–77.

Silver, R. A. 1987b. A Cognitive Approach to Art Therapy. In Approaches to Art Therapy, Judith Rubin (ed). Bruner/Mazel, Inc., NY.

Silver, R. A. 1988a. Screening Children and Adolescents for Depression. American Journal of Art Therapy, 26(4), 119–124.

Silver, R. A. 1988b. Draw-a-Story: Screening for Depression and Emotional Needs. Ablin Press, Mamaroneck, NY.

Vilstrup, K., 1983. Review of Stimulus Drawings and Techniques. American Journal of Art Therapy 22(2) Jan.

Whitmore, J. 1980. Giftedness, Conflict, and Underachievement, Allyn and Bacon, Boston, MA.

# Epilogue References 2000

Allessandrini, C.D.; Duarte, J.L.; Dupas, M.A., Bianco, M.F., 1998. SDT: The Brazilian Standardization of the *Silver Drawing Test of Cognition and Emotion, AR Therapy, Journal of the American Art Therapy Association*, 15 (2) 107-115.

Hunter, G., 1992. *An examination of some individual differences in information processing, personality, and motivation with respect to some dimensions of spatial thinking or problem solving in TAFE students.* Unpublished master's thesis, The University of New England, School of Professional Studies, Armidale, Australia.

Silver R., and Ellison, J., 1995. Identifying and assessing self-images in drawings by delinquent adolescents, *The Arts in Psychotherapy*, 22 (4) 339-352. ERIC EJ 545 763

Silver, R., 1992, 2000. Gender differences in drawings, a study of self-images, autonomous subjects, and relationships, *Art Therapy: Journal of the American Art Therapy Association*. 9 (2) 85-92.

Silver, R., 1993a. Draw A story: Screening for depression and age or gender differences, Florida, Ablin Press Distributors.

Silver, R., 1993b, 2000. Age and gender differences expressed through drawings, A study of attitudes toward self and others. *Art Therapy, Journal of the American Art Therapy Association,* 10 (3) 159-168. ERIC EJ 502 654

Silver, R., 1993c. Assessing the emotional content of drawings by older adults, *American Journal of Art Therapy*, 32, 46-52.

Silver, R., 1996a. Comparing *SDT* scores of deaf and hearing girls and boys, and learning-disabled, hearing-impaired, and hearing girls and boys, *Silver Drawing Test of Cognition and Emotion*. Florida: Ablin Press Distributors.

Silver, R., 1996b, 2000. Sex differences in the solitary and assaultive fantasies of delinquent and nondelinquent adolescents, *Adolescence*, 31 (123) 543-552. ERIC EJ # 535 383

Silver, R., 1996c, 2000. Gender differences and similarities in the spatial abilities of adolescents, *Art Therapy: Journal of the American Art Therapy Association*, 13 (2) 118-120. ERIC EJ 530 390.

Silver, R., 1997a, 2000. Sex and Age differences in attitudes toward the opposite sex, *Art Therapy: Journal of the American Art Therapy Association*, 14 (4), 268-272.

Silver, R., 1997b, 2000. *Stimulus Drawings & Techniques in Therapy, Development, and Assessment*. Florida: Ablin Press Distributors

Silver, R., 1998a, 2000.Gender parity and disparity in spatial skills: Comparing horizontal, vertical, and other task performances, *Art Therapy: Journal of the American Art Therapy Association* 15 (1) pp. 38-45.

Silver, R., 1998b. Correlations between the *SDT* and *DAS, Updating the Silver Drawing Test and Draw A Story Manuals,* FL, Ablin Press Distributors.

Iver, R., 1999a, 2000. *Studies in Art Therapy*, 1962-2000. Florida, Ablin Press Distributors.

Silver, R., 1999b. Differences among aging and young adults in attitudes and cognition, *Art Therapy, Journal of the American Art Therapy Association*, 16 (3), 133-139.

# Index

Abstract thinking, 21–24, 138
Activation patterns for language, art experience to help establish, 11
Adjustment, personal
  role of art experience in, 29–48, 233
  see also Art experience, therapeutic value of
Aesthetic value, of work of art
  determining, 105–106
  scoring of, 134
Affect, in work of art
  evaluating, 134–135
  see also Expressiveness
Aphasia, word combining impaired by, 197
Art education
  conceptions about, 105–108, 233
  objectives of, 81–82, 105, 107
    see also Art education and art therapy, shared objectives of
    see also Art therapy
Art education and art therapy
  ability to associate and represent concepts
  ability to combine (form), 127–129
  ability to represent (creativity), 129–134
  ability to select (content), 124–127
  aesthetic merit, 134
  affect, 134–135
  title of work, 135–138
  issues in
    form versus content, 105–106
    instruction versus spontaneity, 107–108
    therapy versus aesthetics, 98, 106–107

procedures for working with
  handicapped persons, 111–116
  with emotional disturbance, 115–116
  with verbal and visuo-motor impairment, 114–115
  with verbal weaknesses and visuo-motor strengths, 112–113
  with visuo-motor weaknesses and verbal strengths, 113–114
shared objectives of, 100, 103, 234–235
  inviting exploratory learning, 109–110, 113
  providing tasks that are self-rewarding, 110
  reinforcing emotional balance, 110–111
  widening the range of communication, 108–109, 112
viewed as a continuum, 235
Art experience
  enjoyment as keynote of, 110
  importance of atmosphere to, 110, 233
  in lives of handicapped, summary discussion, 231–236
  therapeutic value of
    experiencing control over people and events, 42–43
    expressing unacceptable feelings in an acceptable way, 33–35
    fulfilling wishes vicariously, 29
    obtaining relief from tension, 35–37
    personal involvement, 39–42
    self-monitoring, 38–39
    testing reality, 29–30
    transfer of behavior, 43–48

Art therapy
   objectives of, 105
      see also Art education and art
         therapy, shared objectives of
   training and skill for practice of,
      111
      see also Art education; Art
         experience
Assessment, through the visual arts,
   49–62
   clues to changes, 59
   clues to a child's development,
      57–59
   clues to interests and concerns,
      53–57
   clues to perception of self and
      others, 51–53
Association, concept of, role of in
   learning, 138
Association areas, see
   Neuroanatomy
Atmosphere, factor in art
   experience, 110, 233


Behavior change
   effected by art experience, 43–48
      see also Art experience,
         therapeutic value of
Bourbaki mathematicians, and
   fundamental structures
      recognized by, 117


Clay, modeling of, to develop
   cognitive skill of
      conservation, 150, 181
Cognition
   concepts related to, 117
      concept of class or groups, 117,
         121–140
      sequential order, 117, 141–159
      spatial concept, 117, 161–178
   defined, 9–10
   left and right hemisphere thinking,
      10–11
   modes of thinking, 11
   nonverbal thinking, 5–9
      see also Cognitive skills;
         Visuo-spatial thinking
Cognition, and role of art in
   development of

abstract thinking, 21–24
activating or reinforcing language,
   16–18
establishing patterns for language
   to follow, 11–13
imaginary play, 20–21
learning new words, 14–15
organizing and representing experiences, 9–10
recall, 25–27
transfer of learning, 18–20
Cognitive skills, 117–119, 231–233
   conceptual, 118, 119, 121–140
   sequential, 118, 119, 141–159
   spatial, 118, 119, 161–178
   testing of, statistical analysis, 205
College of New Rochelle, 140, 205,
   225, 227
Columbia University, 205
Communication, through the visual
   arts, 50–51, 106, 108–109,
   233
Conceptual skills, evaluating
   through art experience
      remediation procedures, 138–139
   results of, 139–140
   testing procedures, 122–138
      ability to combine (form),
         127–129
      ability to represent (creativity),
         129–134
      ability to select (content),
         124–127
Conservation
   assessing ability of, 142, 147, 159,
      181–182, 205
   basic to logical thinking, 142
   Sonstroem technique, designed to
      develop, 150, 181
Content (ability to select), 124–127
Creative skills, studies of, 79–100,
   233–235
   assessing handicapped children in
      four schools, 81–83
   demonstration project for
      hearing-impaired children and
         adults, 84–97
   State Urban Education Project,
      97–100, 119, 139, 151, 175
   Fall program, 204
   Spring program, 204
   statistical analyses of, 203–205

see also Torrance Test of
    Creative Thinking
Creative thinking
  fundamental operations of, 122
  transfer of, from art to other
    areas, 109
Creativity (ability to represent),
    129–134


Deaf adults, vocational
    opportunities for, 95–97
Deaf children
  art teachers' opinions about
    teaching, 90–91
  artistic abilities of, 79–100
  see also Hearing-impaired
    children
Description, levels of in the visual
    arts, 99
Development, intellectual
  assessing, see Cognitive skills;
    Creative skills
  contribution of exploratory
    behavior to, 109
  and language, relationship
    between, 5–6
Drawing
  aid to learning, 14, 19
    see also Cognitive skills
  see also Art experience;
    Predictive drawing
Drawing from imagination, 121–140
  statistical analysis of test of,
    205–210
Drawing from observation, 161–178
  statistical analysis of test of,
    218–225
Drawings
  childrens', universal elements in,
    51
  as instruments to evaluate
    cognitive skills, 236
Dyslexic children, patterns of
    abilities in, 118


The Education for All Handicapped
    Children Act, 231
Employment opportunities for the
    deaf, see Vocational
    opportunities for the deaf

Expectations of child's ability, held
    by art therapists and art
    educators, 63–77, 100
  case studies exploring, 64–77
  influence of, on assessment, 84
  nature of, 63–64, 89
Exploratory learning, 109–110, 113,
    233
Expressiveness, in the visual arts,
    87, 88, 89
  and structuring art experience,
    107
  tests of, statistical analysis, 220,
    225


Form (ability to combine), 128–129


Generalization, concept of, 43–45,
    138, 173


Hearing-impaired adults
  aptitudes for art of, 79–100
  interest in art of, 92–95, 235
Hearing-impaired children
  aptitudes for art of, 79–100
  intelligence testing of, 49
  interest in art of, 63, 91–95, 235
  restricted in imaginary play,
    20–21
Hearing impairment, types of, 98
Horizontality and verticality,
    concepts of
  development of, 185
    case study, 12–13
  testing by predictive drawing,
    142–143, 150–159, 232
  statistical analysis of, 211–218


Imagery, basic instrument in
    thinking, 3, 11
Imaginary play, 20–21, 131
Imitation, 99, 106
  see also Representation
Individuality, prerequisite to art
    expression, 106
Intellectual development, see
    Development, intellectual

Intelligence tests, difficulties of
    assessment by, 49

Kinetic Family Drawing technique,
    114, 183

Language
    activation or reinforcement of,
        through visual arts, 16−18
    child's education limited by lack
        of, 72
        case study, 69-74
    equated with intelligence, 63
    inadequacy of, for
        communication, 49
    learning new words through
        drawing, 14
    role of, in self-monitoring, 38
    and thinking, relationship
        between, 5−6
Language disorders, and brain
    damage, 10
Language-impaired children,
    aptitudes for art of, 9,
    79−100
Language impairment
    expressive, 121, 127
        effect on word use, 197
    receptive, 121, 127
        effect on word use, 197
Learning, definition of, 18−19
Learning-disabled children
    aptitudes for art of, 79−100
        statistical analyses of, 225−230
    identifying, 112, 231
    patterns of abilities in, 118
    role of art in intellectual
        development of, see
        Cognitive skills; Creative
        skills

Mamaroneck Artist's Guild, 91
Manhattanville College, Purchase,
    N.Y., 205
Memory, 25−27, 106, 141
    see also Conservation

National Art Education Association,
    109

Neuroanatomy
    activation patterns, 11
    association areas, 11
    left and right hemisphere thinking,
        10−11
Nonverbal behavior, fundamental
    operations underlying,
    121−122
Nonverbal thinking, 5−9

Originality, in the visual arts, 87,
    88, 89, 106, 109, 235

Painting
    as act of involvement, 39−40
    to develop cognitive skills,
        148−150
    see also Art experience
Piagetian developmental theory, 5,
    117, 142−143, 161, 184−85
Predictive drawing, 143−144, 192,
    231−232
    see also Horizontality and
        verticality
Primitive art, symbolic
    representations in, 106
Public Law 94−142, 231

Reading, stimulating through the
    visual arts, 16−18
Recall, see Memory
Representation, ability of, 99−100,
    106, 129−134
Restructuring, 99−100

Self-monitoring, 38−39
Sensitivity, in the visual arts, 87,
    88, 89, 99, 106, 234−235
Sequential order, cognitive skill of,
    117, 141−159, 192, 205
    remediation procedures for,
        148−151
    testing procedures for, 143−147
        manipulative tasks, 144−147
        predictive drawing, 143−144
        results, 151−159
Spatial skills, 161−178, 181, 205
    remediation procedures for,
        172−175

drawing and painting from observation and imagination, 173

drawing other arrangements, 173

manipulative games, 174–175

reversing the arrangements, 173

testing procedures, 166–172

above-below orientation, 169–170

front-back orientation, 170–172

left-right orientation, 168–169

observations, 176–178

results, 175–176

statistical analysis of, 218–225

*see also* Horizontality and verticality

Stroke patients, cognitive and creative skills of, 193–202, 233

State Urban Education Project for language- and hearing-impaired children, 97–100, 119, 139, 151, 175

Fall program, 204

Spring program 205

statistical analyses of, 203–225

drawing from imagination, 205–210

drawing from observation, 218–220

predictive drawing test of horizontal and vertical orientation, 211–218

test of artistic expressiveness and skill, 220–225

test of cognitive skills, 205

Subjectivity, in the visual arts, 42

and artist's sensitivity to criticism, 111

Symbols

meanings of, 37, 135

use of

in art, 6–8, 23, 33, 40, 52–53, 106, 111, 133, 181

in language, 6

Thinking, *see* Abstract thinking; Cognition

Torrance Test of Creative Thinking, 85, 98, 99

comparison of deaf and hearing populations by, 85–86

Transfer of learning, 18–20

Transformation, 100

Verbal behavior, fundamental operations underlying, 121–122, 197

Visuo-motor disorders

art experience for individuals with, 112–115

and brain damage, 10

Visuo-spatial thinking, 109, 232

*see also* Cognitive skills

Vocational opportunities for the deaf in the visual arts, 74–77, 84, 95–97

comments about, 237–247

in ceramics, 237–239

in commercial art, 244

in fine printing, 244–245

in glassblowing, 242

in hand bookbinding, 239–241

in handweaving, 241–242

in metalcrafts, 241

in stained glass, 243

in woodworking, 243–244

Westchester Association for Children with Learning Disabilities, 226

WISC, grouping of subtests on, 118

Printed in the United States
24984LVS00002B/193

9 780595 088867